HBJ SPELLING

SIGNATURE EDITION

GOLD

Thorsten Carlson

Richard Madden

HBJ SPELLING

SIGNATURE EDITION

HBJ **HARCOURT BRACE JOVANOVICH, PUBLISHERS**

Orlando   San Diego   Chicago   Dallas

Acknowledgments

For permission to reprint copyrighted material, grateful acknowledgment is made to the following source:

Harcourt Brace Jovanovich, Inc.: Letter forms from *HBJ Handwriting,* Copyright © 1987 by Harcourt Brace Jovanovich, Inc. Definitions and the pronunciation key in the "Spelling Dictionary" are from the *HBJ School Dictionary.* Copyright © 1985, 1977 by Harcourt Brace Jovanovich, Inc.

COVER DESIGN Graphic Concern, Inc.

ART CREDITS

Key: T, Top; B, Bottom; L, Left; C, Center; R, Right.

Page 4(T), Blaise Zito Assoc.; 4(B), Bill Hartman; 8, Bill Colrus; 9, Blaise Zito Assoc.; 10, Tom Powers; 12, Bob Shein; 13, Bill Colrus; 20, Bob Shein; 21, Tim Lundgren; 26, ALL, 27, 28, Blaise Zito Assoc.; 31, Bill Colrus; 34, ALL, Tom Powers; 38(T), Bill Hartman; 38(B), Bob Shein; 39, Blaise Zito Assoc.; 42(T), Tim Lundgren; 42(B), Bob Shein; 46, ALL, Arthur Friedman; 51, 54, Blaise Zito Assoc.; 56, Ruth Soffer; 57, Tim Lundgren; 60, Bob Shein; 63, Ruth Soffer; 64, Tom Powers; 65, HBJ Photo; 68, ALL, Herb Reed; 69, Bill Colrus; 70, Blaise Zito Assoc.; 72, ALL, Bill Hartman; 73, Tom Powers; 76, ALL, 77, 79, ALL, 80, Blaise Zito Assoc.; 82, Leonard Leibowitz; 86(T), Blaise Zito Assoc.; 86(B), Tim Lundgren; 90(T), Blaise Zito Assoc.; 90(B), Ruth Soffer; 91, Blaise Zito Assoc.; 92, Ruth Soffer; 95, Bob Brower; 98(T), Bill Colrus; 98(B), Ruth Soffer; 102, 103, 105, Blaise Zito Assoc.; 108(T), Bill Colrus; 108(B), Bob Shein; 109, Tim Lundgren; 112, 115, Blaise Zito Assoc.; 116, Bob Shein; 120, Tom Powers; 122, Bill Hartman; 124(T), Bill Colrus; 124(B), 125, Bob Shein; 126, Tim Lundgren; 131, ALL, 132, 135, 136, Blaise Zito Assoc.; 138, ALL, Bill Colrus; 139, Bob Shein; 140, Marjorie Impell; 141, Blaise Zito Assoc.; 142, ALL, Arthur Friedman; 144, Marjorie Impell; 146, Tom Powers; 148, 149, Blaise Zito Assoc.; 150(T), Bill Hartman; 150(B), Tim Lundgren; 156, Meryl Henderson; 151, 154, 155, 157, 158, Blaise Zito Assoc.; 165, Philip Jones; 166, 170, 172, 179, 180, 182, 184, 186, 187, 188, Blaise Zito Assoc.; 190, Philip Jones; 191, Blaise Zito Assoc.; 197, 200, 201, Blaise Zito Assoc.

PHOTO CREDITS

Key: T, Top; B, Bottom; L, Left; C, Center; R, Right.

Cover Photography, Ken Lax; Page 5, Michael Philip Manheim/Photo Researchers; 8, Wally McNamee/Woodfin Camp and Assoc.; 12, Wide World; 14, Granger Collection; 16(T), Elizabeth Marshall/Kiaison; 16(B), HBJ Photo; 17, Focus on Sports; 18, Tom Pix/Peter Arnold; 20(T), John Sotomayor/The New York Times; 25, Nick Basilon/Blaise Zito Assoc.; 30(T), Mark Schorr/DPI; 30(B), Hans Pfetschinger/Peter Arnold; 35, Susan Peterson; 36, Bettmann Archives; 40, Bradley Smith/Photo Researchers; 44, National Geographic Society; 50, Jim Smith/Blaise Zito Assoc.; 52(T), James V. Elmore/Peter Arnold; 52(B), Chris Sorensen/Stock Market; 56(T), John de Visser/Photo Researchers; 58, Lynn Johnson/Black Star; 59, Nick Basilon/Blaise Zito Assoc.; 60, J. Alex Langley/DPI; 61, Lillian Bolstad/Peter Arnold; 64(T), M,PH, Fogden/Bruce Coleman; 66, UPI; 70, Bruno Zehnder/Peter Arnold; 74, David Barnes/Photo Researchers; 78, Farrell Grehan/Photo Researchers; 84, 87, Culver Pictures; 88, George Galicz/Photo Researchers; 94(TL), 94(TR), 94(BR), Granger Collection; 94(BL), John R. Rosenberger/DPI; 100, Bettmann Archives; 104, David Madison/Bruce Coleman; 106, Lawrence Migdale/Photo Researchers; 110, Albert Azzarello/Shostal Assoc.; 111, Jim Smith/Blaise Zito Assoc.; 113, Culver Pictures; 116(T), Historical Pictures Service; 117, Granger Collection; 118, M, Abbey/Photo Researchers; 120, Peter Larsen/Photo Researchers; 129, 130, HBJ Photo/Sam Joosten; 134, Robert A. Isaacs/Photo Researchers; 146, Leonard Lee Rue/Monkmeyer; 147, Richard Hutchings/Photo Researchers; 152, Nick Basilon/Blaise Zito Assoc.; 153, Lee Foster/Bruce Coleman; 169, 170, Jim Smith/Blaise Zito Assoc.; 177, Granger Collection; 177, Jim Smith/Blaise Zito Assoc.; 181(L), Chuck Muhlstock/Focus on Sports, 181(R), Murray Greenberg/Monkmeyer Press; 185, George Gerster/Photo Researchers; 193, Hans Wolfe/Image Bank; 195, Jim Smith/Blaise Zito Assoc.; 196, M,P, Kahl/Photo Researchers; 197, Tom McHugh/Photo Researchers; 198, Jim Smith/Blaise Zito Assoc.

PRODUCTION AND LAYOUT Blaise Zito Associates

Printed in the United States of America
ISBN 0-15-327084-5

Contents

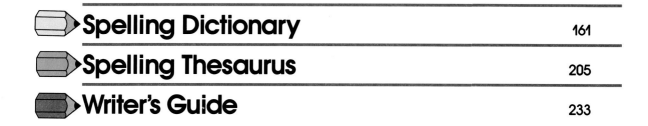

Spelling Dictionary — 161

Spelling Thesaurus — 205

Writer's Guide — 233

Study Steps to Learn a Word

 **SAY** the word. Recall when you have heard the word used. Think about what it means.

 **LOOK** at the word. Find any prefixes, suffixes, or other word parts you know. Think about other words that are related in meaning and spelling. Try to picture the word in your mind.

 **SPELL** the word to yourself. Think about the way each sound is spelled. Notice any unusual spelling.

 **WRITE** the word while looking at it. Check the way you have formed your letters. If you have not written the word clearly or correctly, write it again.

 **CHECK** your learning. Cover the word and write it. If you did not spell the word correctly, practice these steps until the word becomes your own.

Skills Check

A. Write the letter of the misspelled word.

1. **a.** tongue   **b.** ninty   **c.** region
2. **a.** ridiculous   **b.** muscle   **c.** spoonfulls
3. **a.** alligater   **b.** portrait   **c.** umbrella
4. **a.** economy   **b.** acquarium   **c.** independent

B. Write the correct spelling for each pronunciation.

5. /loj′ik/   6. /kə•mit′ē/

7. /di•sēv′/   8. /gi•tär′/

C. The words in each column end with syllables that contain the sounds at the top of the column. Write the correct spelling of the whole word.

/ər/	/əl/	/əm/
9. calend	12. civ	15. embl
10. operat	13. pan	16. den
11. lawy	14. tramp	17. sympt

D. Write a homophone for each word below.

18. principle   19. cereal

20. patients   21. mousse

E. Complete each sentence using one of the words in ( ).

22. We cannot (except, accept) ＿＿ the gift.

23. She wrote the letter on blue (stationery, stationary) ＿＿.

24. The meeting must (proceed, precede) ＿＿ without me.

best score
A. 4

best score
B. 4

best score
C. 9

best score
D. 4

best score
E. 3

F. Add the inflectional ending in ( ) to each word. Write the word.

25. pity + (ed)   **26.** pursue + (ing)

27. omit + (ing)   **28.** benefit + (ed)

G. Add one of these prefixes to each word to form its antonym.

dis-   il-   im-   in-   ir-   non-

29. accurate   **30.** similar

31. essential   **32.** legal

33. regular   **34.** perfect

H. Add the adjective-forming suffix *-able* or *-ible* to each verb. Write the new word.

35. sense   **36.** consider

37. value   **38.** permit

I. Add the noun-forming suffix *-sion* or *-tion* to each verb. Write the new word.

39. appreciate   **40.** confess

41. participate   **42.** extend

J. Complete each sentence using a synonym for the word in ( ).

43. The (inside) _____ of the box was lined with velvet.

44. The (gasoline) _____ gauge in the car reads empty.

45. The doctor (suggested) _____ that I take multivitamins.

46. The (first) _____ owners of the house planted that tree.

K. Write a word from the language indicated for each definition.

47. French   "a soft hat"

48. Spanish   "a flat-topped hill"

49. Latin   "the way out"

50. Spanish   "a riding and roping contest"

1 Prefixes and Suffixes

UNIT WORDS

1. gruesome
2. aloft
3. withdrew
4. handsome
5. clockwise
6. likelihood
7. ashore
8. bewilder
9. falsehood
10. belittle
11. lengthwise
12. adrift
13. befriend
14. withhold
15. worrisome
16. otherwise
17. livelihood
18. withstand
19. likewise
20. astride

The Unit Words

Each Unit word has a prefix or a suffix which has been used to form English words for almost a thousand years. A **prefix** is a word part that is added to the **beginning** of a word to change its meaning or part of speech. A **suffix** is a word part that is added to the **end** of a word to change its meaning or part of speech.

One prefix used in the Unit words is *be-*. When *be-* is added to the noun *friend,* the meaning of the word and the part of speech change. The noun *friend* means "a person one knows well and likes," but the verb *befriend* means "to act as a friend to." In the same manner, when the suffix *-some* is added to the word *worry,* a verb meaning "to be uneasy in the mind," the word becomes *worrisome,* an adjective meaning "causing worry or anxiety." Here are the English prefixes and suffixes found in the Unit words.

PREFIXES	EXAMPLES	SUFFIXES	EXAMPLES
a-	*ashore*	**-hood**	*falsehood*
be-	*bewilder*	**-some**	*gruesome*
with-	*withdrew*	**-wise**	*clockwise*

Spelling Practice

A. Write the Unit word that is formed by adding a prefix to each word.

1. stride
2. drew
3. friend
4. shore
5. drift
6. little
7. hold
8. stand

B. Write the Unit words that have the same meaning as these words.

9. confuse
10. attractive
11. dishonesty
12. in flight
13. horrible
14. troubling
15. income
16. probability

C. Complete these sentences using Unit words that end with -wise.

17. First fold the paper horizontally, and then fold it ____.

18. We'd better hurry; ____ we'll miss the bus.

19. Turn the bulb ____ to fit it into the socket.

20. Since she apologized, you should do ____.

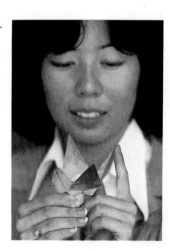

D. When a word ends in a consonant and y, you usually change the y to i before adding a suffix. Add a suffix to each of these words to form a Unit word.

21. worry
22. likely
23. lively

E. Now try a spelling game. Start by writing a Unit word. Then, by subtracting one letter at a time, write a list of new words until you finally write a word of only one letter. You may rearrange the letters at each step, but you may not add new ones. Look at the example.

atlas → last → sat → at → a

24. In six steps, change the word *adrift* into the word *a*.

25. In seven steps, change the word *astride* into the word *I*.

Using the Dictionary to Spell and Write •
The Parts of a Main Entry

The dictionary is an excellent reference tool. It provides us with a great deal of important information about our language that helps us when we write. In order to condense all this information into one volume, the dictionary is written in a kind of shorthand or code. Understanding this code will help you use the dictionary effectively.

Look at the main entries below. Study the labels as you read the entries.

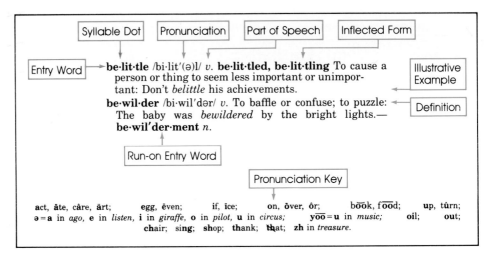

be·lit·tle /bi·lit'(ə)l/ *v.* **be·lit·tled, be·lit·tling** To cause a person or thing to seem less important or unimportant: *Don't belittle his achievements.*

be·wil·der /bi·wil'dər/ *v.* To baffle or confuse; to puzzle: The baby was *bewildered* by the bright lights.—**be·wil'der·ment** *n.*

act, āte, câre, ärt;   egg, ēven;   if, īce;   on, ōver, ôr;   bŏŏk, fōōd;   up, tûrn;
ə = a in *ago,* e in *listen,* i in *giraffe,* o in *pilot,* u in *circus;*   yōō = u in *music;*   oil;   out;
chair;   sing;   shop;   thank;   that;   zh in *treasure.*

A. Find the word *withdrew* in the **Spelling Dictionary.** Then complete these exercises.

1. Under which main entry is *withdrew* listed?

2. Write a sentence using the second definition of *withdraw.*

B. Look up the words *handsome, lengthwise, withhold,* and *worrisome* in the **Spelling Dictionary.** Use the words to complete these exercises.

3. Write the two words that have alternate pronunciations.

4. Write the word that is divided into syllables one way in the written word and another in the pronunciation.

5. Write the word that has a run-on entry word.

Writing on Your Own

Imagine that you are the captain of a ship caught in a storm. Write a journal entry describing the storm and your feelings. Use as many Unit words as you can.

WRITER'S GUIDE For a sample journal entry, turn to page 263.

Spelling on Your Own

Guide words tell you the first and last word on a dictionary page. Copy the pairs of guide words below on a separate sheet of paper. Then write, in alphabetical order, the Unit words that would be found on a dictionary page with each pair of guide words.

actor–bicycle   city–limb   list–wrap

MASTERY WORDS

against
lonesome
neighborhood
ashamed
besides
within

Write the Mastery word that begins with each of these prefixes.

1. be-   **2.** with-   **3.** a- (two words)

Write the Mastery word that ends with the same suffix as each of these words.

4. childhood   **5.** troublesome

Finish these exercises using the Mastery words.

6. Write the Mastery words in alphabetical order.

7. Write a sentence using at least two Mastery words.

BONUS WORDS

aloof
bequeath
abound
withdrawn
tiresome
counterclockwise
cumbersome
belated

Complete these sentences using the Bonus words. Use each word only once.

1. His name was _____ from the list of candidates.

2. Since I forgot your birthday, here's a _____ gift.

3. Mrs. Sanders will _____ her art collection to the museum.

4. Sparrows _____ in the city's parks.

5. This package is too _____ to carry on board the plane.

6. The movie star remained _____ from his fans.

7. Plotting a graph can be a _____ activity.

The prefix *counter-* means "opposite or opposing." Write the definition of *counterclockwise*. Then use a dictionary to find three other words that begin with the prefix *counter-* and use each one in a sentence.

The Sound /ə/

UNIT WORDS

1. competitor
2. strenuous
3. siphon
4. ample
5. tremendous
6. abdomen
7. contagious
8. apparel
9. incidental
10. similar
11. familiar
12. comedian
13. entangle
14. continuous
15. particular
16. intruder
17. courteous
18. sullen
19. peculiar
20. outrageous

The Unit Words

Each of the Unit words has an unaccented final syllable. The vowel sound heard in each final syllable is the weak vowel sound schwa /ə/. Schwa may be written with any vowel letter. In the Unit words, /ə/ is spelled with these letters in the final syllable.

a as in *incidental*
e as in *intruder*
o as in *competitor*
ou as in *tremendous*

Say the words *similar, familiar, particular,* and *peculiar.* They all have the final sounds /ər/, but the sound /y/ is heard before /ər/ in *familiar* and *peculiar.* This sound is spelled with *i*. Remember to include the *i* in words that end with /yər/.

In most of the Unit words that end with /əs/, a vowel letter precedes *ous.* You can tell from the pronunciations of *strenuous, continuous,* and *courteous* what letters come before *ous.* The pronunciations of *contagious* and *outrageous,* on the other hand, provide no clues. The final syllable is pronounced the same in both words, but the spellings are different.

REMEMBER THIS

You won't forget the spelling of *courteous* if you remember that *courteous* originally meant "having the manners of the king's *court.*"

Spelling Practice

A. Complete these exercises using the Unit words.

1. Write the four words that end with /ən/.

2. Write the four words that end with /əl/.

3. Write the two words that end with /yər/.

4. Write the four other words that end with /ər/.

5. Write the two words that have /yo͞o/ before /əs/.

6. Write the word that has /ē/ before /əs/.

7. Write the three other words that end with /əs/.

B. Write the Unit word that is related to each of these words.

8. outrage   **9.** tangle   **10.** continual

11. compete   **12.** courtesy   **13.** comedy

14. intrude   **15.** incident

C. Write a Unit word to complete each of these sentences.

16. When I have a _____ illness, I stay away from everyone.

17. Compared to an ant, a person is _____ in size.

18. The work was so _____ that I didn't think I could last all day.

19. We put our winter wearing _____ back in the closet.

20. Our jackets are _____, but mine has more pockets.

21. The dog's legs were so short that its _____ nearly touched the ground.

Spelling and Language • Synonyms

UNIT WORDS

competitor
strenuous
siphon
—ample
tremendous
abdomen
contagious
apparel
incidental
—similar
—familiar
comedian
—entangle
continuous
particular
intruder
courteous
sullen
peculiar
—outrageous

Words that have the same or nearly the same meaning are **synonyms.** *Bewilder* and *confuse* are synonyms.

You will find a thesaurus in the back of your book. Take a moment to understand its organization and use it when you need a synonym or antonym.

A. Write the Unit word that is a synonym for each of these words.

1. clothing   **2.** strange   **3.** stomach   **4.** polite
5. player   **6.** alike   **7.** sulky   **8.** plentiful

English is a language filled with synonyms. Words borrowed from other languages, invented words, and variations of English words provide a variety of ways to express a thought.

B. Write the Unit word that has a meaning similar to the meanings of the words in each group.

9. everyday, commonplace, known
10. catching, infectious, communicable
11. trespasser, invader, meddler
12. unbelievable, shocking, fantastic

Sometimes you can sharpen your writing by substituting one word for a group of words in a sentence. Look at the sentences below.

The sailors came <u>onto the land</u>.
The sailors came <u>ashore</u>.

C. Write the Unit word that could be substituted for the underlined words in each of these sentences.

13. My watch and yours are <u>just about but not quite the same</u>.
14. Use a tube to <u>draw off</u> the dirty water from the fish tank.
15. You have had <u>more than enough</u> time to finish your report.

Writing on Your Own

Pretend that you have just won a race. Write a letter to a pen pal in another country using some of the Unit words to describe the scene and tell what happened. To help your friend understand what the Unit words mean, define them by using easier synonyms in the sentences, like this: "The course was strenuous, or difficult."

 THESAURUS For help finding synonyms, turn to page 205.

Spelling on Your Own

UNIT WORDS

The Unit words below are misspelled. Write each word correctly.

1. apparal
2. sullin
3. similiar
4. intrudor
5. courtous
6. competiter
7. siphen
8. ampel
9. commedian
10. familar
11. outragous
12. continous
13. contagous
14. particuliar
15. abdomin
16. tremendus
17. strennuous
18. entangel
19. incidentel
20. peculier

MASTERY WORDS

Write the Mastery words that end with these sounds. Then answer the questions.

1. /əl/
2. /ən/
3. /ər/ (two words)
4. /əs/ (two words)
5. Which word has /ən/ and /ər/?
6. Which word has /ər/ and /əs/?
7. Which word has the sound /ē/?
8. Which word has double consonant letters?

Synonyms are words that mean the same or nearly the same thing. Write the Mastery word that is a synonym for each of these words.

9. mistake
10. captive
11. strange
12. unselfish

13. Use one of these words in a sentence: *melon, example.*

> prisoner
> example
> generous
> melon
> error
> curious

BONUS WORDS

Write the Bonus word that is related in meaning to each of these words. Then use each Bonus word in a sentence.

1. pedal
2. pore
3. loiterer
4. futility
5. anonymity
6. oblivious
7. embassy

"Hey, good buddy, copy you wall-to-wall." In CB jargon this means "I hear you loud and clear." A **jargon** is a special vocabulary used by a particular group or profession. List at least three words or phrases that are part of a jargon. Then define each one.

> futile
> pedestal
> anonymous
> porous
> loiter
> ambassador
> oblivion
> jargon

11

3 Confusing Pronunciations

UNIT WORDS

1. restaurant
2. jewelry
3. congratulations
4. missile
5. laboratory
6. twelfth
7. veteran
8. kindergarten
9. literature
10. reference
11. mischievous
12. frightening
13. strength
14. temperature
15. memorable
16. lightning
17. separate
18. boundary
19. beverage
20. privilege

The Unit Words

In the early 1940's, a linguist named Henry Lee Smith, Jr., conducted a program on radio station WOR in New York City entitled "Where Are You From?" Mr. Smith amazed complete strangers by telling them where they were born and brought up. He was able to do this because he was a linguist, a person who studies language and speech patterns. By listening for regional accents and dialects, Mr. Smith could identify a person's origin. How do you pronounce *aunt* or *ten*? Your pronunciation will probably tell something about where you were born or live now.

The way you pronounce the words in this Unit word list may also give away your location, and it may cause spelling problems, too. Do you say /strenth/, /strength/, or /strengkth/? If you say /strenth/, you probably forget to include the letter *g* when you write the word.

To help you spell the Unit words correctly, pronounce each syllable as you say the word. Do not add or leave out syllables or sounds.

REMEMBER THIS

To lighten something is to make it lighter. The *ing* form is spelled *lightening*. There is no *e* in *lightning* that flashes from the sky.

Spelling Practice

A. Most dictionaries give two pronunciations for several of the Unit words. Write the Unit word for each pair of pronunciations. Then write the pronunciation you use.

Be careful! This /bev'ər·ij/ has a high /tem'pər·ə·chər/.

	I	**II**
1.	/tem'pər·ə·chər/	/tem'prə·chər/
2.	/boun'də·rē/	/boun'drē/
3.	/sep'ər·it/	/sep'rit/
4.	/bev'ər·ij/	/bev'rij/
5.	priv'ə·lij/	/priv'lij/
6.	/lit'ər·ə·chər/	/lit'rə·chər/
7.	/res'tə·ränt/	/res'tränt/
8.	/vet'ər·ən/	/vet'rən/

B. Knowing the root of a word is often a clue to the way the word is spelled. The original letters usually remain, although the pronunciation may have changed. Write the Unit word that comes from each of these words.

9. the German word *garten,* meaning "garden"

10. the Latin word *gratus,* meaning "pleasing"

11. the Latin word *labor,* meaning "work"

12. the Old English word *twelf,* meaning "twelve"

13. the Latin word *missilis,* meaning "something thrown"

C. Add a suffix to each of these words to form a Unit word. You may need to drop or change a letter in the base word before adding the ending.

14. jewel   **15.** mischief   **16.** memory   **17.** refer

D. Complete these exercises using the Unit words.

18. Write the two-syllable word meaning "a flash of light."

19. Write the three-syllable word that means "scary."

20. Many words end with a **consonant digraph,** two different consonant letters written together that represent one consonant sound. Write the Unit word that ends with two consonant digraphs. Then write one other English word that ends with the same two digraphs.

13

Proofreading • A Science Report

Anne wrote this report for her science class. Now she must correct her work and write her final copy. Anne made nine spelling mistakes and five mistakes in capitalization. Read the science report carefully.

1. Find Anne's spelling mistakes.

2. Find her capitalization mistakes.

What a frightning experience it must have been for our early ancestors as they watched an electrical storm. They must have been biwildered by the great flashes of light and the tremendis booms of thunder that rolled across the sky.

It was not until benjamin franklin conducted his memarable experiment in 1752 that the mystery of the origins of lightening was solved. After attaching an iron key to a silk kite, Franklin sent the kite aloof during a thunderstorm. lightning traveled down the wire. As Ben Franklin touched the key, an electrical shock raced through his finger.

Today Scientists believe that electricity is created in a cloud as its water droplets become charged and then seperat into layers. The flashes of lightning occur between negatively and positively charged areas. These flashes may appear in the sky in a perticular shape, such as a zigzag, a chain, or a ball. The flash may also be seen as a solid sheet of light traveling across the Horizon. Scientists use generators to produce lightning for study in a labratory setting.

3. Now write the nine misspelled words correctly. Then write the words with capitalization mistakes correctly.

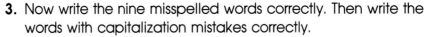

Writing on Your Own

Imagine that your club is presenting awards to two outstanding members of your community at a dinner. You have been asked to introduce the winners at the party. One is an expert at launching space vehicles and the other is a respected kindergarten teacher. Write a short comparison paragraph to introduce them. Tell how their work is similar and compare the importance of their fields. Use six or more Unit words in your speech.

WRITER'S GUIDE For a sample comparison paragraph, turn to page 260.

Benjamin Franklin

Spelling on Your Own

Write each Unit word. Next to each word, write the number of syllables you hear as you pronounce it. Check your syllable counts in a dictionary.

MASTERY WORDS

drowned
favorite
scenery
nuclear
library
probably

Write the Mastery word that is related in meaning to each word.

1. probable   **2.** scene   **3.** drown
4. favor   **5.** librarian

Finish these exercises using the Mastery words.

6. Write the name of a kind of energy.

7. Write the word that has only one syllable.

Lisa wrote this letter to her friend Chris.

8. Find Lisa's six spelling mistakes.

June 4, 19____

Dear Chris,

    For my last diving lesson, we went to my favrite bay. I wore tanks that looked like the hull of a nuclar sub. You should see the scenry there. It looks just like the pictures in liberry books. When I came up, I probly looked like a dround rat!

       Love,

       Lisa

---

9. Write the six misspelled words correctly.

BONUS WORDS

temperamental
perspiration
breadth
preferable
incidentally
introductory
pursuit
disastrous

Write the Bonus word that is related to each word.

1. pursue   **2.** prefer   **3.** temper   **4.** disaster
5. perspire   **6.** incident   **7.** introduce

Don't forget to pronounce the *d* in *breadth*. *Breadth* comes from the Middle English word *brede,* "broad." Look up the words *bread* and *breath* in a dictionary. What words do they come from? Use *breadth, bread,* and *breath* in a paragraph.

The /ə/ and Shifting Accents

UNIT WORDS

1. record
2. duplicate
3. project
4. associate
5. exhibition
6. exhibit
7. atom
8. atomic
9. residence
10. reside
11. admiration
12. admire
13. disposition
14. dispose
15. distribution
16. distribute
17. civilization
18. civilize
19. composition
20. compose

The Unit Words

The word *record* is pronounced two different ways. Read these sentences.

> The group is working on a new <u>record</u>.
> They will <u>record</u> it next week.

Used as a noun, *record* is pronounced /rek′ərd/ and has a schwa /ə/ in the unaccented second syllable. Used as a verb, it is pronounced /ri·kôrd′/ and has the sounds /ôr/ in the accented second syllable. Any vowel letter can spell the schwa sound. To help you remember the spelling for the schwa in /rek′ərd/, think of the vowel sound you hear in the accented second syllable for the verb /ri·kôrd′/. The /ôr/ reminds you that /rek′ərd/ is spelled with **o.**

You can use the same method to spell /ə/ in many words. To spell a word with /ə/, think of another word with the same root. You can often hear the vowel sound clearly. Look at this pair of words, for example.

/rez′<u>e</u>·dəns/   /ri·zīd′/
res<u>i</u>dence   res<u>i</u>de

To spell the unaccented second syllable of *residence,* listen to the vowel sound you hear in the accented second syllable of *reside,* /ī/. The /ī/ in *reside* reminds you that the first /ə/ in *residence* is spelled with an **i.**

16

Spelling Practice

A. Write the spelling for each pronunciation. Then write the related Unit word that helps you decide how to spell the underlined /ə/ in each pronunciation.

1. /ad′mə·rā′shən/   **2.** /ek′sə·bish′ən/   **3.** /dis′trə·byōō′shən/

4. /dis′pə·zish′ən/   **5.** /siv′ə·lə·zā′shən/   **6.** /rez′ə·dəns/

7. /kom′pə·zish′ən/   **8.** /at′əm/

B. The pronunciations of some words change depending on how the words are used in sentences. Write the letter of the pronunciation that best completes each sentence. Then write the Unit word that matches the pronunciation. For example, the answer for **9** is *b–*record.

a. /ri·kôrd′/   **b.** /rek′ərd/

9. Hank Aaron holds the lifetime _____ for home runs.

10. Myra will _____ the attendance today.

c. /ə·sō′shē·āt/   **d.** /ə·sō′shē·ət/

11. I can't _____ his face with his name.

12. Dr. Wallace's _____ is on call this weekend.

e. /prə·jekt′/   **f.** /proj′ekt/

13. I am working on my science _____ tonight.

14. You must _____ your voice so that we can hear you.

g. /d(y)ōō′plə·kāt/   **h.** /d(y)ōō′plə·kət/

15. Please _____ these papers on the copy machine.

16. The bank keeps a _____ record of your deposits.

Hank Aaron

C. Write the Unit word that is related in meaning to each group of words.

17. home, dwelling   **18.** create, make up   **19.** appreciation, approval

20. divide, give out   **21.** character, personality

Spelling and Language • Parts of Speech

Words are the basic ingredients of language. Individual words carry meaning. Often the way a word is used with other words affects the word's meaning. The word *plant,* for example, has several meanings. You need to know how *plant* is used in a sentence before you can determine its exact meaning. We classify words into parts of speech according to their function in a sentence. Three of the parts of speech are defined below.

Noun   A word used to name a person, place, thing, or idea

Verb   A word used to express an action or state of being

Adjective   A word used to describe a noun or pronoun

Complete each sentence using Unit words. Write *noun, verb,* or *adjective* above each word you write to show its function in the sentence.

1. Michael will ____ the writing paper so that you may begin to work on your English ____.

2. A nucleus and one or more electrons ____ an ____.

3. The blizzard of 1979 brought a ____ snowfall to our area.

4. Archaeologists studying early Egyptian ____ learned that a pyramid served as a tomb and not as a royal ____.

5. I greatly ____ anyone who can wake up with a sunny ____ on such a cold and rainy morning.

Writing on Your Own

Pretend you are a teacher planning a social studies contest for the students in your school. Write a how-to paragraph about the contest. Explain what kinds of projects are eligible, how students can enter, how their work will be judged, and what the prizes will be. Use six or more Unit words in the contest guidelines. Choose at least one word that can be both a noun and a verb. Use the word in at least two sentences to show the different meanings.

WRITER'S GUIDE For a sample how-to paragraph, turn to page 259.

18

Spelling on Your Own

UNIT WORDS

Write the Unit words in alphabetical order. Then try to write a synonym next to each of the Unit words. Several of the words may be used as a noun or as a verb. For these words, try to write a synonym for each use of the word.

MASTERY WORDS

invitation
preparation
confidence
dividend
information
graduate

Each Mastery word has the schwa /ə/ sound heard at the beginning of *above.* Usually, this sound is not heard clearly when you say a word. In addition, /ə/ may be spelled with any vowel letter. Sometimes thinking of a related word will help you decide which vowel represents /ə/.

Write the Mastery word that is related in meaning to each word.

1. prepare **2.** inform **3.** graduation
4. divide **5.** invite **6.** confide

Remember that **guide words** are the two words in dark print or color at the top of a dictionary page. Guide words tell you the first and last words on the page.

7. Write the two Mastery words that would be the guide words if the six Mastery words were the only words listed on one dictionary page.

The word *graduate* may be used as a noun or as a verb. Look up *graduate* in the **Spelling Dictionary.**

8. Write a sentence using *graduate* as a noun.
9. Write a sentence using *graduate* as a verb.

BONUS WORDS

delegate
articulate
deliberate
alternate
inspiration
inspire
coincidence
coincide

1. Four Bonus words may be used as more than one part of speech. Write the words. Then write sentences using each word as noun, verb, or adjective. You will need to write nine sentences in all.

2. Two Bonus words are formed by adding suffixes to two other Bonus words. Use all four words in a paragraph.

3. The word *inspire* has the Latin root *spir,* "breathe." *Inspire* often means "breathe life into." Write as many other words as you can that have the root *spir.* Then use three of the words in sentences.

5 More Shifting Accents

UNIT WORDS

1. custody
2. custodian
3. minor
4. minority
5. abolition
6. abolish
7. practical
8. practicality
9. diplomat
10. diplomacy
11. moral
12. morality
13. human
14. humanity
15. comparable
16. compare
17. consolation
18. console
19. moderate
20. moderation

P.S. 26 TAKEN INTO CUSTODY

NEW YORK CITY, March 28 —Annette Higgins has been appointed custodian of the annex of Public School 26 in the Bronx today. She is the only female custodian in the New York City public school system. Mrs. Higgins and her staff are responsible for maintaining the school building, its heating system, and the outside grounds.

The Unit Words

When you read the headline, what did you think had happened to P.S. 26? The use of *custody* in the headline is a play on words. The word *custody* suggests something different from "care taking." But in fact *custody* and *custodian* are related words. They both came from the Latin word *custos*, "guardian." Words that have the same root often have related meanings and similar spellings.

When you are uncertain of the spelling of a word, remember that a related word can often help you. Look at these words.

cus /tə/ dy   cus /tō/ dian

The sound /ō/ in the second syllable of *custodian* tells you that the /ə/ in the second syllable of *custody* is spelled with **o**.

CUS·to·dy
cus·TO·di·an

Spelling Practice

A. Write the spelling for each of these pronunciations. Then write the Unit word that helps you identify the letter that spells the underlined /ə/ in each pronunciation.

1. /môr′əl/   **2.** /dip′lə•mat/   **3.** /prak′ti•kəl/   **4.** /ab′ə•lish′ən/

B. Complete these sentences using the Unit words.

5. Playing on a school team is not _____ to playing on a professional team.

6. As a _____ for losing in the school election, Tara's friends treated her to a pizza.

7. Eating salt in _____ will benefit your health.

8. Only a _____ of the student population can walk to school.

9. That store sells expensive clothing, but this store has clothing at _____ prices.

C. Write the Unit word for each of these clues. If you do the puzzle correctly, the circled letters will spell a Unit word.

10. examine for similarities   Ⓞ __ __ __ __ __ __

11. a person   __ Ⓞ __ __ __

12. comfort another   __ __ __ Ⓞ __ __ __

13. useful; functional   __ __ __ __ Ⓞ __ __ __ __

14. not important   __ __ __ Ⓞ __

15. a caretaker   __ __ __ __ __ __ Ⓞ __ __ __

16. the human race   __ __ __ __ __ __ __ Ⓞ

17. Write the Unit word spelled by the circled letters.

Don't confuse the words *moral* and *morale* /mə•ral′/. The word *morale* means "a state of mind, especially concerning courage, confidence, and enthusiasm."

D. Complete each of these sentences using *moral* or *morale*.

18. The coach tried to raise the team's _____.

19. His parents had taught him to lead a _____ life.

UNIT WORDS

custody
custodian
minor
minority
abolition
abolish
practical
practicality
diplomat
diplomacy
moral
morality
human
humanity
comparable
compare
consolation
console
moderate
moderation

rare¹ /râr/ *adj.*
  rar·er, rar·est
  Not often seen or
  found.
  —**rare'ly** *adv.*
rare² /râr/ *adj.*
  rar·er, rar·est
  Not cooked thor-
  oughly.

Using the Dictionary to Spell and Write •
Pronunciations and Homographs

Each entry word in a dictionary is followed by a pronunciation. The **pronunciation** represents the sounds of the spoken word.

The dictionary shows alternate pronunciations for some words. Sometimes these pronunciations reflect differences in regional speech. In other cases, the pronunciation varies according to the word's part of speech. The words *separate* and *moderate,* for example, may be used as either verbs or adjectives. You pronounce each of these words one way when you use it as a verb and another way when you use it as an adjective.

A. Look up *separate* and *moderate* in the **Spelling Dictionary.** Complete each sentence pair using the correct pronunciation of *separate* or *moderate.* Write the letter of the correct pronunciation by the sentence.
  a. /mod'ə·rāt/   **b.** /mod'ər·ət/
1. The chairperson should be someone with _____ views on the topic.
2. Susan was asked to _____ the class discussion.
  c. /sep'ə·rāt/   **d.** /sep'ər·it/
3. I used dividers to _____ my class notes.
4. Last year I used two _____ notebooks.

B. Write the Unit word that fits each set of pronunciations.
5. /hyo͞o·man'ə·tē/ or /yo͞o·man'ə·tē/   **6.** /kom'pər·ə·bəl/ or /kom'prə·bəl/

Homographs are words that are spelled alike but have different meanings and sometimes different word histories. The words *rare,* "valuable," and *rare,* "not well cooked," are homographs. Sometimes homographs are pronounced differently, as in *minute,* "sixty seconds," and *minute,* "very tiny."

C. Look up *moral* and *console* in the **Spelling Dictionary.** On a separate sheet of paper, use each homograph of *moral* in a sentence that clearly shows its meaning. Then write a sentence using *console* when it is pronounced /kən·sōl'/.

Writing on Your Own

Imagine that you are a community planner. You are working to help a community where medical care and clean drinking water are urgently needed. However, you can do only one thing at a time. Decide which problem you would tackle first. Then write several paragraphs in which you describe both courses of action and try to persuade the members of the community to support your plan. Use at least eight of the Unit words in your persuasive paragraphs.

Spelling on Your Own

Copy this chart. Then write each Unit word under the correct heading. You will have to write some words more than once. For example, *moderate* will be written under **Verbs** and **Adjectives.**

Nouns	Verbs	Adjectives

MASTERY WORDS

Write the Mastery word that is related in meaning to each word.

1. nationality   **2.** conserve   **3.** political
4. medical   **5.** industrial   **6.** preside

We usually do not capitalize the word *president.* However, when the word refers to the head of a nation, it is often capitalized. Finish each sentence using the word *president.*

7. Antonio was elected _____ of the class.

8. The senators met with the _____ in the Oval Office.

One Mastery word is misspelled in each of these groups of words. Write it correctly.

9. drowned, consavation, graduate

10. against, generous, nationel

11. favorite, medacine, information

12. prisoner, indistry, lonesome

medicine
national
president
conservation
industry
politics

BONUS WORDS

Complete each sentence using related Bonus words.

1. The book has an _____ of the _____ Amelia Earhart and her airplane.

2. _____ to the flood, funds for a dam had a low _____.

3. A _____ film was made about a rare _____.

E pluribus unum is the motto of the United States. These Latin words mean "One out of many." The words *plural, plurality,* and *pluribus* have the root *plur.* The English words *plus* and *surplus* also come from this root. Write a definition for *plural, plurality, plus,* and *surplus.* Then use each word in a sentence.

plural
plurality
document
documentary
illustration
illustrious
prior
priority

Review

Follow these steps when you are unsure of how to spell a word.

- **Say** the word. Recall when you have heard the word used. Think about what it means.
- **Look** at the word. Find any prefixes, suffixes, or other word parts you know. Think about other words that are related in meaning and spelling. Try to picture the word in your mind.
- **Spell** the word to yourself. Think about the way each sound is spelled. Notice any unusual spelling.
- **Write** the word while looking at it. Check the way you have formed your letters. If you have not written the word clearly or correctly, write it again.
- **Check** your learning. Cover the word and write it. If you did not spell the word correctly, practice these steps until the word becomes your own.

UNIT 1

astride
bewilder
handsome
otherwise
withdrew
likelihood
lengthwise
withhold
livelihood
withstand

UNIT 1   Follow the directions using words from Unit 1.
Write the words that include these prefixes or suffixes.

1. a-
2. -wise (two words)
3. be-
4. with- (three words)
5. -hood (two words)
6. -some

Write the word that is a synonym for each of the following.

7. confuse
8. attractive
9. removed
10. income
11. keep back

UNIT 2

tremendous
comedian
similar
incidental
contagious
competitor
familiar
continuous
particular
outrageous

UNIT 2   Using words from Unit 2, write the words that end with these sounds.

12. /əs/ (four words)
13. /lər/ (two words)
14. /yər/
15. /ər/
16. /əl/
17. /ən/

UNIT 3 One Unit 3 word is misspelled in each of these groups. Find the word. Then write the misspelled word correctly.

18. otherwise   frightning   incidental

19. comedian   jewlry   particular

20. labratory   contagious   familiar

21. beverage   vetran   withhold

22. temprature   twelfth   boundary

23. seprate   outrageous   otherwise

24. project   restaraunt   similar

25. withdraw   strenth   familiar

26. litrature   moral   atomic

27. record   incidental   congradulations

UNIT 3

laboratory
frightening
restaurant
congratulations
separate
jewelry
veteran
literature
strength
temperature

UNIT 4 Follow the directions using words from Unit 4. Write the words that are from the same word family as the words below.

28. reside   **29.** civilize

30. compose   **31.** admire

32. exhibit

33. Write the word that adds *-ic* to a noun to make an adjective.

34. Write the word that is a verb related to the noun *distribution.*

UNIT 4

exhibition
residence
composition
civilization
project
atomic
admiration
distribute
record
duplicate

Project, record, and *duplicate* can be used as nouns or verbs. Use these Unit 4 words to complete the sentences below. Then write *n.* or *v.* by the word to show how it was used.

35. I will ____ the report for my English ____.

36. We will ____ the film on the screen and play the ____ that goes with it.

37. We need another tape player to ____ a ____ of my favorite song.

25

Complete each sentence with a word that is related to the underlined word in each sentence.

38. The <u>practicality</u> of a picnic lunch makes it ____ to take the car.

39. <u>Humanity</u> must conserve the earth's resources for the future of the ____ race.

40. Aesop taught <u>morality</u> by telling a story with a ____.

41. A ____ of players will make the <u>minor</u> leagues.

42. The ____ prize did not <u>console</u> the loser.

43. The <u>diplomat</u> was not known for his ____.

44. The <u>custodian</u> had ____ of his grandchild.

45. The price of the TV was ____, but the quality did not <u>compare</u>.

46. The <u>abolitionists</u> worked to ____ slavery in the United States.

47. If you are eating in <u>moderation</u>, you will take only a ____ amount of food.

WORDS IN TIME

The word *human* had somewhat humble beginnings. It actually is related to the word *humble. Human* comes from the Latin word *humanus,* which is related to the word *humus,* meaning "earth or ground." What do you think the people who used the word *humanus* considered essential to human life?

Spelling and Reading
An Interview

Read the following interview. Notice the questions the interviewer asks.

Clown magazine spoke with comedian Hardy Harhar in his California beachfront home. Although Harhar is known for his outrageous behavior and costumes, offstage we found him to be a quiet, handsome man with surprisingly low-key taste in clothes.

Clown: How did you decide to make laughter your livelihood, Hardy?

Harhar: Andrea, I've always had tremendous admiration for people who bring joy to this world. I like to laugh myself, and laughter, as they say, is contagious. So I decided I'd spread joy by making people laugh.

Clown: That's wonderful, Hardy. Tell me, what do you think of the state of comedy today?

Harhar: Well, some of these younger comics are tremendous. They put the veterans to shame. But I'm a competitor. I'll survive. I'll tell you, though, at my age you can't tour as much. Continuous travel wears you down.

Clown: Do you get tired of hotel rooms and restaurant food?

Harhar: Yes, but the admiration of my fans makes up for it. They're my one big consolation.

Clown: I understand you have a new project. Can you tell me about it?

Harhar: I'm making a video, which I hope to distribute next year.

Clown: Congratulations! Well, Hardy, how about giving me a sample of your humor?

Harhar: Sorry, Andrea. I'd tell a joke, but I've got to make like a tree and leave!

Write the answers to these questions.

1. What reason does Hardy Harhar give for becoming a comedian?
2. Why does Hardy Harhar's low-key taste in clothes surprise the interviewer?
3. How does Harhar use his sense of humor to end the interview?
4. Why do you think Harhar chose a video as his next project?

Underline the review words in your answers. Check to see that you spelled the words correctly.

Spelling and Writing
An Interview

Words to Help You Write

otherwise
likelihood
livelihood
tremendous
familiar
continuous
congratulations
separate
strength
residence
project
admiration
practical
diplomacy

Think and Discuss

Many people like to read what a famous person has to say. To provide this kind of information, a writer conducts an interview with the person. An interview is a conversation in which the writer asks questions and the other person gives answers. The writer then records what was said in the interview in a special kind of article. Look back at the interview on page 27. Who is the subject of the interview? Why might people be interested in this person?

An interview often begins with a paragraph of general information that describes the subject and the setting of the interview. What information does the writer give in the introductory paragraph on page 27? Notice that the rest of the article presents only questions and answers, with labels to show who is speaking. This is called a question-and-answer format. What might be some of the advantages of this format?

A good interview requires careful preparation. First the writer must make an appointment with the subject and find out how much time will be allowed for the interview. Next the writer needs to plan questions that will draw out the information the audience is interested in. Look at the questions the interviewer asks on page 27. Why do you think the writer felt readers would be interested in these questions?

As the subject is interviewed, the writer takes careful notes on the answers he or she gives. In a question-and-answer format, the answers are the exact words of the subject. Why is this important?

Apply

Ask one of your classmates to pose as a well-known character from a book, and conduct an **interview** with him or her. Write the results of the interview for a class newspaper. Follow the writing guidelines on the next page.

Prewriting

Think about what you'd like to ask a well-known character from a book.
- Make a list of questions you want to ask.
- Ask a classmate to pretend to be the character.
- Arrange a time to interview your classmate.
- Conduct the interview. Take notes on the answers your subject gives.

Composing

Use the notes from your interview to write the first draft of an article for a class newspaper. Use a question-and-answer format.
- Write a paragraph of general information. Tell when and where you conducted the interview and whom you interviewed.
- Record the questions you asked during the interview.
- Record your subject's answers as accurately as possible.
- Look back at the notes from your interview. Have you left out any of your questions or the subject's answers?

Revising

Read your article and show it to a classmate. Follow these guidelines to improve your work. Use the editing and proofreading marks on this page to indicate corrections.

Editing

- Make sure your questions are relevant. Do they draw out the information you and your readers would most like to know about the character?
- Make sure you recorded your subject's answers accurately.

Proofreading

- Check your spelling and correct any mistakes.
- Check your capitalization and punctuation.

 WRITER'S GUIDE If you need help with capitalization or punctuation, turn to pages 268 and 269.

Copy your story onto clean paper. Write carefully and neatly.

Publishing

Share your interview with your classmates. Compare the questions and answers in your interview with those in the interviews your classmates conducted.

Editing and Proofreading Marks	
≡	capitalize
⊙	make a period
∧	add something
⋏	add a comma
⅋ ⅋	add quotation marks
⌿	take something away
◯	spell correctly
¶	indent the paragraph
/	make a lowercase letter
∿ tr	transpose

7 Plurals

UNIT WORDS

1. antennas
2. alumni
3. alumnae
4. crises
5. parentheses
6. formulas
7. indexes
8. data
9. pastries
10. personalities
11. authorities
12. theories
13. strategies
14. allergies
15. raspberries
16. mysteries
17. essays
18. surveys
19. attorneys
20. displays

The Unit Words

The word *antenna* has two plural forms. Look at these sentences.

> Television antennas crowded the skyline.

> The ant waved its antennae excitedly.

Antenna is a word borrowed from Latin. The most common way to form the plural of a Latin or Greek noun in English is to add *s* or *es: antenna—antennas.* However, when you use *antenna* in its more specialized scientific sense, you keep the original Latin plural form: *antenna— antennae.*

Several other Latin and Greek words, such as *formula* and *index,* also have two plural forms. The plurals of these words are usually written as *formulas* and *indexes,* but you may occasionally see *formulae* or *indices* used.

For some Latin and Greek words, the original forms are preferred. The words *crisis, alumnus* ("male graduate"), *alumna* ("female graduate"), and *datum* are examples. The plurals of these words are *crises, alumni, alumnae,* and *data.*

Remember these rules for forming the plural of nouns that end with *y.*

1. Add *s* to words that end with a vowel and *y.*

2. Otherwise, change *y* to *i* and add *es.*

30

Spelling Practice

A. Write the plural form of each of these Latin and Greek words. Then answer the question.

1. index
2. formula
3. crisis
4. datum
5. alumnus
6. alumna
7. parenthesis
8. What are the two plural forms of *antenna*?

B. Write the Unit word that is a synonym for each of these words. Then write the singular form of each Unit word you wrote.

9. lawyers
10. exhibits
11. compositions
12. overviews
13. tactics

C. Complete this spoof of a nursery tale using Unit words that end with *ies.*

One of the world's great __14__ was solved when the local __15__ discovered who had stolen the __16__ baked by the Queen of Hearts all on a summer's day. For hour upon hour, the King's ministers discussed their learned __17__ about how the crime had been committed. Noted detectives were called in to provide foolproof __18__ for capturing the thief. Psychologists, tests in hand, sought to detect criminal tendencies in the __19__ of the palace staff members.

In the end, it was the Knave of Hearts's own __20__ that gave him away. Loud sneezes echoed through the marble halls. The sergeant-at-arms quickly traced the violent explosions to the pantry. There sat the embarrassed knave, his face and hands stained bright red by the juice of the __21__ that had filled the tarts. And thus the case was closed!

Spelling and Language •
Possessive Nouns and Pronouns

UNIT WORDS

antennas
alumni
alumnae
crises
parentheses
formulas
indexes
data
pastries
personalities
authorities
theories
strategies
allergies
raspberries
mysteries
essays
surveys
attorneys
displays

The **possessive** form of a word shows ownership. To form the possessive of a singular noun, you add an apostrophe and s.

Maria's jewelry   Les's record

To form the possessive of a plural noun ending with s, you add only an apostrophe.

the Thomases' residence
the comedians' jokes

To form the possessive of a plural noun that does not end with s, you add an apostrophe and s.

the women's businesses

A. Write the plural form of each of these nouns. Then write the plural possessive form. For example, the correct answer for **1** would be *competitors* and *competitors'*.

1. competitor   2. attorney   3. alumnus
4. authority   5. alumna   6. laboratory

B. Possessive personal pronouns do not need an apostrophe. Rewrite each sentence using the correct spelling of the possessive pronoun.

7. The insect injured (its, it's) antennae.
8. Those mysteries are (her's, hers).
9. (Whose, Who's) essays are on my desk?

Writing on Your Own

Write a business letter to your city council to tell why you nominate "Betty's Bookstore and Cafe" for the year's Best Business Award. Include several possessive nouns and pronouns in your letter. These Unit words may provide ideas for your letter: *pastries, personalities, raspberries, mysteries,* and *essays.*

 WRITER'S GUIDE For a sample business letter, turn to page 262.

Spelling on Your Own

On a separate sheet of paper, complete these exercises using the Unit words.

1. Write the seven Unit words that form the plural by adding *s* or *es*.
2. Write the eight words that form the plural by changing *y* to *i* and adding *es*.
3. Write the three words that have plural forms that end in *a, ae,* or *i.*
4. Write the two words that have a singular form and plural form both ending in *s.*

MASTERY WORDS

groceries
valleys
chimneys
diaries
movies
highways

Write the Mastery word that is the plural form of each of these words.

1. valley   2. diary   3. grocery
4. highway   5. chimney   6. movie

Remember that careful pronunciation can help you spell a word correctly.

7. Write the letter that matches the correct pronunciation of a word.

a. /chim′in·ē/   b. /chim′nē/

8. Now write the word that matches the pronunciation.

A verb must agree with its subject in number. You must use a plural verb with a plural subject. Here's an example: "The children are hungry." Choose the word in ( ) that is correct in each sentence. Then write the sentence.

9. Two movies (is, are) playing at the drive-in.
10. The two highways (meets, meet) near my house.

BONUS WORDS

criteria
hypotheses
trivia
buoys
celebrities
tributaries
appendixes
decoys

Write the Bonus word that is based on the same base word as each of these words. Then use each Bonus word in a sentence.

1. trivial   2. contribute   3. celebrate   4. critic
5. buoyant   6. hypothetical   7. suspend

A decoy is a person or object used as a lure to trap prey. Write a short story entitled "The Decoy."

8 Words with *-ery* and *-ary*

UNIT WORDS

1. extraordinary
2. revolutionary
3. contemporary
4. pottery
5. shrubbery
6. elementary
7. voluntary
8. surgery
9. cemetery
10. imaginary
11. secondary
12. archery
13. gallery
14. embroidery
15. honorary
16. refinery
17. hereditary
18. flattery
19. primary
20. hatchery

The Unit Words

Adjectives are words that flash in bright lights across the American landscape. They jump out at us from newspapers, billboards, and the television screen. Adjectives are used frequently by advertising copywriters and salespeople. Have you seen phrases similar to these?

> extraordinary cleaning power
>
> revolutionary design concept
>
> a fresh, contemporary fragrance

Adjectives are often formed by adding a suffix to a root or base word. The suffix *-ary* is an adjective-forming suffix.

The suffix *-ery* is a noun-forming suffix. It sometimes adds the meaning "a place where something is done." A refinery is a place where a crude material such as petroleum is refined. The suffix *-ery* can also mean "the act or art of." Embroidery is the art of embroidering.

REMEMBER THIS

The word *extraordinary* is usually pronounced /ik•strôr′də•ner′ē/, but it is made up of two words that are very familiar: *extra* + *ordinary*. The Latin word *extra* means "beyond." An extraordinary event, then, is beyond the ordinary.

Spelling Practice

A. Write the Unit word that is a synonym for each of these words.

1. needlework **2.** simple **3.** bushes

4. compliments **5.** first **6.** graveyard

B. Write the Unit word that has the same root as each of these groups.

7. volunteer, voluntarily **8.** imagine, imagination

9. inherit, heredity **10.** refine, refinement

11. surgeon, surgical **12.** honor, honorable

C. Write the Unit word that fits each definition.

13. a sport using bows and arrows

14. a breeding place for fish

15. coming after the first one

D. Complete these paragraphs using the Unit words.

Maria Montoya Martinez, an American Indian potter, spent most of her ninety-four years in San Ildefonso Pueblo, New Mexico. However, the beauty of her blackware __16__ is known throughout the world. In recognition of her __17__ talent, Maria Martinez received many awards.

Maria became seriously interested in making pots in 1907 when she first saw the black pottery shards dug up by archaeologists near her home. Although Maria's work is based on the traditional shapes and designs of the old pots, her work has a sleek, __18__ look. Julian Martinez, Maria's husband, is credited with discovering the __19__ process that re-creates the black color of the ancient shards. Sometimes __20__ creatures or other designs are painted on the pots before they are fired. Someday you may have the opportunity to see an exhibition of Maria Martinez's pottery in a museum or an art __21__.

Maria Montoya Martinez

35

Using the Dictionary to Spell and Write •
Multiple Definitions

UNIT WORDS

extraordinary
revolutionary
contemporary
pottery
shrubbery
elementary
voluntary
surgery
cemetery
imaginary
secondary
archery
gallery
embroidery
honorary
refinery
hereditary
flattery
primary
hatchery

Many entry words in the dictionary have more than one definition. Each definition is numbered. Most dictionaries arrange the definitions so that the most common meaning is given first. But the most common meaning may not be the one that fits the context of the sentence you are reading or writing. So you must keep searching until you find the correct meaning.

A. Look up the word *revolutionary* in the **Spelling Dictionary.** Write the number of the definition that matches the meaning of *revolutionary* in each of these sentences.

1. Henry Ford's use of the assembly line was *revolutionary.*
2. In 1776, the patriot leaders signed a *revolutionary* document.
3. *Revolutionaries* gathered to plan their strategy.
4. The *Revolutionary* War began in Massachusetts.
5. The *revolutionary* motion of the carousel made me dizzy.

B. Now look up the word *compose.* Write the number of the definition that matches the meaning of *compose* in each sentence.

6. Mozart began to *compose* music before he was five years old.
7. After forgetting my lines, I *composed* myself and began again.
8. Wood looks solid, but it is *composed* of millions of tiny atoms.
9. The lawyer was *composed* as he spoke before the jury.

A dictionary often provides an illustrative sentence or example after the definition of a difficult word or concept. The **illustrative sentence** or **example** gives you a further clue to the meaning of the word.

C. Look up *elementary* and *contemporary* in the **Spelling Dictionary.**

10. Write an illustrative sentence for the second definition of *elementary.*
11. Write an illustrative sentence for the third definition of *contemporary.*

Wolfgang Amadeus Mozart as a child

Writing on Your Own

Write several paragraphs for a class booklet called "Careers." Choose at least four careers and discuss the skills they require and the education needed. Use as many Unit words as you can. Choose at least one word with multiple definitions. Use the word at least twice in your paragraphs to show the different meanings of the word.

WRITER'S GUIDE For help revising your paragraphs, use the checklist on page 256.

Spelling on Your Own

UNIT WORDS

The letters *ary* or *ery* are missing from the Unit words below. Decide on the correct spelling and write each word on a separate sheet of paper.

1. element___   2. hatch___   3. volunt___   4. imagin___
5. shrubb___   6. flatt___   7. second___   8. honor___
9. heredit___   10. refin___   11. surg___   12. contempor___
13. embroid___   14. gall___   15. pott___   16. extraordin___
17. prim___   18. cemet___   19. arch___   20. revolution___

MASTERY WORDS

nursery
machinery
stationery
stationary
vocabulary
temporary

Write the Mastery word for each of these definitions.

1. not long lasting   2. mechanical devices
3. children's room   4. the words you know
5. writing paper   6. not moving

The words *stationery* and *stationary* sound alike, but they are spelled differently. They also have different meanings. Remember that *stationery* and *paper* are both spelled with *er*. It will help you use the correct spelling for the word you mean.

Finish each sentence with the word *stationery* or *stationary*.

7. The bus remained ___ in the traffic jam.

8. Juan bought a new pen at the ___ store.

BONUS WORDS

customary
auxiliary
arbitrary
preliminary
drudgery
bribery
mockery
adversary

Write the Bonus word that is a synonym for each word.

1. toil   2. ridicule   3. unreasoned   4. usual
5. helpful   6. enemy   7. introductory   8. graft

The Latin prefix *pre-* you find in *preliminary* means "before." List at least five other words that begin with *pre-*. Then write sentences using *preliminary* and five of the other words you wrote.

9 Homophones

UNIT WORDS

1. canvas
2. canvass
3. guerrilla
4. gorilla
5. cite
6. site
7. complimentary
8. complementary
9. flare
10. flair
11. peer
12. pier
13. council
14. counsel
15. duel
16. dual
17. hoard
18. horde
19. current
20. currant

MILLER PROMISES TO CANVAS THE NEIGHBORHOOD

The Unit Words

The cartoonist has created a funny image by substituting the word *canvas* for its homophone, *canvass*. **Homophones** are words that sound alike but have different meanings and often are spelled differently. The word *homophone* comes from the Greek word parts *homo*, "same," and *phone*, "sound."

Knowing the roots of homophones can frequently help you decide which spellings and meanings go together. The word *guerrilla*, for example, comes from the Spanish word *guerra*, meaning "war." *Gorilla*, on the other hand, was the name given by the Greeks to a mythical tribe of hairy beings.

The word *site* comes from the Latin word *situs*, "a place." *Situate* also has this root. *Cite* comes from the Latin *citare*, "to summon or rouse." *Excite* is a related word.

REMEMBER THIS

You won't forget the spelling of the homophone *complementary* if you remember the related word *complete*.

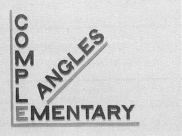

38

Spelling Practice

A. Write the two Unit words for each of these pronunciations.

1. /sīt/ **2.** /kan'vəs/ **3.** /hôrd/

4. /kom'plə·men'tər·ē/ **5.** /kûr'ənt/ **6.** /gə·ril'ə/

B. Write the Unit word for each description. Be sure to choose the correct homophone.

7. a lighted torch **8.** look closely **9.** advice

10. a talent **11.** a fight **12.** a dock

13. double **14.** a group that meets to make decisions

C. Complete each sentence with a pair of Unit homophones.

15. Jonathan tried to _____ into the murky water beneath the old _____.

16. My _____ favorite recipe in the cookbook is the one for _____ pie.

17. The huge _____ silently watched the _____ building a campsite in the jungle.

18. The candidate wished she had worn _____ sneakers as she began to _____ the neighborhood for votes.

19. The city _____ followed the mayor's _____ and passed the bill.

20. The real estate agent was able to _____ every available building _____ in town.

21. The king tried to protect his _____ of gold from the _____ of people outside the castle.

Using the Dictionary to Spell and Write •
Etymologies

UNIT WORDS

canvas
canvass
guerrilla
gorilla
cite
site
complimentary
complementary
flare
flair
peer
pier
council
counsel
duel
dual
hoard
horde
current
currant

An **etymology** is a word history. The word *etymology* comes from the Greek words *etymon* and *logia*. When combined, these words mean "the study of words." An etymology shows how the meaning and spelling of a word have developed. The Words in Time features in this book give you the etymologies of many words.

You can also find etymologies in many dictionaries. Dictionary etymologies are usually written in abbreviated form. These abbreviations are explained in a key found at the front of the dictionary. Look at the key below. Use it to help you complete the exercises.

F French	Gk Greek	L Latin
fr. from	It Italian	OE Old English

Read this etymology for *compliment*. Then complete the exercise.

> **com·pli·ment** /*n.* kom′plə·mənt, *v.* kom′plə·ment/ [F *com-pliment*, fr. It *complimento*, a courtesy]

1. The word *compliment* came into English without a change in spelling or meaning. It came directly from the _____ language.

2. The abbreviation *fr.* means _____.

3. The original word *complimento* comes from the _____ language.
   Look up the words *current, currant, dual,* and *duel* in the **Spelling Dictionary.** Then complete these exercises.

4. The word *dual* comes from a Latin adjective, *dualis,* which means _____.

5. A fight between two people is called a _____.

6. *Current* comes from a Latin word meaning _____.

7. *Raisin de Corauntz* was the original name of the fruit we call a _____.

Writing on Your Own

Write a silly mystery story for your classmates. Use as many Unit words as you can. Choose a title that has a pair of homophones. Here's an example: "The Case of the Current Currant."

WRITER'S GUIDE For a sample paragraph from a story, turn to page 265.

Spelling on Your Own

UNIT WORDS

Copy this chart. Then write each Unit word under the correct heading. You will need to write some words more than once. Use the **Spelling Dictionary** if you need help.

Nouns	Verbs	Adjectives

MASTERY WORDS

Write the Mastery word that is a synonym for each word.

1. stop   **2.** rope   **3.** rule   **4.** rough

Homophones are words that sound alike but often are spelled differently. They also have different meanings. Write the Mastery word that is a homophone for each of these words.

5. roomer   **6.** paws   **7.** course
8. chord   **9.** jeans   **10.** rain

Use a Mastery word and its homophone to finish each of these sentences.

11. The _____ holding Angelo's guitar broke as he strummed the first _____.

12. Mrs. Eng's _____ heard a _____ that the Lees were moving.

13. Rocky, a dog who traveled 800 miles to join its master, didn't _____ even when its _____ hurt.

14. On the day the king began his long _____, not a drop of _____ fell on the kingdom.

15. "Of _____," said Kathy, "you must use _____ sandpaper to remove those layers of paint."

> **genes**
> **pause**
> **cord**
> **coarse**
> **reign**
> **rumor**

BONUS WORDS

1. Write each Bonus word. Then write a homophone for each word.
2. Use each pair of homophones in a sentence.
3. The English word part *fore* means "before." A *foreword* consists of the words that come before the first chapter of a book. Write at least three other words that begin with *fore.* Then use all four words in sentences.

> **waive**
> **strait**
> **foreword**
> **colonel**
> **gait**
> **bloc**
> **feint**
> **callous**

10 Easily Confused Words

UNIT WORDS

1. *personal*
2. *personnel*
3. *adapted*
4. *adopted*
5. *respectively*
6. *respectfully*
7. *statute*
8. *statue*
9. *later*
10. *latter*
11. *partition*
12. *petition*
13. *formerly*
14. *formally*
15. *persecute*
16. *prosecute*
17. *access*
18. *excess*
19. *immigrate*
20. *emigrate*

The Unit Words

The words *personal* and *personnel* sound very similar, even though they have different stress patterns. Their spellings are also similar, but their meanings are different. The word *personal* is an adjective. It often means "private," as in the phrase "a personal matter." *Personnel*, a noun, means "employees."

Our office <u>personnel</u> may not make <u>personal</u> phone calls.

The words *adapt* and *adopt* also sound similar. Was the movie adapted or adopted from the novel? *Adapt* means "to change for a new use or to adjust to new conditions." The movie was *adapted*. *Adopt* means "to take as one's own."

The puppy we <u>adopted</u> has <u>adapted</u> well to its new home.

The words *respectively* and *respectfully* both come from the Latin verb *respicere,* "to look at." Their meanings in English, however, are very different. *Respectfully* means "with respect, courteously." *Respectively* means "in the order given."

The knight bowed <u>respectfully</u> to the king, queen, and lords <u>respectively</u>.

Spelling Practice

A. Write the Unit word for each definition.

1. at a future time
2. changed to fit a new use
3. take to court
4. courteously, politely
5. the second of two
6. took as one's own
7. in the order given
8. mistreat, oppress

B. Write the two Unit words that could be substituted for the underlined words in each sentence.

9. People in the past dressed in fancy clothes when attending a party.

10. A counselor was hired to help employees with their private problems.

11. We all signed the formal request to have the dividing wall between our desks removed.

12. A law was passed to erect a bronze figure in front of the courthouse.

C. *Immigrate* and *emigrate* have the Latin root *migrare,* "to wander." The prefixes *im-* and *e-* add the meanings "in" and "out" respectively. Use these words to complete these sentences.

13. After the war, many refugees wished to ____ to the United States.

14. These people chose to ____ from their homelands to seek a new life.

D. *Access* and *excess* stem from the Latin verb *cedere,* "to go." *Ac + cess* = "to go to or to approach." *Ex + cess* = "to go beyond or to surpass." Use these words to complete these sentences.

15. We ate to ____ over the Thanksgiving holiday.

16. The snow made ____ to the highway difficult.

17. This card gives you ____ to all of our facilities.

18. Never take ____ baggage on a backpacking trip.

Proofreading • A Business Letter

Cynthia was so anxious to mail this letter that she forgot to proofread it. Her letter has nine mistakes in spelling and five mistakes in the punctuation and capitalization of a business letter. Read the letter carefully.

1. Find Cynthia's spelling mistakes.
2. Find the places where Cynthia made capitalization and punctuation mistakes. Write those lines correctly.

UNIT WORDS

personal
personnel
adapted
adopted
respectively
respectfully
statute
statue
later
latter
partition
petition
formerly
formally
persecute
prosecute
access
excess
immigrate
emigrate

---

33 Longview Road
San Diego CA 92111
February 19, 19__

ms. Christine Choi
Personal Department
The San Diego Zoo
San Diego, CA 92199

Dear Ms. Choi;

I would like to apply for the job of zookeeper's assistant that was advertised in the classified section of my newspaper. I understand that this position is voluntery and that there will be no financial benefits. However, I have always been fascinated by apes, and it will be an extrordinary privlige to work in the guerrilla house and to associete with veteran zoologists. In fact, I am currantly studying animal behavior in school and have read all Jane van Lawick-Goodall's books about her work.

I am a student, but I can work latter in the afternoon, on weekends, and during vacations. I would be happy to come in for an interview.

Respectively Yours
Cynthia Brown

---

3. Write the nine misspelled words correctly.

Writing on Your Own

Write a letter to a personnel director to apply for a job. Introduce yourself, mention the job, give reasons why you should be hired, and ask for an interview. Be direct, confident, and polite. Use Unit words.

 WRITER'S GUIDE For help editing and proofreading, see the marks on page 257.

Spelling on Your Own

UNIT WORDS

Write ten sentences. Use a pair of easily confused words in each sentence. For example: <u>Formerly</u>, I wore jeans every day, but now I dress more <u>formally</u> for my after-school job.

MASTERY WORDS

quite
quiet
empire
umpire
desert
dessert

Write the Mastery word for each description.

1. without noise

2. a baseball official

3. a sweet eaten at the end of a meal

4. lands ruled by one person

5. completely; entirely

Homographs are words that are spelled alike but often have different meanings. Sometimes homographs are pronounced differently. Look up *desert* in the **Spelling Dictionary.** Then finish these exercises.

6. Write a sentence to show the meaning of *desert*[1].

7. Write a sentence to show the meaning of *desert*[2].

Sometimes two words have the same letters placed in a different order. For example, the letters *a, e, r,* and *t* may be used to spell the words *tear* and *rate.*

8. Use all the letters in the word *deserts* to spell a Mastery word.

9. Use the letters *e, i, u, q,* and *t* to spell two Mastery words.

BONUS WORDS

insure
assure
libel
liable
martial
marital
evade
invade

Which Bonus word might you use when you are talking about these topics?

1. making false statements

2. self-defense techniques

3. protecting property

4. making a promise

5. not answering a question

6. marriage

7. attacking a country

8. possible weather changes

Write a paragraph about a courtroom trial. Use as many Bonus words as you can.

11 Inflectional Endings

UNIT WORDS

1. throbbing
2. compelled
3. signaled
4. appealed
5. leveled
6. sprawling
7. propelled
8. controlled
9. labeled
10. canceled
11. scrapped
12. rebelled
13. modeling
14. revealed
15. dragging
16. patrolling
17. crammed
18. rivaled
19. repelled
20. hauled

The Unit Words

Even people writing love letters must follow the rules for doubling consonants when adding *ed* and *ing*. Some of the verbs in this letter illustrate the rules for writing inflected verb forms.

When a verb ends with *one* vowel and *one* consonant,

- double the final consonant if it is a one-syllable word.

  | throb | throbbed | throbbing |

- double the final consonant if it is a two-syllable word and the final syllable is accented.

  | compel | compelled | compelling |

- do not double the final consonant if the first syllable is accented.

  | signal | signaled | signaling |

When a verb ends with two consonants or with two vowels and a consonant, do not double the final consonant.

| sprawl | sprawled | sprawling |
| appeal | appealed | appealing |

Spelling Practice

A. Add *ed* or *ing* to each of these one-syllable verbs to form a Unit word.

1. scrap   **2.** drag   **3.** throb
4. cram   **5.** sprawl   **6.** haul

B. The final syllable is accented in each of these verbs. Add *ed* or *ing* to each word to form a Unit word.

7. repel   **8.** control   **9.** patrol
10. rebel   **11.** propel   **12.** compel
13. reveal   **14.** appeal

C. Complete each of these sentences using a word you wrote for **7–14.**

15. The mayor _____ to the voters to support his reforms.

16. The dense fog _____ the helicopter pilot to make an emergency landing in a parking lot.

17. The skunk's strong odor _____ its enemy.

18. When the fog lifted, the distant mountain tops were _____.

D. The final syllable is not accented in these verbs. Add *ed* or *ing* to each one and write a Unit word.

19. cancel   **20.** level   **21.** model
22. rival   **23.** label   **24.** signal

E. A Rhyme Styme is a riddle with two rhyming words for the answer. For example: What do you call a plan made by nine baseball players? A team scheme! Complete these Rhyme Stymes using the uninflected forms of some Unit words.

25. What do you call a piece of paper torn from an atlas page?

        A _____   _____!

26. What do you call young sheep studying together for a test?

        A _____   _____!

27. What do you call a truckload of round objects used in games?

        A _____   _____!

Using the Dictionary to Spell and Write •
Multiple Definitions and Idioms

Jeannette is *cramming* for her math exam.
Don't *cram* too much stuffing into the turkey.
Aldo *crammed* the ticket into his pocket.

The word *cram* has a different meaning in each of these sentences. The meanings are related, but they are not the same. You cannot accurately define a word with multiple definitions unless you know the context in which it is used.

A. Look up the word *rival* in the **Spelling Dictionary.** Write the number of the definition that matches the meaning of *rival* in each sentence.

1. Nothing can *rival* the smell of freshly baked bread.
2. Could a *rival* team ever win the loyalty of our fans?
3. Chris Evert faced her *rival* across the tennis court.
4. The networks *rivaled* each other for the highest ratings.

B. Look up the word *model* in the **Spelling Dictionary.** Note that *model* can be a verb or a noun. For each sentence, write *V* if *model* is a verb or *N* if it is a noun.

5. Mr. Swenson's tractor is the latest *model* available.
6. The U.S. Congress is *modeled* on the English Parliament.
7. The artist built a *model* before beginning the sculpture.
8. Did Whistler's mother *model* for his famous painting?

An **idiom** is an expression that has a specialized meaning. The meaning of an idiom is usually quite different from the meaning of the separate words that make up the idiom. For example, the idiom *beside oneself with grief* does not mean "standing next to oneself with sadness." Instead, the idiom means "very upset." Idioms often appear at the end of an entry. Learning the meanings of idioms can be useful when you write.

Writing on Your Own

Do you prefer to shop in separate stores or in a shopping mall? Why do you think one is better than the other? Write a letter to your Community Planning Board. Ask them to encourage the building of more separate stores or a larger shopping mall. Use five or more Unit words in your letter. Choose at least one word with multiple definitions. Use the word at least two times to show the different meanings.

SPELLING DICTIONARY If you need to check the meanings of some words, turn to page 161.

Spelling on Your Own

UNIT WORDS

Write sentences using all of the Unit words. Use as many of the words as you can in each sentence and underline each Unit word. See how few sentences you can write.

MASTERY WORDS

Add *ed* to each of these words to form a Mastery word.

1. stun   **2.** prowl   **3.** dial

4. conceal   **5.** panel   **6.** channel

Finish each sentence. Add *ed* or *ing* to the word in ( ).

7. With Julie's help, I (panel) _____ our den in one day.

8. The farmer tried (channel) _____ water from the river into the fields.

9. I have been (dial) _____ your phone number all day.

10. The tiger (prowl) _____ restlessly through the jungle.

11. Tim (conceal) _____ his surprise at the news.

Add *ed* or *ing* to *stun* to write the synonym for each of these words.

12. astonished   **13.** beautiful

Try this spelling game. Start with a three-letter word. Add one letter at each step until you write a five-letter Mastery word without the *ed* ending. Use the clues to help you.

14. something used for cooking

15. part of a window

16. a Mastery word without *ed*

> concealed
> prowled
> paneled
> channeled
> dialed
> stunned

BONUS WORDS

Write the Bonus word that is a synonym for each word.

1. banished   **2.** withered   **3.** hardened   **4.** scattered
5. canceled   **6.** surpassed   **7.** compelling   **8.** fraying

The Latin root *pel* means "drive." Write the three Bonus and three Unit words that have this root.

> impelling
> expelled
> dispelled
> congealed
> annulled
> shriveled
> unraveling
> excelled

12 Review

UNIT 7

data
essays
allergies
displays
mysteries
alumni
crises
pastries
theories
attorneys

Follow these steps when you are unsure of how to spell a word.

- **Say** the word. Recall when you have heard the word used. Think about what it means.
- **Look** at the word. Find any prefixes, suffixes, or other word parts you know. Think about other words that are related in meaning and spelling. Try to picture the word in your mind.
- **Spell** the word to yourself. Think about the way each sound is spelled. Notice any unusual spelling.
- **Write** the word while looking at it. Check the way you have formed your letters. If you have not written the word clearly or correctly, write it again.
- **Check** your learning. Cover the word and write it. If you did not spell the word correctly, practice these steps until the word becomes your own.

UNIT 7 Follow the directions using words from Unit 7.

1. Write three plural words in which s is added to the final y.

2. Write four plural words in which the final y changes to i before es is added.

Write the plural of these words.

3. crisis   4. alumnus

5. datum

UNIT 8

elementary
primary
flattery
cemetery
imaginary
revolutionary
voluntary
surgery
secondary
refinery

UNIT 8 Follow the directions using words from Unit 8.
Write the word associated with each word or phrase.

6. graves   7. war in 1776

8. not first   9. oil

10. fairy tales   11. compliments

12. not paid   13. election

14. What kind of school do fourth graders go to?

15. What is it that doctors perform in an operating room?

**Follow the directions using words from Unit 9.
Write the homophone for each word below.**

16. cite   **17.** counsel

18. dual   **19.** peer

20. complementary   **21.** horde

22. currant   **23.** guerrilla

24. canvas   **25.** flair

26. What is another word for *recent*?

27. What lives in a zoo?

28. Where does a boat dock?

**Follow the directions using words from Unit 10.
Finish the paragraph.**

Zack decided to __29__ to the United States. When he saw the __30__ of Liberty, he was grateful to be in his __31__ country. He had __32__ lived in a country with less freedom. Zack hoped that his whole family would be able to join him __33__.

Write the words that are often confused with the following words.

34. access   **35.** persecute

36. personnel   **37.** respectively

38. partition   **39.** adapted

WORDS IN TIME

Person, the root of the word *personal,* comes from the Latin word *persona,* which means "mask." In ancient times, actors in plays wore face masks to suggest the human or animal they were portraying. The word *persona* also survives today. Why do you think people use the word *persona* to describe the social front a person presents to others?

controlled
revealed
rebelled
labeled
compelled
leveled
propelled
patrolling
hauled
modeling

UNIT 11 Follow the directions using words from Unit 11.
Add *ed* to the following base words.

40. rebel   **41.** label

42. compel   **43.** level

44. reveal   **45.** control

46. haul   **47.** propel

Add *ing* to the following base words.

48. patrol   **49.** model

50. What word is the opposite of *hidden*?

51. What is another word for *marked*?

52. What is another word for *forced*?

Write sentences using each word or pair of words.

53. propelled

54. controlled, hauled

55. revealed, rebelled

56. labeled

57. leveled

The word *control* may be used as a verb or as a noun. Follow the directions using the word *control*.

58. Write a sentence using *control* as a verb.

59. Write a sentence using *control* as a noun.

Spelling and Reading
A Letter of Opinion

Read this letter of opinion. Notice how the writer expresses and supports her opinion.

650 Ocean Drive
Shoreham, Florida 33162
April 7, 19——

Heading

Editor
Shoreham *Reader*
Shoreham, Florida 33162

Inside Address

Dear Editor:

Salutation

   I strongly disagree with the city council's decision to make the Shell Beach pier the site of a new shopping mall. I want to urge the city council to consider two other local sites.

   One of the sites is the foundation of the old shoe factory. This location, formerly called North Heights, would be an excellent site for the mall for several reasons. First, the land has already been leveled. Second, building the mall on an existing foundation would reduce the cost of the project.

   Another good location would be north of the cemetery at Second Street, where the old elementary school was just torn down. Once the rubble is hauled away, that spot would be perfect because the new highway goes right past it.

   Building a mall on one of these other sites instead of at Shell Beach would not disturb our precious wildlife. Moreover, it would still leave us with a place to meet our friends and relax.

Body

Respectfully yours,

Jill Martin

Closing

Signature

Write the answers to the questions.

1. With what decision does the writer disagree?
2. What other sites does Jill suggest for the mall?
3. If the decision were yours, which of the two sites suggested by Jill would you pick for the shopping mall? Why?

Underline the review words in your answers. Check to see that you spelled the words correctly.

Spelling and Writing
A Letter of Opinion

Words to Help You Write

data
crises
theories
elementary
primary
volunteer
council
site
current
personal
respectfully
later
controlled
revealed
labeled

Think and Discuss

As in all persuasive writing, the purpose of a letter of opinion is to convince an audience to share the writer's opinion on an issue. Before writing a letter of opinion, the writer should first be aware of who the audience will be. Who will be the audience of Jill's letter on page 53?

A letter of opinion has the same form as a business letter. It has a heading, salutation, body, closing, and signature. The body of the letter contains an introductory paragraph with a topic sentence that expresses the writer's opinion or states a position. What is the topic sentence in the first paragraph of Jill's letter on page 53? This first paragraph might also contain a general statement about the writer's reasons for his or her opinion. What general statement does Jill provide for her readers that indicates how she will support her opinion?

The other paragraphs in the body of the letter should state a specific reason for the writer's opinion and provide facts to support it. What facts does Jill offer to persuade her readers that her suggestions for alternative sites are good ones?

Look at the last paragraph of Jill's letter. Notice that she repeats briefly the most important reasons for her opinion. Why might this be an effective way to end a letter of opinion?

Apply

Write a **letter of opinion** to your school newspaper that states your opinion on some issue. Follow the writing guidelines on the next page.

Prewriting

Choose an issue you are concerned about. Decide how you feel about it. Be sure to consider issues related to events at your school.

- Make a two-column chart. Label the columns *Feelings* and *Facts.*
- Fill in your chart with notes about your opinion on the issue and facts that support your opinion.

Composing

Use your chart to write your letter.

 WRITER'S GUIDE For information on the correct form for your letter, turn to page 262.

- Identify the issue you want to discuss and express your opinion about.
- Explain the reasons why you believe as you do, and offer facts to support your opinion.
- Summarize your stand on the issue in your concluding paragraph.

Revising

Read your letter and show it to a classmate for a first reaction. Follow these guidelines to improve your work. Use the editing and proofreading marks on this page to indicate corrections.

Editing

- Make sure you stated your opinion and your reasons for having that opinion.
- Make sure you have presented facts to support your opinion.
- Check that your letter is clear and convincing to your audience.
- Make sure you chose words that are appropriate for your audience.

Proofreading

- Check your spelling and correct any mistakes.
- Check your capitalization and punctuation.

Copy your story onto clean paper. Write carefully and neatly.

Publishing

Share your letter with your class. Ask your classmates if they agree with you, and if so, whether it is because they found your letter convincing.

	Editing and Proofreading Marks
≡	capitalize
⊙	make a period
∧	add something
⋀	add a comma
ᵛᵛ	add quotation marks
ℛ	take something away
◯	spell correctly
ℋ	indent the paragraph
/	make a lowercase letter
∼tr	transpose

13 Words with Greek Roots

UNIT WORDS

1. sphere
2. atmosphere
3. hemisphere
4. photocopy
5. photography
6. photogenic
7. thermal
8. thermos
9. thermometer
10. thermostat
11. astronaut
12. astronomy
13. astrology
14. disaster
15. graphite
16. stenographer
17. bibliography
18. geography
19. geometry
20. geology

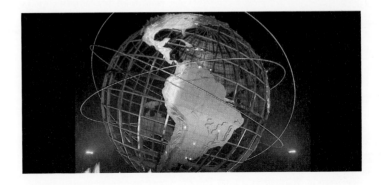

The Unit Words

The English language has borrowed many words from ancient Greek. Some Greek loan words entered our language unchanged. Generally, however, the root of the loan word was used to form a new English word. The Greek word *sphaira*, for example, which means "ball," became our word *sphere*. The Greek prefix *hemi-*, meaning "half," was added to form the new word *hemisphere*. The word *atmosphere*, "the mass of air surrounding the earth," was created by adding the Greek word *atmos*, "vapor," to *sphere*.

The chart below lists some common Greek roots and their meanings.

ROOT	MEANING	EXAMPLE
astro	"star"	*astronaut*
geo	"earth"	*geography*
graph	"write, describe"	*graphite*
photo	"light"	*photocopy*
sphere	"ball, globe"	*hemisphere*
therm	"heat"	*thermos*

REMEMBER THIS

There is no *f* in the Greek alphabet. The sound /f/ in Greek is represented by the letters *ph*. English words that come from Greek roots and have the sound /f/ spell that sound *ph*, as in *graph*, *photo*, *Philadelphia*, and *phantom*.

Polaris
LITTLE DIPPER

BIG DIPPER

Spelling Practice

A. For each word below, write the Unit words that have the same Greek root.

1. *aster,* "a star-shaped flower" (four words)

2. *spheroid,* "an object resembling a ball" (three words)

3. *photometer,* "an instrument that measures light" (three words)

B. Use the four Unit words that contain the Greek root meaning "heat" to complete the paragraph below.

I've resolved to help conserve the world's energy supply. Next winter, when the __4__ registers below freezing, I'll control my urge to turn the __5__ up a degree or two. Instead, I'll snuggle into my __6__ underwear, fill a __7__ with hot cocoa, and smile.

C. Complete each sentence with a Unit word. Each word has one of these roots.

biblio, "book"   *log,* "study"   *meter,* "measure"
naut, "sailor"   *steno,* "shortened, narrow"

8. A _____ is a person who writes in shorthand.

9. _____ is the study of the earth's history through its rocks.

10. _____ was originally used to measure the earth's surface.

11. A list of books is a _____.

12. An instrument used to measure heat is a _____.

13. An _____ is someone who "sails among the stars."

D. Complete these exercises using the Unit words.

14. The suffix *-ite* sometimes means "a mineral or rock." Write the word that means "a mineral used for writing."

15. Write the word that has two Greek roots that together mean "to describe the earth."

57

Proofreading • A Social Studies Report

Nina wrote this report for a social studies assignment. Now she must edit and proofread her work before handing in her final copy. Nina has made eight mistakes in spelling and five mistakes in capitalization. Read the social studies report carefully.

1. Find Nina's spelling mistakes.
2. Find Nina's capitalization mistakes.

UNIT WORDS

sphere
atmosphere
hemisphere
photocopy
photography
photogenic
thermal
thermos
thermometer
thermostat
astronaut
astronomy
astrology
disaster
graphite
stenographer
bibliography
geography
geometry
geology

Antarctica: The Unknown Land

Antarctica is the continent around the South Pole. If you visit antarctica, be sure to take your tharmal long johns. In the dead of winter, which in the Southern Hemmisphere is in June, the thermmometer along the coast drops below −40°F. A broken thermostatt here can lead to death. But the atmossphere of Antarctica is dry. At the South Pole, only four to six inches of snow falls a year.

Antarctica was discovered by Captain cook in 1772, but it was not until about 1840 that it was found to be a continent. Soon, several explorers began making expeditions to Antarctica to try to discover more about the gography of the area and to try to reach the South Pole. Roald Amundsen of norway set out on October 20, 1911, and arrived at the pole on December 14. robert Scott of Great Britain started November 1 and reached the pole on january 18, 1912. His party, however, met with dizaster on the return trip, and no one was able to return home.

Today, scientists study the geollogy of Antarctica, searching for natural resources and monitoring the movement of the polar ice caps. They also gather data on weather and the oceans.

---

3. Write the eight misspelled words correctly. Then write the five words with capitalization errors correctly.

Writing on Your Own

What explorers have you studied in your social studies or history classes? Choose one or two explorers and write a brief research report for class about what the explorers discovered and the hardships they endured. Check the history section in the library to help you find information.

 WRITER'S GUIDE For a sample paragraph from a research report, turn to page 264.

Spelling on Your Own

UNIT WORDS

Write each Unit word next to the meaning of its Greek root.

1. "star"

2. "earth"

3. "ball"

4. "light"

5. "write"

6. "heat"

MASTERY WORDS

autograph
autobiography
biography
telegraph
telegram
photo

Study these Greek roots and their meanings: *graph*, "write, describe"; *auto*, "self"; *bio*, "life." Then write a Mastery word for each definition below.

1. the description of someone's life

2. the description of your own life

3. your own signature

Finish these exercises using the Mastery words.

4. The Greek root *tele* means "far." Write the Mastery words that have the root *tele*.

5. In words with Greek roots, the sound /f/ is spelled with *ph*. Write the Mastery words that have /f/.

BONUS WORDS

astrophysics
ecosphere
seismograph
choreographer
astronomical
geological
photosynthesis
thermonuclear

Use Bonus words to complete these exercises.

1. A _____ history of our continent may be studied in the Grand Canyon.
2. The _____ recorded an earthquake along the San Andreas fault.
3. The insect population has reached _____ proportions.
4. Space travel has helped advance the science of _____.
5. The hydrogen bomb is a _____ weapon.
6. Does Mars have an _____ capable of sustaining life?
7. The _____ created a dance for the TV special.
8. Plants form carbohydrates by the process of _____.

14 More Words with Greek Roots

UNIT WORDS

1. antibiotic
2. biology
3. synthetic
4. hydroelectric
5. diagonal
6. antonym
7. synonym
8. hydrant
9. dialect
10. antidote
11. mythology
12. sympathetic
13. diagnosis
14. dehydrate
15. dermatology
16. antiseptic
17. synagogue
18. diagram
19. zoology
20. symbolize

The Unit Words

Many of the words you will study in this unit did not exist when ancient Greek was spoken, yet they have their roots in that language. Most of the words name and describe recent scientific and technical processes and discoveries.

Scientists have practically created a new language using ancient Greek prefixes and roots. If you know the Greek word parts, you can understand unfamiliar technical words and spell new words correctly.

The chart below lists the Greek prefixes and roots found in the Unit words.

PREFIX	MEANING	EXAMPLE
anti-/ant-	"against; opposite"	*antibiotic*
dia-	"through; across"	*diagonal*
sym-/syn-	"together; with"	*synthetic*

ROOT		
hydr	"water"	*hydrant*
log/logy	"word; study of"	*biology*

REMEMBER THIS

The word *diagonal* has the sound /ə/ in the third syllable. To help you remember which vowel letter spells /ə/, think of other words that have the Greek root *gon*, "angle," such as *polygon* and *hexagon*. You hear /o/ in the root of both words. Therefore, you know that *diagonal* is also spelled with **o**.

60

Spelling Practice

A. Write the Unit words that have the same prefix as each of these words.

1. *antibodies* (four words)   **2.** *symphony* (five words)

3. *diameter* (four words)

B. Write the Unit words that have the same suffix as this word.

4. *psychology* (four words)

C. Complete these sentences using the Unit words that have the Greek root that means "water." You will need to add an inflectional ending to two of the Unit words.

5. In 1976, many fire _____ were painted red, white, and blue.

6. _____ power is one way to meet our growing energy demands.

7. The soup package contains noodles and _____ vegetables.

D. Write the synonym for each of these words.

8. sterile   **9.** artificial

10. illustration   **11.** represent

12. dry   **13.** slanted

E. Write the antonym for each of these words.

14. poison   **15.** unfriendly

F. Write the plural form of each of these words. Remember to check the plural form of unfamiliar Greek or Latin words in a dictionary.

16. antibiotic   **17.** synagogue

18. mythology   **19.** diagnosis

20. synonym   **21.** hydrant

Spelling and Language • Vocabulary Building

UNIT WORDS

antibiotic
biology
synthetic
hydroelectric
diagonal
antonym
synonym
hydrant
dialect
antidote
mythology
sympathetic
diagnosis
dehydrate
dermatology
antiseptic
synagogue
diagram
zoology
symbolize

In this lesson, you will be asked to build words from Greek prefixes and roots. Some of the words you will write are not Unit words. Use a dictionary to help you spell these words.

anti, "against"	*sym/syn,* "together"	*geo,* "earth"
astro, "star"	*graph,* "write"	*derm,* "skin"
bio, "life"	*myth,* "legend"	*zoo,* "animal"

A. Remember, the Greek root *logy* means "study of." Use the list above to help you write a word for each definition.

1. the study of life

2. the study of animals

3. the study of the skin

4. the study of the earth

5. the study of the stars

6. the study of handwriting

7. stories about gods and heroes

B. The Greek root *path* means "feelings" or "disease." Use the Greek roots and prefixes listed above to help you write a word for each definition.

8. the study of disease   **9.** sharing feeling with someone

10. having a dislike of or an opposition toward

C. The Greek root *onym* means "name; meaning." Write the word that fits each definition.

11. a word that has the same meaning as another

12. a word that has the opposite meaning from another

Writing on Your Own

Imagine you are a reporter working for a newspaper in the year penicillin was first discovered or in the year a vaccine for poliomyelitis was perfected. Write a news story for a national newspaper telling about the important medical breakthrough.

 WRITER'S GUIDE For a sample paragraph from a news story, turn to page 266.

Spelling on Your Own

UNIT WORDS

Arrange the Unit words in vertical columns so that a word or message can be read horizontally. Look at the example. Create as many puzzles as you can.

F		B		C	
A	S	M	O	A	D
M	E	E	T	M	E
E	T	A	H	E	N
			T		O	T

MASTERY WORDS

Finish these exercises using the Mastery words.

ecology
symptom
diameter
symbol
hydrogen
antipollution

1. Write the two words with the prefix *sym,* "together."

2. Write the word with the prefix that means "against."

3. Write the word that means "the measure across a circle."

Finish these sentences using the Mastery words.

4. Water is made up of oxygen and ____.

5. ____ is the study of how people and animals live in their surroundings.

6. Fever may be a ____ of the flu.

7. Our flag is a ____ of our country.

8. The ____ of a nickel is larger than that of a dime.

9. ____ devices help to keep our air clean.

One word in each group is misspelled. Write that word correctly.

10. photo, telegram, symtom

11. autograph, hydragen, biography

12. symble, telegraph, umpire

13. ecology, antepollution, diameter

BONUS WORDS

anthropology
meteorology
symmetrical
etymology
synopsis
synchronize
hydraulic
hydrofoil

Write the Bonus words that have the same Greek prefix or root as each of these Unit words.

1. symbolize (3 words)   2. hydrant (2 words)   3. biology (3 words)

Many objects are symmetrical. Write a short description of a symmetrical object. Try to make your reader experience the object with more than one of the five senses.

15 Verb Suffixes

UNIT WORDS

1. petrify
2. qualify
3. clarify
4. nominate
5. communicate
6. discriminate
7. notify
8. unify
9. abbreviate
10. imitate
11. mystify
12. concentrate
13. modify
14. terrify
15. evaluate
16. investigate
17. specify
18. refrigerate
19. contaminate
20. justify

The Unit Words

If the cat scared the mouse, and the dog frightened the cat, what petrified the forest? The humor in this question depends on the two meanings of the word *petrify*. The answer, of course, is that mud, volcanic ash, and sand petrified the forest millions of years ago.

Petrify comes from two Latin words: *petra,* "rock or stone," and *facere,* "to make." The original meaning of *petrify* is "to turn to stone." Later a second meaning, "to make rigid or motionless with fear or surprise," developed. Our language is alive and changing. It is certainly not petrified.

Look at the Unit words. Notice that all the Unit words are verbs. You can often recognize a verb by looking at the final letters of a word. The suffixes *-ify* and *-ate* are frequently added to a root or base word to form a verb.

petr + ify = petrify
nomin + ate = nominate

Spelling Practice

A. Write the Unit word that is related to each of these words.

1. discrimination   **2.** mystery   **3.** communication   **4.** justice
5. investigation   **6.** terror   **7.** concentration   **8.** specific

An **analogy** shows a similarity between two sets of ideas. "*Duel* is to *fight* as *throb* is to *beat*" is an analogy. *Duel* and *fight* are synonyms. *Throb* and *beat* are also synonyms. The two word pairs have similar relationships. Word pairs in an analogy can also be antonyms. An example is "*Numerous* is to *few* as *costly* is to *inexpensive.*"

B. Complete the following analogies using the Unit words.

9. *Sphere* is to *globe* as *pollute* is to _____.

10. *Former* is to *latter* as *dilute* is to _____.

11. *Advise* is to *counsel* as *alter* is to _____.

12. *Dirty* is to *antiseptic* as *divide* is to _____.

13. *Recent* is to *current* as *scare* is to _____.

14. *Blazed* is to *flared* as *copy* is to _____.

15. *Scare* is to *frighten* as *harden* is to _____.

C. The words in analogies below have a different kind of relationship to each other than the words in **9–15.** Think about the relationship between these words. Then complete the analogies using the Unit words.

16. *Dignity* is to *dignify* as *quality* is to _____.

17. *Simple* is to *simplify* as *note* is to _____.

18. *Peace* is to *pacify* as *clear* is to _____.

19. *Separation* is to *separate* as *evaluation* is to _____.

20. *Donor* is to *donate* as *refrigerator* is to _____.

21. *Imitation* is to *imitate* as *nomination* is to _____.

22. *Celebration* is to *celebrate* as *abbreviation* is to _____.

D. Use Unit words to finish the sentences below.

23. Scary stories do not usually _____ me.

24. Spiders and other bugs _____ my brother so he cannot move!

25. We'll never win if we don't _____ the team.

Spelling and Language • Adding *ed* and *ing*

UNIT WORDS

petrify
qualify
clarify
nominate
communicate
discriminate
notify
unify
abbreviate
imitate
mystify
concentrate
modify
terrify
evaluate
investigate
specify
refrigerate
contaminate
justify

Follow these rules when adding *ed* and *ing* to verbs.

1. When a word ends in a consonant and *e*, drop the *e*.

    imitate   imitated   imitating

2. When a word ends in a consonant and *y*, change *y* to *i* and add *ed*. Do not change the *y* when adding *ing*.

    modify   modified   modifying

3. When a word ends in a vowel and *y*, keep the *y*.

    survey   surveyed   surveying

Add *ed* or *ing* to the Unit words to complete this paragraph. Each Unit word may be used only once.

Scientists are currently __1__ reports of a UFO sighting in the Arizona desert. Local authorities __2__ the governmental agencies immediately when they heard that an object had been seen. The authorities __3__ that a team of experts must be sent to the area at once. Although the scientists are still studying the evidence and are __4__ it as best they can, no explanations have been given. The scientists admit that they are __5__ by the event. Is this merely a case of mass hysteria, or were beings from other worlds truly __6__ with us?

Usually, when you see a word that ends with *ed* or *ing* in a sentence, you can assume that the word is used as a verb. Sometimes, however, words with these endings are used as adjectives. This sentence shows two examples.

The <u>mystified</u> audience watched the <u>disappearing</u> hat trick.

Writing on Your Own

Imagine that you have just watched a debate between candidates for your school's student government. One candidate clearly addressed important issues, while the other avoided them. Write a persuasive paragraph for the school newspaper to try to convince students to vote for the candidate who honestly tackled the issues. Use eight or more Unit words in your persuasive paragraph. Add *ed* or *ing* to some verbs.

WRITER'S GUIDE For a sample persuasive paragraph, turn to page 260.

Spelling on Your Own

The verb-forming suffix is missing from each Unit word below. Think of the missing letters. Then write the complete word.

1. qual___
2. communic___
3. just___
4. discrimin___
5. clar___
6. abbrevi___
7. un___
8. not___
9. imit___
10. concentr___
11. mod___
12. evalu___
13. investig___
14. myst___
15. terr___
16. refriger___
17. petr___
18. spec___
19. contamin___
20. nomin___

MASTERY WORDS

appreciate
insulate
translate
magnify
purify
identify

Finish each of these sentences using a Mastery word.

1. The Dunlops plan to ___ their house to save fuel.

2. We must ___ the water before drinking it.

3. A microscope lens will ___ these tiny cells.

4. A name tag will ___ your pet if it is lost.

5. We ___ all your help.

6. Ana will ___ my story into Spanish.

Write each of these Mastery words adding *ed* and *ing.*

7. appreciate   8. insulate   9. magnify   10. purify

BONUS WORDS

saturate
escalate
renovate
meditate
amplify
signify
liquefy
stupefy

Write the Bonus word that is related to each of these words. Then circle the two words that end with *-efy.*

1. liquid
2. ample
3. significant
4. renew
5. stupendous
6. meditation
7. saturation

The verb *escalate* was formed by dropping the suffix *-or* from *escalator,* a trademark for moving stairs. This process is called **back-formation.**

8. Look up *edit, diagnose, donate,* and *televise* in a dictionary. What words were these words made from?

9. Use *escalate* and the four other words created by back-formation in sentences.

16 More Shifting Accents

condem**n**

condem**n**ation

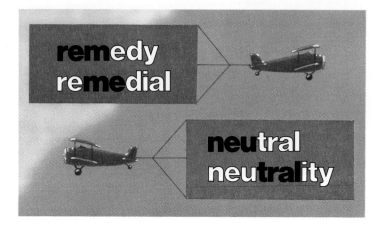

rem**edy**
re**me**dial

neutral
neutra**li**ty

The Unit Words

Words that have the same root are called related words. The root of a word carries the basic meaning. The prefixes and suffixes add additional meanings. Look at the words *immortal* and *immortality* below. Notice how they have grown from the Latin root *mort*, meaning "death."

im ("not") + mort ("death") + al = immortal
immortal + ity = immortality

Look at the pairs of related words at the top of the page. Each pair of words has the same root. Say the pairs aloud. Listen for the shift in the accented syllable when a suffix is added to the first word in each pair. The vowel sound heard in the accented syllable of the second word helps you remember the spelling of the /ə/ in the unaccented syllable of the first word.

Say *condemn* and *condemnation* aloud. Did you notice that the "silent" letter in *condemn* is sounded when the accent shifts in *condemnation*? Thinking of related words is an excellent key to becoming a better speller.

Spelling Practice

A. The letter that spells /ə/ is missing in the final syllable of each of these Unit words. Write the word. Then write the related Unit word that provides the clue to the spelling of the missing /ə/.

1. vit____l   **2.** neutr____l   **3.** fat____l   **4.** immort____l

5. leg____l   **6.** loc____l   **7.** regul____r

B. Write the Unit word for each of these pronunciations. Then write the related Unit word that helps you identify the spelling of /ə/ in each pronunciation.

8. /kən·dem′/   **9.** /rem′ə·dē/   **10.** /fan′tə·sē/

A **malapropism** /mal′ə·prop′iz′əm/ is a mix-up in the use of words that is often quite funny. A word that has a similar sound is used instead of the correct word. These verbal slips are named after Mrs. Malaprop, a comic character in a play called *The Rivals.* Here is an example of a malapropism: "My friends were very synthetic about my problem." Of course, the writer meant to use *sympathetic,* not *synthetic,* in the sentence.

C. Each underlined word in the paragraphs below is an example of a malapropism. Write the correct Unit word.

> Dr. Harty stepped before the reporters and TV cameras. "I'm happy to report that The Creature's breathing is <u>singular</u> (**11**) again," he said, "and its other <u>vinyl</u> (**12**) signs are stable. We have found a <u>recipe</u> (**13**) for each medical problem. Fortunately, the Earth's atmosphere has not proved <u>faithful</u> (**14**) to it."
>
> Top <u>vocal</u> (**15**) reporter Robin Newsome called out, "Doctor, do you foresee any <u>lethal</u> (**16**) problems for the government in keeping The Creature here?"

D. Write the synonym for these words.

17. convict   **18.** dream

Proofreading • A Health Education Report

UNIT WORDS

immortal
immortality
remedy
remedial
neutral
neutrality
local
locality
legal
legality
vital
vitality
fatal
fatality
fantasy
fantastic
regular
regularity
condemn
condemnation

Elena wrote this report for her health education class. Now she must proofread her work before handing in the final copy. Elena made twelve spelling mistakes. She also omitted an apostrophe or used one incorrectly five times. Read the report carefully.

1. Find Elena's spelling mistakes.
2. Find the words in which apostrophes are used incorrectly or omitted.

How to Live Longer

Ponce de Leon searched endlessly for the fountain of youth. But he consentrated his efforts in the wrong area's of the New World. He should have investegated the tiny village of Vilcabamba, high in the Andes mountains of Ecuador. There the locol inhabitants live well beyond the average persons life span.

Doctors are mystifyed by the vytality desplaied by the villagers. Some researchers site the regularty of the residents routines as the reason for their long lives. The farmers climb miles into the mountains every day to tend their fields. There are few tensions and distractions. Meals are simple. Vilcabambans consume about 1,200 calories a day. Their meals consist mainly of grain, yucca root, beans, and potatoes. They also eat many oranges and bananas.

The fantastick climate and the uncantaminated water of the rivers and mineral springs may also increase the life expectancy of the people of Vilcabamba. When a Vilcabamban suffers from a cold or other minor illness, the usual remidy is herbal tea.

We cant all move to the mountains of Ecuador, but its possible to modefy some of our habits in order to live more healthful lives.

---

3. Write the twelve misspelled words correctly. Then write the five words with apostrophe mistakes correctly.

Writing on Your Own

Imagine that you have just started exercising regularly. Write a friendly letter to a friend explaining what a good effect the exercise is having on you. Use as many Unit words as you can.

WRITER'S GUIDE For a sample friendly letter, turn to page 261.

Spelling on Your Own

UNIT WORDS

1. List the Unit words that are adjectives. Then list the words that are nouns.
2. Write the three suffixes that identify the nouns on the Unit word list.
3. Write the suffix that identifies most of the adjectives on the Unit word list.
4. Write the two Unit words that are verbs.

MASTERY WORDS

original
originality
muscle
muscular
democracy
democratic

Finish these exercises using the Mastery words.

1. Write the Mastery words in alphabetical order.

2. Write the word that is pronounced /mus′əl/. Then underline the consonant letter in the word you wrote that does not stand for a sound.

3. Write the related Mastery word that helps you remember the "silent" letter in the word you wrote for **2.**

Finish each pair of sentences with two related Mastery words. The first sentence in each pair needs a noun to complete it. The second sentence needs an adjective.

{
4. People elect government officials in a ____.

5. Public elections are necessary in a ____ country.
}

{
6. Exercise can strengthen every ____ in your body.

7. You must exercise to build a strong, ____ body.
}

{
8. We admire Margaret's creativity and ____.

9. Margaret's ____ ideas helped us win an award.
}

BONUS WORDS

tyranny
tyrannical
syllable
syllabication
frugal
frugality
solemn
solemnity

Complete these sentences with related Bonus words.

1. ____ is the method used to divide a word into more than one ____.
2. He served us a ____ meal; I call such ____ "starvation."
3. Our forefathers fought against ____ so that we would not have to live under a ____ ruler.
4. Her ____ words were fitting for the ____ of the occasion.

Words that come from Greek, such as *tyranny* and *syllable,* often have the sound /i/ spelled with **y.** Write a list of five words other than the Bonus words that have /i/ spelled with **y.** Then use the five words in sentences.

17 Mathematics Words

UNIT WORDS

1. digit
2. geometric
3. algebra
4. polygon
5. pentagon
6. cylinder
7. pyramid
8. parallelogram
9. perimeter
10. horizontal
11. perpendicular
12. vertical
13. segment
14. tangent
15. coordinate
16. median
17. exponent
18. proportion
19. axis
20. mathematics

The Unit Words

Early in human history, people realized the importance of numbers. Fingers and toes were probably the first calculators. The word *digit* comes from the Latin word *digitus,* "a finger or toe."

The Egyptians and the Chinese developed practical systems of mathematics, which they used to measure fields and to construct buildings. The greatest advances, however, occurred during the height of ancient Greek civilization. Philosophers and mathematicians such as Pythagoras, Euclid, Archimedes, and Ptolemy created the abstract mathematical systems we use today. The Romans, in turn, enlarged upon these systems. Consequently, most mathematical words have Greek or Latin roots.

After the fall of the Roman Empire, interest in mathematics was kept alive by the Arabs. The word *algebra* comes from two Arabic words: *al,* "the," and *jabr,* "reduction of fractions."

Spelling Practice

A. Write the Unit word that comes from each of these Latin words.

1. *vertex,* "top"

2. *medius,* "middle"

3. *horizon,* "boundary; the horizon"

4. *perpendiculum,* "plumb line"

5. *digitus,* "finger or toe"

6. *segmentum,* "a cut-off piece"

7. *tangere,* "to touch"

8. *pro portione,* "as a due share"

9. *exponere,* "to indicate"

10. *ordinare,* "to arrange"

B. Complete these exercises using the Unit words.

11. Two words have the Greek root *meter,* "measure." Write these words.

12. Two words have the Greek root *gon,* "angle." Write these words.

13. Words from Greek often have /i/ spelled with *y.* Write the three words that follow this spelling pattern.

14. The Greek word *gramme* means "line." Write the word that names a geometric figure that has parallel lines or sides.

15. The Greek word *axon* means "axle," the bar on which a wheel turns. Write the word that names the imaginary line on which the earth turns.

16. The Greek word *mathema* means "a lesson." Write the Unit word that is derived from *mathema.*

17. Write the word that comes from Arabic.

C. Write the five four-syllable Unit words that begin with these letters:

18. *c*

19. *h*

20. *m*

21. *g*

22. *p*

Using the Dictionary to Spell and Write •
Changes in Word Meanings

Samuel Johnson, who completed his famous dictionary in 1755, wrote, "No dictionary of a living tongue can ever be perfect, since while it is hastening to publication, some words are budding, and some are falling away."

Just as new words are constantly appearing, the meanings of existing words are changing as well. It is important to know the meaning of a word in order to use it correctly when writing. Sometimes the meaning of a word is changed from a general meaning to a specialized one. *Hound,* for example, at one time was the name for any kind of dog. Today *hound* is used only for certain breeds. The word *dog,* on the other hand, once meant a small lapdog, but today the word is applied to most canines.

A. For each of these sentences, write *S* if the underlined word has a specialized meaning or *G* if it has a more general meaning.

1. Find the length of the segment AB.
2. The flowers look out of proportion with that vase.
3. A large segment of our population lives in urban areas.
4. The median number in the series 1, 2, 3, 4, 5 is 3.
5. A proportion states that two ratios are equal.
6. The car nearly hit the median strip on the roadway.

B. Look up these words in the **Spelling Dictionary:** *cylinder, exponent, perimeter,* and *tangent.* Each word has a specialized meaning and a general meaning. Write the word that has a general meaning that fits each sentence.

7. Frank Lloyd Wright was an _____ of modern architecture.
8. While lecturing about ancient Japanese culture, the speaker went off on a _____ about his trip to Tokyo.
9. The highway circled the _____ of the city.
10. Justin packed the poster in a cardboard _____.

A house designed by Frank Lloyd Wright

Writing on Your Own

Pretend you are teaching a ten-year-old friend some geometry. Choose three of the following figures: *polygon, pentagon, cylinder, pyramid, parallelogram.* Draw a picture of each one and write a paragraph to describe it. Use as many of the Unit words as you can.

 WRITER'S GUIDE For a sample of a descriptive paragraph, see page 259.

Spelling on Your Own

Write the Unit words in alphabetical order. Circle the five nouns that name geometric shapes. Underline the four adjectives that describe lines.

MASTERY WORDS

Write the Mastery word that is related to each word.

1. graphic   **2.** measuring   **3.** averaged

4. radiator   **5.** angular (two words)

Write the Mastery word that ends with the same sound as each of these words.

6. laugh   **7.** curious   **8.** symbol (two words)

Look up *radius* in the **Spelling Dictionary.** Then finish the exercises.

9. Write the preferred plural form of *radius.*

10. Which language does *radius* come from?

Finish these sentences using the Mastery words.

11. What is Willie Mays's lifetime batting _____?

12. Fred took careful _____ before he built the desk.

13. My sister drew a circle _____ to show her budget.

14. Our house is shaped like a _____.

Look at the Mastery word list. Two words are out of alphabetical order.

15. Write the two words in the correct order.

| angle |
| average |
| graph |
| measurements |
| rectangle |
| radius |

BONUS WORDS

Write the Bonus word that is related to each word.

1. equal   **2.** theory   **3.** quadruplet   **4.** hyphen   **5.** isometric

Write the Bonus word that is a synonym for each word.

6. sharp   **7.** blunt, dull

Congruent comes from the Latin *congruere,* "to agree." "His jeans were *incongruous* with his tuxedo jacket." What do you think *incongruous* means?

| equilateral |
| theorem |
| congruent |
| obtuse |
| acute |
| hypotenuse |
| isosceles |
| quadrilateral |

18 Review

UNIT 13

disaster
geometry
atmosphere
bibliography
thermometer
sphere
thermos
astronaut
stenographer
geography

Follow these steps when you are unsure of how to spell a word.

- **Say** the word. Recall when you have heard the word used. Think about what it means.
- **Look** at the word. Find any prefixes, suffixes, or other word parts you know. Think about other words that are related in meaning and spelling. Try to picture the word in your mind.
- **Spell** the word to yourself. Think about the way each sound is spelled. Notice any unusual spelling.
- **Write** the word while looking at it. Check the way you have formed your letters. If you have not written the word clearly or correctly, write it again.
- **Check** your learning. Cover the word and write it. If you did not spell the word correctly, practice these steps until the word becomes your own.

UNIT 13 Write the words that have root words with these meanings. Use words from Unit 13.

1. "star" (two words)
2. "earth" (two words)
3. "ball" (two words)
4. "heat" (two words)
5. "write" (three words)

UNIT 14

mythology
antiseptic
synthetic
diagonal
dehydrate
antibiotic
antonym
synonym
sympathetic
diagram

UNIT 14 Finish these sentences. Use words from Unit 14.

6. Put _____ on that cut.
7. Draw a _____ line from corner to corner.
8. This cloth is not natural; it is _____.
9. Hera is a goddess in Greek _____.
10. *Ashamed* is an _____ for *proud.*
11. *Applaud* is a _____ for *clap.*
12. You will _____ the animals if you don't give them plenty of water.
13. My aunt is very _____ and understands how I feel.
14. I will draw you a _____ so that you will understand.
15. The doctor gave me an _____ to fight my sickness.

76

UNIT 15 Follow the directions using words from Unit 15.
Finish these sentences.

16. Some parrots learn to _____ human speech.
17. Bees _____ with a kind of body language.
18. Adjectives describe or _____ nouns.
19. Scientists _____ mysteries of outer space.
20. Can you _____ coming home so late?
21. Please _____ your parents when you arrive.

Write the word that has the same base word as each word below.

22. qualification   23. refrigerator   24. terrific   25. specific

Take away *ed* or *ing* from each of these verbs to make a Unit 15 word.

26. justified   27. communicating

UNIT 15

modify
justify
communicate
imitate
investigate
qualify
notify
terrify
refrigerate
specify

UNIT 16 Follow the directions using words from Unit 16.
Write the words that are in the same word family as these words.

28. fatality   29. legality   30. fantasy   31. vital

Write a synonym for each of these words.

32. ordinary   33. wonderful   34. cure   35. doom

Write an adjective that describes each item.

36. a movie you think is wonderful
37. a document drawn up by a lawyer
38. a color such as beige, white, or gray
39. your neighborhood or town

UNIT 16

fantasy
legal
neutral
condemn
fatal
remedy
local
vitality
fantastic
regular

WORDS IN TIME

The verb *terrify* and the adjective *terrific* both come from the Latin word *terrificus,* meaning "causing terror." If a movie terrifies you, you are frightened. If a movie is terrific, you think it is great. If you like scary movies, you might even say that the terrific movie terrified you! Over the years, how has the meaning of *terrific* changed?

UNIT 17

perimeter
segment
vertical
proportion
mathematics
geometric
cylinder
pyramid
perpendicular
median

UNIT 17 Follow the directions using words from Unit 17. Write a word that comes from each of these Latin or Greek words.

40. vertex

41. mathema

42. perimetros

43. pro portione

44. cylindrus

Write a word that fits each definition.

45. in the middle

46. little piece

47. upright

48. meet at right angles

49. around the edge

50. study of numbers

51. ancient Egyptian tomb

52. perfect relationship of parts in a whole

53. having to do with geometry

Finish these sentences.

54. We walked around the ____ of the field.

55. The car pulled over to the ____.

56. Did you know that ____ is my favorite subject?

57. My street is ____ to your street.

58. Put the book in a ____ position.

59. The fun house mirror made things look out of ____.

60. She only saw a small ____ of the movie.

61. Write the two words that have /i/ spelled with *y*.

62. Write the two words that are antonyms for *horizontal*.

63. Write the seven words that are nouns.

Spelling and Reading
A News Story

Read the following news story from a school newspaper. Notice what kind of information is given about the earthquake in each paragraph.

QUAKE ROCKS TAYLOR

An earthquake along the Santa Rita fault system hit the Taylor area at 6:45 A.M. The quake registered 6.5 on the Richter scale. A spokesperson for the Red Cross says that no fatal injuries have been reported. However, the quake set off a fire at the Festive Fabric warehouse. Molly Rosenblum, a stenographer at the warehouse, was treated at the scene for smoke inhalation. The quake also cracked a segment of the freeway bypass at the perimeter of Taylor.

Arthur T. Brown, owner of Festive Fabrics, said the quake may put him out of business. "It was the fire that got us, not the quake itself," he said. "We had a lot of synthetic fabrics in the building. I can't specify how much we lost, but I doubt we can come back. It boils down to mathematics: we lost more than we can replace." Festive Fabrics employs 30 people in the Taylor area.

Meanwhile, 13-year-old Taylor resident Alan Barnes claims his dogs predicted the quake. "They felt something in the atmosphere," said Alan. "One minute they showed no vitality at all. The next minute they were making a fantastic racket. I went out to investigate, but I couldn't see what they were barking at. Then I remembered reading somewhere that animals can feel this type of disaster coming."

Write the answers to the questions.

1. According to this news story, what damage did the earthquake do?
2. What news from the Red Cross did the writer mention?
3. Who may lose their jobs as a result of the earthquake?
4. If you were a reporter covering the story of the earthquake, who else might you interview?

Underline the review words in your answers. Check to see that you spelled the words correctly.

Spelling and Writing
A News Story

Think and Discuss

A news story gives clear, concise information about a current event. The event must be interesting, important, or unusual.

The most important facts in a news story go in the first, or **lead,** paragraph. This paragraph should explain *what* happened, *when* it happened, *where* it happened, *who* was involved, *why* the event happened and sometimes *how* the event happened. Look at the first paragraph of the news story on page 79. How does it answer the questions *who, what, where, when,* and *why*? Why do you think the writer chose not to tell *how* the event happened?

The second and third paragraphs of the news story on page 79 form the **body.** They give additional details of interest about the event. In a good news story, the details in the second paragraph should be more important than those in the third paragraph. How is this true of the news story on page 79?

The **headline,** or title, of a news story briefly summarizes the event. A headline usually contains a strong verb. What verb is used to make the headline of this story effective?

Apply

Write a **news story** about a recent event in your area that was important, interesting, or unusual. Imagine that the story will be published in your community or local paper. Follow the writing guidelines on the next page.

Prewriting

Think of various events you might write about. Choose the event you think is most newsworthy.

- List the questions *who, what, when, where, why,* and *how* in a notebook. Leave space at the bottom of the page for extra details.
- If possible, talk to people who were present at the event. Ask them for information that answers the six questions in your notebook.
- At the bottom of the page, jot down additional details that you learn from the people who talk to you. Try to get some exact quotes.

Composing

Use your notes to write your news story.

- Write a lead paragraph that answers these questions about the event: *who, what, when, where, why,* and *how.*
- In the body, write paragraphs with interesting details about the event. Arrange the paragraphs in order from most to least important.
- Sum up your story in a short headline with a strong verb.

 THESAURUS For help finding vivid verbs, turn to page 205.

Revising

Read your news story and show it to a classmate. Follow these guidelines to improve your work. Use the editing and proofreading marks on this page to indicate corrections.

Editing

- Make sure your lead paragraph contains the most important information about the event.
- Make sure the body gives details that add interest to your account.
- Check that your paragraphs are in order from most to least important.
- Make sure your headline is brief, clear, and accurate.

Proofreading

- Check your spelling, capitalization, and punctuation.

Copy your story onto clean paper. Write carefully and neatly.

Publishing

Share your story with your classmates. Ask them if your story is clear and if there are any details you might have added.

<table>
<tr><td colspan="2">**Editing and Proofreading Marks**</td></tr>
<tr><td>≡</td><td>capitalize</td></tr>
<tr><td>⊙</td><td>make a period</td></tr>
<tr><td>∧</td><td>add something</td></tr>
<tr><td>⋏</td><td>add a comma</td></tr>
<tr><td>ᵛ ᵛ</td><td>add quotation marks</td></tr>
<tr><td>ℯ</td><td>take something away</td></tr>
<tr><td>◯</td><td>spell correctly</td></tr>
<tr><td>Ⴔ</td><td>indent the paragraph</td></tr>
<tr><td>/</td><td>make a lowercase letter</td></tr>
<tr><td>∼ tr</td><td>transpose</td></tr>
</table>

19 Tricky Spellings

UNIT WORDS

1. heir
2. mortgage
3. drought
4. bough
5. thorough
6. khaki
7. bankruptcy
8. attempt
9. aerial
10. fascinate
11. nuisance
12. adolescent
13. maneuver
14. debt
15. doughnut
16. conceive
17. vehicle
18. amateur
19. lieutenant
20. gauge

I take it you already know
Of tough and bough and cough and dough?
Others may stumble but not you,
On hiccough, thorough, lough, and through.
Well done! And now you wish, perhaps,
To learn of less familiar traps?

Beware of heard, a dreadful word
That looks like beard and sounds like bird,
And dead: it's said like bed, not bead—
For goodness sake don't call it "deed"!
Watch out for meat and great and threat.
(They rhyme with suite and straight and debt.)
A moth is not a moth in mother
Nor both in bother, broth in brother,
And here is not a match for there
Nor dear and fear for bear and pear,
And then there's dose and rose and lose—
Just look them up—and goose and choose,
And cork and work and card and ward,
And font and front and word and sword,
And do and go and thwart and cart—
Come, come, I've hardly made a start!
A dreadful language? Man alive!
I'd mastered it when I was five!

T.S.W.

The Unit Words

As this poem humorously shows, English pronunciation and spelling can sometimes be tricky. George Bernard Shaw, an Irish-born English writer, once jokingly said that the word *fish* could easily be spelled *ghoti*: /f/ as in *rough*, /i/ as in *women*, and /sh/ as in *nation*.

The Unit words have some unusual letter combinations. Study them well. When you have mastered these spellings, you will have mastered some of the most challenging words in English.

ghoti

Spelling Practice

A. Four Unit words are spelled with *ough*. Write the Unit words in which *ough* spells the vowel sound heard in each of these words.

    1. cow (two words)   **2.** snow (two words)

B. Write the spelling for each of these pronunciations. Then underline the "silent" consonant in each word.

  3. /det/   **4.** /vē′i·kəl/   **5.** /kak′ē/   **6.** /môr′gij/

SPELLING DICTIONARY If you need help, use the pronunciation key on page 162.

C. Write two Unit words in which each of these sound groups is heard.

  7. /âr/   **8.** /n(y)o͞o/   **9.** /sē/   **10.** /ənt/

D. Complete these exercises using the Unit words.

11. Write the two words that have three pronounced consonants in a row.

12. Write the word that has /ā/ spelled with *au*.

E. Complete these sentences using the Unit words.

13. My grandmother's stories about the past _____ me.

14. *The Adventures of Tom Sawyer* is a novel by Mark Twain about the lives of two pre-_____ boys in a small town in Missouri.

15. To be eligible to compete in the Olympics, you must be an _____, not a professional athlete.

16. With a skillful _____, the pilot landed the damaged plane safely.

17. The software company ran out of money and had to file for _____.

18. The gas _____ registers full, but the tank is empty!

19. I gave my room a _____ search, but I couldn't find the tape anywhere.

20. I borrowed some money from my aunt, and she is letting me work off my _____ by mowing her lawn.

heir
mortgage
drought
bough
thorough
khaki
bankruptcy
attempt
aerial
fascinate
nuisance
adolescent
maneuver
debt
doughnut
conceive
vehicle
amateur
lieutenant
gauge

Spelling and Language • Spelling Variations

> Whan that Aprille with his shoures sote
> The droughte of Marche hath perced to the rote

These lines begin *The Canterbury Tales,* a poem written by Geoffrey Chaucer in the fourteenth century. The spellings are strange, but you can probably understand most of the words. In modern English, the lines read:

> When April with its showers sweet
> The drought of March has pierced to the root

English spelling has changed over the centuries. Even today the American spellings of certain words are different from the British spellings. *Maneuver* (American) and *manoeuvre* (British) are examples. Changes in spelling are still occurring. Perhaps you have seen some of these modern variations: *lite, foto, slax, Bar-B-Q..* In New York, a major highway is called the Governor Thomas E. Dewey *Thruway.*

Many people have offered suggestions for simplifying English spelling and removing some of its irregularity. These people would like words to be spelled exactly as they sound. Do you recognize the words *enuff, wimmen,* and *tung*?

Some of the words in these paragraphs are written in a simplified style.

1. Read the paragraphs carefully. Find the "new" spellings.

During the 1930's, a severe drout laid waste to the plains of the United States. Lack of rain for a short period of time can be a newsense. A prolonged shortage of rain is a dizaster. It's hard to gaje or conseeve of the damage it can create. Aireal fotografs taken at the time show no signs of green. Even the bows on the trees were covered with brown dust.

Farmers lost their crops year after year as the rains failed to arrive. Finally, many were so greatly in det that they could no longer pay their morgages and were forced to abandon their land. Drivers in v-ickles of every description manuvered the roads, looking for work and a new beginning.

2. Write the accepted spellings for the twelve words you found.

Writing on Your Own

Find out as much as you can about auto loans and mortgages. Then write a comparison paragraph for a pamphlet that a bank can send its customers. Tell how mortgages and auto loans are alike. Explain the ways in which they are different too. Use these Unit words: *mortgage, debt, vehicle, bankruptcy.*

 WRITER'S GUIDE For a sample comparison paragraph, turn to page 260.

Spelling on Your Own

UNIT WORDS

Write sentences including all of the Unit words. Use as many of the words as you can in each sentence. See how *few* sentences you can write.

MASTERY WORDS

yolk
prompt
seize
aisle
exhaust
throughout

Write the Mastery word that has the vowel sound heard in each of these words.

1. odd   **2.** new   **3.** cold   **4.** tree
5. paw   **6.** ice   **7.** now

Write the words in which these letters are not pronounced.

8. gh   **9.** h   **10.** l

Homophones sound alike but are spelled differently. Write the Mastery word that is a homophone for each word.

11. seas   **12.** I'll

Finish this paragraph using the correct homophone of the two in parentheses.

(Threw out, Throughout) __13__ history, people have sailed the seven (seas, seize) __14__. Some, perhaps, hoped to find a romantic desert (isle, aisle) __15__. But I'd set sail immediately if I thought I could find a place that serves a soft-boiled egg without a runny (yoke, yolk) __16__.

BONUS WORDS

succumb
subtle
cryptic
ecstasy
knoll
naive
alien
wretched

Write the Bonus word for each of these meanings.

1. a mound   **2.** innocent   **3.** delicate
4. unhappy   **5.** foreign   **6.** great happiness
7. yield

Use the Bonus words to complete these exercises.

8. The word *cryptic* comes from the Greek word *krypte,* "a vault or hidden cave." Write a definition for *cryptic.* Then use your knowledge of Greek roots to decipher the meaning of the word *cryptogram.*

9. Use the eight Bonus words to write a story entitled "A Cryptic Message."

20 Latin Prefixes

UNIT WORDS

1. *projector*
2. *progress*
3. *protrude*
4. *provide*
5. *abnormal*
6. *absurd*
7. *abrupt*
8. *absorb*
9. *adjacent*
10. *adhesive*
11. *advantage*
12. *attachment*
13. *extinct*
14. *exception*
15. *exclusive*
16. *expectation*
17. *suburb*
18. *submerge*
19. *subtraction*
20. *substitute*

The Unit Words

You are probably very familiar with the machine in the picture. But even if you had never seen it before, its name, *projector,* could help you understand this machine's function.

The word *projector* is made up of three parts, and each part has a meaning. The prefix *pro-* means "forward." The root *ject* means "throw." The suffix *-or* means "one who does." Combined, these parts make a word that means "something that throws (an image) forward."

The prefix *pro-* and four other Latin prefixes are found in the Unit words. Here are the other four prefixes and their meanings.

ab-, "away from"
    ab + rupt ("break") = *abrupt*

ad-, "to"
    ad + hes ("stick") + *ive* = *adhesive*

ex-, "out from"
    ex + cept ("take") + *ion* = *exception*

sub-, "under"
    sub + merge ("plunge") = *submerge*

Spelling Practice

Charlie Chaplin

A. The prefix *sub-* means "under." It can also mean "near" or "instead of." Complete each sentence with a Unit word beginning with *sub-*.

1. In emergency first aid, a straight stick can _____ for a splint.

2. Sea otters _____ themselves in the ocean when danger threatens.

3. Appletown is a quiet _____ of New City.

4. Ellen made two errors in _____ on the math test.

B. The prefix *ab-* means "away from" or "on account of." Finish these sentences using Unit words that have *ab-*.

5. A paper towel will _____ moisture.

6. The car came to an _____ stop at the intersection.

7. A temperature of 104°F is _____ in humans.

8. Charlie Chaplin looked so _____ in his outfit that we immediately began to laugh.

C. Write the Unit words that have the prefix *pro-* and roots with these meanings.

9. *trud,* "thrust"   10. *gress,* "go"

11. *ject,* "throw"   12. *vid,* "see"

D. Write the Unit words with the prefix *ad-* that have these meanings. The prefix *ad-* changes to *at-* in one word.

13. next to   14. sticky   15. benefit   16. fondness

E. Write the Unit word that is related to each of these words.

17. exclude   18. except   19. expect   20. extinguish

F. Substitute *pro-, ab-, at-, sub-,* or *ex-* for the prefix in each word and write a Unit word.

21. intrude   22. distraction   23. disrupt   24. reception

25. objector   26. institute   27. emerge   28. congress

29. detachment   30. inclusive

87

Proofreading • A Current Events Report

UNIT WORDS

projector
progress
protrude
provide
abnormal
absurd
abrupt
absorb
adjacent
adhesive
advantage
attachment
extinct
exception
exclusive
expectation
suburb
submerge
subtraction
substitute

Geraldo wrote this current events report for his social studies class. Now he must correct his work and write his final copy. Geraldo made nine spelling mistakes and two mistakes in the punctuation of abbreviations. Read the current events report carefully.

1. Find Geraldo's eleven mistakes in spelling and punctuation.

The Peregrine Falcon

The peregrine falcon was doomed! It was the expection that the species would be exstinct by the end of the twentieth century. These fasinating birds of prey were being systematically wiped out. The veicle for this mass destruction was DDT, a pesticide that was once used freely by farmers. DDT. remains in the body. The falcons, at the top of the food chain, were contamanated by the DDT stored in the bodies of their prey. Even a small, consentrated amount of DDT can weaken eggshells and cause them to crack before the chicks are hatched. The results are fatal.

In 1972 the use of DDT was outlawed. At the same time, Cornell University and other laboratories around the US. and Canada began to breed peregrine falcons in captivity. Young falcons bred in the laboratory were shipped to special training cites. There they were cared for until they were experienced enough to substetute their own kill for the food pervided by attendants. After their release, the falcons were able to breed and rear their young in the wild. Peregrine falcons have returned to the skies.

---

2. Write the nine misspelled words correctly.

3. Write the incorrectly punctuated abbreviations correctly.

Writing on Your Own

Imagine that you are a talented model-builder. The hobby shop where you buy your supplies has asked you to share some tips with less experienced model-builders. Write one or two paragraphs to explain how to avoid some common problems in model-building. Use as many Unit words as you can.

 WRITER'S GUIDE For a sample how-to paragraph, turn to page 259.

Spelling on Your Own

 UNIT WORDS

Write the Unit word that would come next in alphabetical order after each word below. For example, the word that would come next after *abdomen* is *abnormal*.

1. abdomen	**2.** abolish	**3.** absent	**4.** abstract
5. address	**6.** adios	**7.** adult	**8.** adverb
9. evil	**10.** exchange	**11.** exist	**12.** extend
13. prepare	**14.** prohibit	**15.** protect	**16.** proud
17. style	**18.** subscribe	**19.** substitution	**20.** subtropical

MASTERY WORDS

Write the Mastery words that begin with these prefixes.

1. ab-   **2.** ad-   **3.** pro-   **4.** sub-   **5.** ex-

Complete each of these sentences using two Mastery words.

6. What is the correct ____ for ordering a magazine ____?

7. The fire chief's ____ was to cover your face and walk quickly to the nearest ____.

8. Do you have a reasonable ____ for your ____ on Friday?

Find the misspelled word in each group. Then write the word correctly.

9. explaination, exit, aisle

10. throughout, proceedure, yolk

11. advice, exhaust, subsciption

12. seize, prompt, absense

> explanation
> advice
> procedure
> absence
> subscription
> exit

BONUS WORDS

Sometimes the final letter of a prefix is changed or dropped when the prefix is added to a word. The meaning of the prefix, however, remains the same. Think of the meaning of each Bonus word. Then write the Bonus word or words that have the same prefix as each of these Unit words. Use the **Spelling Dictionary** to help you.

1. abrupt   **2.** adhesive   **3.** exception

4. progress   **5.** submerge

Use each Bonus word in a sentence that shows the meaning of the prefix.

> accentuate
> apprehend
> abstain
> avert
> emerge
> procession
> suppress
> emit

21 Words with Latin Roots

UNIT WORDS

1. spectacular
2. spectator
3. inspector
4. suspect
5. verdict
6. prediction
7. contradict
8. dictate
9. educational
10. conduct
11. deduction
12. reduction
13. attentive
14. intention
15. tendency
16. intently
17. attraction
18. extract
19. distraction
20. contraction

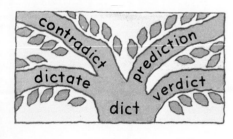

The Unit Words

Someone once said that you can read the history of a nation in its newspaper headlines. Perhaps it is also true that you can read the history of its language as well. Nine of the ten words in the headlines above have Latin roots. Only the word *soon* does not.

Latin has had a great influence on the English language. Almost half the words in the English vocabulary have Latin roots.

Each of the Unit words has one of five common Latin roots. The chart below lists these roots and their meanings.

ROOT	MEANING	EXAMPLE
dict	"say"	*dictate*
duc/duct	"lead"	*conduct*
spect	"look at"	*spectator*
tend/tent/tens	"stretch"	*attention*
tract	"pull"	*attraction*

Spelling Practice

A. For each of these words, write the four Unit words that have the same or a related Latin root.

1. *tractor,* "a vehicle used to pull a plow or other piece of equipment"

2. *viaduct,* "a bridge that leads over a roadway or valley"

3. *tent,* "material stretched over a frame"

B. Complete this paragraph using the four Unit words that have the Latin root meaning "look at."

    The police __**4**__ sat at her desk and sighed deeply. She imagined the joys of sitting in the warm sun, the taste and aroma of popcorn, and the noisy excitement of the crowd at the ballpark. How she wished that she, too, were a __**5**__ at that __**6**__ doubleheader that was now taking place. "Oh well," she said aloud, "I expect that I'll miss many more baseball games before the evidence against the __**7**__ is complete."

C. The Latin root *dict* means "say or speak." Write the Unit word that fits each of these definitions.

8. say the opposite of

9. give orders

10. a forecast

11. a judgment, a decision

D. The prefix *con-* means "with or together." Write the Unit words that have these meanings.

12. to guide or lead together

13. a shortened or pulled-together word

Spelling and Language • Vocabulary Building

The Romans were master builders of roads, bridges, and other structures. They also were skilled word builders. The Romans developed a large vocabulary by adding prefixes to base words. We do the same in English today. This kind of word building is called **derivation.**

In this lesson you will build words from Latin prefixes and roots. Some of the words you will write are not Unit words. Use a dictionary to help you spell these words.

ad-, "to"   *con-,* "together"   *dis-,* "away from"   *ex-,* "out of"
   pro-, "forward"   *re-,* "back"   *sub-,* "below"

A. Remember that the Latin root *tract* means "pull." Use *tract* and the prefixes above to help you write a word that fits each of these meanings. The prefix *ad-* changes to *at-* before a root beginning with *t.*

1. pull toward   **2.** pull out of   **3.** pull away from

4. pull together   **5.** pull below   **6.** pull forward

7. pull back

B. Add the prefix in ( ) to the root *duc/duct,* "lead," to form words to complete these sentences. In some cases you will also have to add a suffix. Remember that *duct* becomes *duce* in many English verbs.

8. (pro) Our drama club will _____ the musical _____ of Maurice Sendak's *Really Rosie.*

9. (intro) As an _____ to the play, the director will _____ the actors.

10. (con) A visiting _____ will _____ our local orchestra for the opening performance.

Writing on Your Own

Compile a class booklet of biographies with the title "Famous People." Choose a famous person from history, the arts, or sports and write a short biography of that person. If possible, use an encyclopedia or other reference source to find information about the person. Use as many Unit words as you can.

WRITER'S GUIDE For a sample paragraph from a biography, turn to page 267.

Spelling on Your Own

UNIT WORDS

Write the Unit words that have these base words.

1. attract   **2.** inspect   **3.** contract   **4.** attend
5. deduct   **6.** reduce   **7.** distract   **8.** predict
9. educate   **10.** tend   **11.** intent (2 words)

Now write the Unit words that are the base words for these words.

12. contradiction   **13.** dictation   **14.** extraction
15. conductor   **16.** suspicion   **17.** spectacularly

Write sentences using the words *spectator* and *verdict.*

MASTERY WORDS

product
dictionary
pretend
expect
extend
distract

Write the Mastery word that fits each group of words.

1. production, produce   **2.** distraction, distractedly

3. pretender, pretense   **4.** extended, extension

5. expectation, expectant

Complete these exercises using the Mastery words.

6. Choice of words and pronunciation is called *diction.* A book that helps you use and pronounce words is called a _____.

7. Things that draw your attention *attract* you. Things that keep you from concentrating _____ you.

Write the Mastery words that have these meanings.

8. make longer   **9.** look forward

10. make believe   **11.** something made

BONUS WORDS

speculation
contender
abduct
aspect
retract
addictive
tendon
induction

1. Use each Bonus word in a sentence that illustrates the word's meaning.

2. Copy and complete this chart by writing as many words as you can that have each Latin root listed. Begin with Bonus words. Then add other words.

dict	duct	spect	tend	tract

3. Use both of the Bonus words with the root *tend* in one sentence.

22 More Latin Roots

UNIT WORDS

1. manuscript
2. inscription
3. scribble
4. prescription
5. description
6. manual
7. manicure
8. manipulate
9. fragment
10. fracture
11. fragile
12. frail
13. reverse
14. inverted
15. controversy
16. convertible
17. multiplication
18. application
19. replica
20. pliable

Book of the Dead, Egypt

Codex Zouche-Nutall, Mexico

The Unit Words

One hundred thousand words in the English language were created from only fourteen Latin and Greek roots. You have already studied five of these fourteen roots. They are the Greek roots *graph* and *log* and the Latin roots *duc/duct, spect,* and *tend/tent/tens.* Two more of the fourteen roots are included in this unit: *plic,* "fold," and *script,* "write."

Sometimes a Latin root has two or more forms, as in *scrib/script.* Any of these forms may be found in an English word.

scribble   inscription

The chart lists other Latin roots found in the Unit words.

ROOT	MEANING	EXAMPLES
frag/fract	"break"	*fragment/fracture*
man/manu	"hand"	*manicure/manual*
plic/pli	"fold"	*replica/pliable*
vert/vers	"turn"	*invert/reverse*

Inscription in the Colosseum, Rome

94

Spelling Practice

A. Write the Unit word that is a noun form of each verb.

1. inscribe   **2.** apply   **3.** prescribe   **4.** describe

B. Four of the Unit words have a common root, *vert/vers,* meaning "turn." Complete each of these sentences using a word that has this root. The underlined words in each sentence are clues to the correct word.

5. _____ your steps and <u>turn</u> <u>back</u> in the other direction.

6. The _____ began when the senator <u>turned</u> <u>against</u> the majority opinion and opposed the bill.

7. When a fraction is _____, it is <u>turned</u> <u>into</u> its reciprocal.

8. When you open the _____ sofa completely, it <u>turns</u> <u>into</u> a comfortable bed.

C. Two of the Unit words have the meaning "delicate, weak, or easily broken." However, they are used to describe different things. Complete each sentence with the appropriate word.

9. Our dog is growing very old and _____ .

10. The crystal vase is delicate and very _____ .

D. Each word or term below includes the English word *hand.* For each word, write a word with the Latin root *man/manu* that is related in meaning.

11. handbook   **12.** handle

13. hand care   **14.** handwritten

E. Write the Unit word that is a synonym for each word.

15. doodle   **16.** reproduction

17. a chip   **18.** flexible

19. crack   **20.** changeable

21. dispute   **22.** opposite

F. The root *plic* also has the form *ply,* as in the word *reply.* Complete each of these sentences with a Unit word that has the root *plic.* The *ply* form is given as a clue.

23. To <u>apply</u> for the job, you must submit an _____.

24. The job requires someone who has learned the _____ tables and can <u>multiply</u> quickly.

manuscript
inscription
scribble
prescription
description
manual
manicure
manipulate
fragment
fracture
fragile
frail
reverse
inverted
controversy
convertible
multiplication
application
replica
pliable

Using the Dictionary to Spell and Write •
Multiple Definitions

When you write, you need to know all the meanings of a word. Many entry words in the dictionary have more than one meaning. Most dictionaries arrange the definitions so that the most common meaning is given first. But the most common meaning may not be the one that fits the context of the sentence. Keep looking until you find the correct meaning.

A. Look up the word *manual* in the **Spelling Dictionary**. Write the number of the definition that matches the meaning of *manual* in each sentence.

1. Irene carefully read the instruction <u>manual</u> before connecting her new stereo system.

2. Our class learned the <u>manual</u> alphabet so that we could communicate more easily with Jerry.

3. Over the summer Tom worked as a <u>manual</u> laborer.

4. Yukari drives a car with a <u>manual</u> transmission.

Sometimes, as the meanings of words develop, a word takes on a meaning that is very different from its original meaning. Remember that the word *terrific* used to have the negative meaning of "terrible." Now its most common meaning is "wonderful."

B. For each sentence below, write the letter *N* if the underlined word has a socially negative meaning or *P* if it has a more positive meaning.

5. The artist was able to <u>discriminate</u> between colors that looked identical to the untrained eye.

6. Unfair voting laws that <u>discriminated</u> against some people have been abolished in the state.

7. Jake found that he could not <u>manipulate</u> people by sulking.

8. Tina tried to <u>manipulate</u> a spinning wheel.

 SPELLING DICTIONARY Remember to use your **Spelling Dictionary** when you write.

Writing on Your Own

Pretend that you are a writer with a great idea for a how-to book for people your age. Your book will be called *One Hundred Unusual Ways to Decorate a T-shirt*. Write the instructions for one idea for decorating a T-shirt. Use some Unit words. Choose at least one word with multiple definitions. Use the word at least twice to show the different meanings.

 WRITER'S GUIDE For help revising your paragraph, use the checklist on page 256.

Spelling on Your Own

UNIT WORDS

Copy the chart below. Write each Unit word under the correct root. One word will be written twice. Then write other words that you know to complete the chart. For example, *manually, manicurist,* and *manufacture* might be added to the *man/manu* column. See how many words you can think of.

frag/fract	man/manu	plic/pli	scrib/script	vert/vers

MASTERY WORDS

Finish these exercises using the Mastery words.

1. Write the two words that have the Latin root meaning "hand."
2. Write the three words that have the Latin root meaning "turn."
3. Write the word that means "part of a whole."

Write the Mastery word that could be used instead of the underlined word in each of these sentences.

4. Only a <u>portion</u> of the student body takes the bus.
5. I read a <u>poem</u> by Ogden Nash in my English book.
6. Rebecca and I had a long <u>talk</u> as we cooked dinner.
7. Mrs. Williams asked the witness to give his <u>story</u> of the crash.
8. That company has gone into the <u>making</u> of wooden boxes.
9. The <u>employers</u> and the workers met last Friday.

**management
fraction
version
verse
conversation
manufacturing**

BONUS WORDS

1. The root *plic* comes from a Latin word meaning "fold." The word part *plex* is a form of the root *plic* and means "entangled." Write the Bonus words with *plic* and *plex.*
2. Write the definition of *maintenance.* The word comes from the Latin roots *manu,* "hand," and *tend,* "hold." Write another Bonus word with the root *man/manu.*
3. Three Bonus words come from the root *vers/vert,* meaning "turn." Write each word and use it in a sentence.
4. The root of *refract* has the meaning "break." Write a short paragraph explaining what the *refraction* of light means.

**versatile
maintenance
diversion
refract
revert
implicate
perplexed
emancipated**

97

23 Synonyms and Antonyms

UNIT WORDS

1. irritate
2. soothe
3. donation
4. complicate
5. urged
6. counterfeit
7. contribution
8. encouraged
9. enthusiastic
10. hindrance
11. apparent
12. inexact
13. obstacle
14. vigorous
15. simplify
16. indifferent
17. evident
18. precise
19. energetic
20. authentic

February 9
My brother Len was really irritating tonight. He played records while I was trying to study my math. The loud opera music irritated me. I asked him to put on some nonirritating rock instead. That made him irritated. We both sat there irritated with each other.

The Unit Words

Good writers avoid repetition by using synonyms and antonyms. Writers find a great many synonyms and antonyms in a thesaurus. The word *thesaurus* is Latin for "treasure." The most famous thesaurus was written more than a hundred years ago by P. M. Roget. The modern version contains about 250,000 words arranged according to meaning. Look at the thesaurus entries below. You will find *irritate* listed in category 885.2—verbs that mean "to aggravate." Category 886 gives you antonyms for words in 885. *Soothe* is listed in this group. *Irritate* and its antonym *soothe* are both on the Unit spelling list. All the words on this list can be paired into synonyms or antonyms.

885. AGGRAVATION	886. RELIEF
.2 VERBS **aggravate, worsen, make worse;** exacerbate, embitter, sour; deteriorate; intensify, heighten, sharpen, make acute or more acute, bring to a head, deepen, increase, enhance, amplify, enlarge, magnify, build up; augment; rub salt in the wound, add insult to injury, pour oil on the fire, heat up [informal], hot up [slang]; **exasperate, annoy,** irritate 866.13, 14; provoke, be an *agent provocateur*.	.5 VERBS **relieve, give relief; ease,** ease matters; **reduce,** diminish, lessen, abate; **alleviate, mitigate, palliate,** soften, pad, cushion, assuage, allay, appease, mollify, subdue, soothe; salve, pour balm into, pour oil on; poultice, foment, stupe; slake, slacken; lull; **dull, deaden,** dull or deaden the pain, numb, benumb, anesthetize; temper the wind to the shorn lamb, lay the flattering unction to one's soul.

Spelling Practice

A. Write the two Unit words that are synonyms for each of these words.

1. obvious   **2.** obstruction   **3.** coaxed

4. offering   **5.** strenuous

B. Write the Unit word that is a synonym for each of these words. Then write the Unit word that is an antonym for the word.

6. forged   **7.** eager   **8.** accurate

9. calm   **10.** streamline

C. Choose two of the synonyms you wrote for **6–10.** Use those words to complete these exercises.

11. Write two sentences, each using one of the words you chose.

12. Write the same sentences again, but this time substitute antonyms for the two Unit words you chose.

D. Remember that the Latin root *pli* or *plic* means "fold." Two Unit words have this root. Write a Unit word for each of the meanings below.

13. to fold many strands together, entangle

14. to make into one fold or strand, disentangle

E. Avoid repetition in the following sentences by substituting a Unit word that is a synonym for each underlined word.

15. It was apparent that the biking trip would be canceled, because dark clouds were <u>apparent</u>.

16. I urged the leader to set another date for the trip, and my friend <u>urged</u> her to as well.

17. We were ready for some vigorous exercise, and sitting around the fireplace didn't sound at all <u>vigorous</u>.

Proofreading • A Reading Log Entry

Marianne wrote this entry in her reading log. Now she must proofread it. Marianne made nine spelling mistakes. She also omitted three quotation marks and made two other punctuation errors. Read Marianne's log entry carefully.

1. Find the misspelled words and the missing punctuation marks.

For this assignment, I read an anthology of short stories. My favorite was "The Necklace." It is about a desaster in the life of Mathilde Loisel, the wife of a poor clerk.

Mathilde spent her days absorbbed in dreaming about luxuries she could not afford. One day, in spite of many obstacles, her husband obtained an invitation to a ball. Instead of being enthusastic, Mathilde complained that she had nothing to wear.

"Here, buy a new dress with this money I have saved," her husband erged. "And you can borrow some jewelry from your wealthy friend, Madame Forestier."

Madame Forestier agreed to lend Mathilde her spectacular diamond necklace. When Mathilde returned from the ball, however, she discovered that she had lost the necklace. It was aparrent that the Loisels would have to replace the jewels. They borrowed enough money to purchase a presise repalica of the costly necklace. As a result, they spent the next ten years struggling to repay the loans.

One afternoon, Mathilde met her friend in the park. She decided to reveal the truth at last. Madame Forestier stared intintly at the worn-out woman. Oh, my poor Mathilde", she said The necklace was not authentic. It was not even a good counterfit. It was made of glass!

2. Write the nine misspelled words correctly.

Writing on Your Own

Write a book report for a reading log that you are keeping for your English class. Use some Unit words to tell about a story or book that you have recently read.

WRITER'S GUIDE For a sample book report, turn to page 263.

Guy de Maupassant, author of "The Necklace"

Spelling on Your Own

UNIT WORDS

Use each Unit word and an antonym for that word in a sentence. The antonym you use should not be a Unit word. Here is an example: "Andrea felt *energetic* when she began the bike trip, but by evening she was thoroughly *exhausted*."

MASTERY WORDS

forward
backward
rival
foe
confessed
admitted

Finish these exercises using the Mastery words.

1. Write the two words that mean "enemy."

2. Write the two words that mean "acknowledged guilt."

3. Write the word that means "in reverse."

4. Write the word that means the opposite of *backward*.

An **analogy** shows the relationship between two sets of words. "*Poem* is to *verse* as *conversation* is to *talk*" is an analogy. *Poem* and *verse* are synonyms. They mean the same thing. *Poem* and *verse* have the same relationship to each other as *conversation* and *talk* do.

Finish each of these analogies using the Mastery words. Think of the relationship between the first pair of words to complete each analogy.

5. *Pretended* is to *imagined* as *confessed* is to _____.

6. *Up* is to *down* as *backward* is to _____.

7. *Confession* is to *confessed* as *admission* is to _____.

8. *Down* is to *downward* as *back* is to _____.

9. *Exit* is to *doorway* as *foe* is to _____.

BONUS WORDS

refuge
sanctuary
terminate
originate
ominous
threatening
unreliable
trustworthy

1. Write the Bonus words. Then look up each word in a thesaurus or a standard dictionary. Write a synonym or an antonym for each of the words. Do not use a Bonus word as your answer.

2. Write sentences using the eight Bonus words. If you can, include in your sentence either the synonym or antonym that you wrote for **1.**

3. Look up *ominous, threaten, trustworthy,* and *reliable* in the **Spelling Dictionary**. Write the name of the language from which each word comes.

24 Review

UNIT 19

fascinate
nuisance
gauge
vehicle
thorough
mortgage
attempt
debt
adolescent
lieutenant

Follow these steps when you are unsure of how to spell a word.

- **Say** the word. Recall when you have heard the word used. Think about what it means.
- **Look** at the word. Find any prefixes, suffixes, or other word parts you know. Think about other words that are related in meaning and spelling. Try to picture the word in your mind.
- **Spell** the word to yourself. Think about the way each sound is spelled. Notice any unusual spelling.
- **Write** the word while looking at it. Check the way you have formed your letters. If you have not written the word clearly or correctly, write it again.
- **Check** your learning. Cover the word and write it. If you did not spell the word correctly, practice these steps until the word becomes your own.

UNIT 19 **Follow the directions using words from Unit 19. Write the accepted spellings for the words written in a simplified style. Underline the letters in your answers that are silent.**

1. v-ickle
2. thorow
3. fasinate
4. nucents
5. morgaj
6. det
7. Write the word that is a title for an officer.
8. Write the word that is a synonym for *teenager.*

Write a word that can be used in place of the underlined word.

9. I am going to <u>try</u> this dive.
10. The tire <u>instrument</u> showed that the tire needed air.

UNIT 20

advantage
exception
progress
provide
substitute
absurd
adjacent
extinct
suburb
absorb

UNIT 20 **Using words from Unit 20, write two words that have these prefixes.**

11. *sub-,* "under or near" (two words)
12. *pro-,* "forward" (two words)
13. *ab-,* "away from" (two words)
14. *ad-,* "to" (two words)
15. *ex-,* "out of" (two words)

UNIT 21 **Follow the directions using words from Unit 21.**
Write the word or words that have these Latin roots.

16. *spect,* "see" (two words)
17. *tract,* "pull" (two words)
18. *dict,* "say" (two words)
19. *duc/duct,* "lead" (two words)
20. *tend,* "stretch" (two words)

Complete these sentences.

21. We didn't want to stay for the second ___ at the movies, because we had already seen it.

22. Instead, we went home and watched a show about earthquakes on ___ TV.

23. A scientist on the show made a ___ that our area would have an earthquake within the next twenty years.

24. This part of the country has several fault lines, so I ___ the forecast is correct.

UNIT 22 **Follow the directions using words from Unit 22.**
Write the word or words that have the same Latin root as each of these words.

25. conversation (two words)
26. describe (three words)
27. fraction (three words)
28. manufacture
29. pliable

Complete these sentences.

30. I read the ___ that came with my bike.

31. It warned that some of the parts of the gears were quite ___, so I was careful with them.

32. The ___ on the rim of the bike tires told how much air to put in the tires.

33. I first put the handlebars on backwards and had to ___ them.

34. After I got the bike together, I rode to the pet shop to leave my ___ for an after-school job.

UNIT 21

contraction
tendency
suspect
conduct
spectator
verdict
educational
intention
attraction
prediction

UNIT 22

prescription
manual
fracture
reverse
application
inscription
description
fragment
fragile
convertible

UNIT 23   Follow the directions using words from Unit 23. Rewrite each sentence using an antonym for the underlined word or words.

contribution
encouraged
apparent
irritate
authentic
enthusiastic
obstacle
simplify
evident
complicate

35. The museum had a <u>fake</u> Rembrandt painting.

36. The guides could <u>confuse</u> an explanation of the paintings.

37. It was <u>unclear</u> what we should do after leaving the museum.

38. To <u>simplify</u> matters, we decided to take a walk downtown.

Rewrite each sentence using a synonym for the underlined word.

39. The club members were <u>interested</u> in helping to build a new playground.

40. Everyone made a <u>donation</u> to the building fund.

41. It was <u>obvious</u> that we could raise enough money.

42. The only <u>hindrance</u> to our plan was that the members didn't have enough time to work on the project.

43. Their busy schedules often seem to <u>annoy</u> them.

44. Everyone was <u>urged</u> to attend the next meeting.

WORDS IN TIME

English is a language rich in synonyms because it contains so many words borrowed from other languages. The word *obstacle* comes from the Latin verb *obstare*, "to stand in the way." *Hindrance*, on the other hand, comes from the Old English word *hindrian*, "to put behind or to keep back."

Spelling and Reading
A Research Report

Read this research report about hot-air balloons. Notice how the writer has ordered the facts.

History and Uses of Hot-Air Balloons

Can you imagine floating silently in an open basket a mile above the countryside? People have been making the attempt for hundreds of years, and today it has become almost commonplace. This paper will briefly discuss the history of the hot-air balloon and its modern uses.

During the thirteenth century, scientists dreamed of sending metal spheres into the air. In 1783 the Montgolfier* brothers substituted cloth for metal and sent King Louis XVI's historian 80 feet into the air over Paris. This was the first real flight of a human in a hot-air balloon.

In the United States, the first scientific recording of air pressure at great heights was made during a balloon flight in 1784. In 1793 President Washington stood among the spectators of an ascent in Philadelphia. Not quite a century later, an enthusiastic American named Thaddeus Lowe telegraphed a message to President Lincoln using a wire that stretched from his balloon to a ground receiver.

Great progress has been made in the use of hot-air balloons since these early attempts at flight. Scientists fascinated by the advantages balloons provide soon learned that they could carry instruments for studying cosmic rays and for forecasting the weather. When modern weather balloons reach a certain height, the pressure of the gas inside explodes the balloon, and parachutes float the instruments safely to earth.

As we look back, it is evident that what might have been absurd during the thirteenth century is an everyday occurrence in the twentieth. What contributions will hot-air balloons make in the next century? Right now, no one can say for sure.

*The name *Montgolfier* is pronounced /Mōn·gôf·yā′/.

Write your answers to the questions.

1. What is the topic of this research report?
2. What famous person attended the 1793 hot-air balloon flight in Philadelphia?
3. What does the writer say that implies there were balloon flights before 1783?

Underline the review words in your answers. Check to see that you spelled the words correctly.

Spelling and Writing
A Research Report

Words to Help You Write

fascinate
thorough
advantage
provide
conduct
description
encouraged
apparent
irritate
simplify

Think and Discuss

A research report is a written record of study on a particular topic. Length is not usually important; an interesting report might be as short as five paragraphs or as long as an entire book. The key to writing such reports is good organization, which begins with a suitably narrow topic. If the report will contain five paragraphs, for example, the writer should plan to discuss no more than three points. A longer report will obviously allow coverage of more material. Writing an outline is a good way to help you organize the main ideas and supporting details in your report.

Research reports generally have three parts: an **introduction,** a **body,** and a **conclusion.** The introduction should contain a topic sentence that tells what the report will cover. It should also include some general information on the topic. On which topic is the model report written? The body of the report contains facts derived from the writer's research—at least one paragraph for each main point discussed. The conclusion often summarizes what has been reported in the body. How might you describe the three main points in this report? How does the conclusion of the report tie together all the information the writer has given?

Once the report is finished, the writer usually composes a suitable title. This is easily done by compressing the information in the introduction into four or five words. What alternate title might have been given to the model report?

Apply

Now get ready to write a **research report** of your own. Follow the writing guidelines on page 107.

Prewriting

Give some thought to a topic you would enjoy researching. Then narrow your topic according to the length of your report.

- Find some books and magazines that contain information on your topic. Take brief notes, including the name of each book and the pages from which the notes came.
- Make a brief outline that helps you organize your information. Be sure that your outline includes one part for the introduction and one part for the conclusion. It should also include one part for each of the main points to be covered in the body of your report.

Composing

Refer to your outline as you write your first draft.

- Write an introduction. Be sure your topic sentence explains clearly what the report will be about. Give a hint about the facts you will use.
- Write the body of your report. Again, follow the order you determined in your outline. Tie the paragraphs together with transitions such as *in addition, however, in contrast,* and *for example.*
- Write your conclusion. Summarize the main points.
- Add a title that reflects the topic of your work.

Revising

Read your research report and show it to a classmate. Follow these guidelines to improve your work. Use the editing and proofreading marks on this page to indicate corrections.

 WRITER'S GUIDE For help in revising your report, see the checklist on page 256.

Editing

- Be sure your report has an introduction, a body, a conclusion, and a title.
- Be sure the body of your report contains at least one paragraph for each main point you discuss.

Proofreading

- Check your spelling, capitalization, and punctuation.

Copy your research report onto clean paper. Write carefully and neatly.

Publishing

You might want to design a cover for your research report and display it with those of your fellow students on a classroom table.

Editing and Proofreading Marks

☰	capitalize
⊙	make a period
∧	add something
⋀	add a comma
ⱽ ⱽ	add quotation marks
‿	take something away
◯	spell correctly
⌤	indent the paragraph
/	make a lowercase letter
∼ tr	transpose

---

25 Words with *ant* and *ent*

The Unit Words

Are you a *hesitant* speller, or are you a *confident* and *competent* speller? If you are *observant,* you will have noticed that the four italicized words end with the letters *ant* or *ent.* If you say the words aloud, you will hear that each word ends with the sounds /ənt/—whether the word is spelled with *ant* or *ent.*

There are no easy rules to guide you in learning the correct spellings for the words in this unit. Each Unit word ends with the sounds /ənt/, so you cannot tell from the pronunciation if it is spelled with *a* or *e.* You need to study the words carefully and memorize their spellings.

REMEMBER THIS

The sound /sh/ is sometimes spelled with the letters *ci.* To spell the sound /sh/ with *ci* in the word *efficient* /i·fish′ənt/, remember to include two *i*'s around the *c.*

108

Spelling Practice

A. Write the spelling for each of these pronunciations.

1. /in'sə·dənt/   **2.** /vā'kənt/   **3.** /in'fənt/

4. /kən·tes'tənt/   **5.** /kon'fə·dənt/   **6.** /ûr'jənt/

7. /mag·nif'ə·sənt/   **8.** /i·fish'ənt/

B. Write the Unit word that names a person who does each of these things.

9. occupies a house   **10.** applies for a job

11. participates in an activity

C. Write the Unit word that describes each of these people or things.

12. someone who hesitates   **13.** someone who observes carefully

14. something that is found in abundance

D. Write the Unit word that is an antonym for each of these words.

15. faltering   **16.** ally   **17.** crude

18. seldom   **19.** independent   **20.** incapable

Adverbs are used to modify verbs. An adverb tells how, when, or where. You can often form an adverb by adding -ly to the end of an adjective.

E. Add -ly to each of these adjectives to form adverbs. Write the adverbs.

21. hesitant   **22.** abundant   **23.** elegant

24. urgent   **25.** fluent   **26.** frequent

27. confident   **28.** efficient   **29.** competent

F. For each of these Latin roots, write a Unit word formed from it. An English word with the same root is given as a clue.

30. *plic* "fold" application   **31.** *flu* "flow" fluid
32. *vac* "empty" vacation   **33.** *pon/pos* "put" oppose

109

Spelling and Language •
Adding -ence, -ency, -ance, or -ancy

There are no rules to help you decide whether a word is spelled with *ent* or *ant*. However, if you know that a word such as *dependent* is spelled with *ent*, then you can assume that the suffixes in related words are also spelled with e: *dependence* and *dependency*. Similarly, if a word such as *occupant* ends with *ant*, a related form will also be spelled with a: *occupancy*.

A. Write a word ending with *-ence* or *-ance* that is related to these words.

1. incident
2. elegant
3. abundant
4. confident
5. observant
6. adolescent
7. magnificent
8. evident
9. indifferent
10. competent
11. dependent
12. resident

B. Complete each sentence with a word ending with *-ency* or *-ancy* that is related to the word in ( ).

13. Is there a (vacant) _____ in your apartment building?

14. There was (urgent) _____ in the rescue worker's voice.

15. Jed's (fluent) _____ in Spanish was helpful in his job.

16. The first months of (infant) _____ are important in a child's development.

17. We will need to work with greater (efficient) _____ if we expect to meet our deadline.

18. The graph indicates the (frequent) _____ of rainfall over a ten-year period.

19. That apartment building maintains 100 percent (occupant) _____ because it is a very nice place to live.

UNIT WORDS

hesitant
confident
competent
observant
vacant
urgent
occupant
fluent
infant
dependent
abundant
frequent
contestant
opponent
participant
efficient
applicant
magnificent
elegant
incident

Writing on Your Own

Imagine that you are a member of the drama club. At a recent meeting, the club's members disagreed about whether the audience should pay to attend. To resolve the argument, the club's president asked everyone to write a persuasive paragraph about what should be done. Describe the advantages of both a free performance and one at which a donation is required. Then tell the members what you think they ought to do. Use eight or more of the Unit words. Try to use the suffixes *-ence, -ency, -ance,* and *-ancy*.

WRITER'S GUIDE For a sample persuasive paragraph, turn to page 260.

Spelling on Your Own

UNIT WORDS

Write the eight Unit words that are nouns in one column. In a second column, write the fourteen adjectives. You will need to write two words twice. Then select a word from the adjective column to form a phrase with each noun. For example, you might write "the hesitant infant."

MASTERY WORDS

Finish these exercises with Mastery words.

1. Write the three words that end with *ant*.

2. Write the three words that end with *ent*.

3. Write a sentence using one word you wrote for **1** and one word you wrote for **2**.

Write the Mastery word that is an antonym, or opposite, of the underlined word in each sentence.

4. The weather is usually <u>nasty</u> at this time of year.

5. The paint left a <u>temporary</u> stain on Jill's jeans.

Write the Mastery word that can be substituted for the underlined word in each sentence.

6. The <u>collision</u> took place at Elm and Grove streets.

7. The undercover <u>spy</u> secretly hid the papers.

Write the spelling for each of these pronunciations.

8. /ə·koun'tənt/   **9.** /ak'sə·dənt/

BONUS WORDS

Write the two Bonus words that come from each of these Latin words.

1. *consistere,* "to stand together"

2. *deficere,* "to fail"   **3.** *belligerare,* "to wage war"

Write the Bonus words that contain these sounds.

4. /sh/ spelled with *ci*   **5.** /j/ spelled with *g*

The word *buoyant* has two meanings. Write a short paragraph using each meaning of *buoyant.* Include the word *buoyancy* in the paragraph as well.

26 Words That End with /īz/

The Unit Words

The verbs above would surely have puzzled a reader a hundred years ago. New words have rapidly been invented to keep pace with advances in twentieth-century living. But word-making is not new; people have been creating words since language began.

One of the easiest ways to form new words in English is to add a suffix to an existing word. The suffix -ize, for example, can be added to a noun or an adjective to form a verb.

critic (n.) + ize = criticize

sterile (adj.) + ize = sterilize

Only about thirty commonly used English verbs end with the suffix -ise. Most of the verbs that end with the sounds /īz/ are spelled with **ize**. *Paralyze* and *analyze* are the only two words you are likely to use that have /īz/ spelled **yze**.

REMEMBER THIS

Sometimes people use rhymes or jingles to help them remember how to spell difficult words. Here is a jingle to help you remember the *hy* spelling in *hypnotize*.

Why, oh why, do you surmise,
Is there a *y* for /i/ in *hypnotize*?

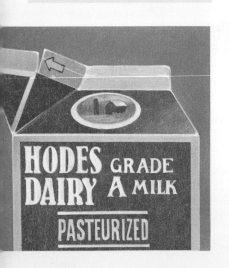

HODES GRADE
DAIRY A MILK
PASTEURIZED

Spelling Practice

Louis Pasteur

A. Change each of these nouns into a verb that ends with *-ize*. Then complete the exercise.

1. critic   **2.** apology   **3.** sympathy   **4.** economy

5. Write the verb that is formed by adding *-ize* to the name of a French chemist who invented a sterilization process.

B. Change each of these adjectives into a verb that ends with *-ize*.

6. sterile   **7.** special

C. In words with Greek roots, the sound /i/ or /ī/ is often spelled **y.** The sound /f/ is often spelled **ph.** Use the Unit words to complete these exercises.

8. Write the two words in which /i/ is spelled with *y.*

9. Write the two words in which /ī/ is spelled with *y.*

10. Write the word in which /f/ is spelled with *ph.*

D. Write the Unit word that comes from each Latin word.

11. *supervidere,* "to oversee"

12. *revisere,* "to look again"

13. *improvidere,* "to fail to foresee"

14. *despicere,* "to look down"

15. *compromittere,* "to make a mutual promise"

E. Write an inflected form of a Unit word that could be substituted for each underlined word in the paragraph. Use each word only once.

   The rapid system of mail delivery known as the Pony Express was <u>invented</u> (**16**) in 1860. The route, <u>arranged</u> (**17**) into relay stations between Missouri and California, involved great risk. The firm that ran the Pony Express <u>realized</u> (**18**) the hazards and <u>asked</u> (**19**) for "small, daring young men, preferably orphaned." When the transcontinental telegraph system was completed in 1861, the need for rapid mail delivery ceased. The short life of the Pony Express was over.

Spelling and Language • Noun-Forming Suffixes

UNIT WORDS

criticize
sterilize
revise
analyze
advertise
apologize
devise
paralyze
sympathize
despise
specialize
supervise
recognize
compromise
hypnotize
pasteurize
improvise
economize
organize
emphasize

Nouns are words that name people, places, things, or ideas. Some nouns are formed by adding a noun-forming suffix to a verb: *dictate + ion = dictation*. Other nouns are created by adding a noun-forming suffix to a base or root word: *frag + ment = fragment*.

A. Write the verb from which each noun was formed.

1. advertisement   **2.** organization   **3.** supervisor

4. sympathizer   **5.** improvisation   **6.** sterilization

7. revision   **8.** pasteurization

B. The noun-forming suffix *-ist* means "one who does." It is often added to a base or root word. Add *-ist* to the base or root of each of these verbs to form a noun. Use the **Spelling Dictionary** if you need help.

9. specialize   **10.** hypnotize

11. economize   **12.** colonize

13. When you add *-ist* to a word that ends with *yze*, the spelling of *-ist* changes to *yst*. Write the noun that means "one who analyzes."

C. Sometimes *-ist* is added to a noun. Write the word that is formed when *-ist* is added to each noun.

14. journal   **15.** column   **16.** manicure

D. Write the noun from which each word is formed.

17. abolitionist   **18.** revisionist   **19.** biologist

20. essayist   **21.** moralist   **22.** manicurist

Writing on Your Own

Write a humorous poem for a favorite teacher called "Things to Learn." In each line use one or two of the Unit words to help you describe something you want to learn. Use as many Unit words as you can. Try to use some words with the suffixes *-ion, -ment,* and *-ist.*

 WRITER'S GUIDE For a sample poem, turn to page 267.

Spelling on Your Own

UNIT WORDS

Each Unit word below is incomplete. Think of the letters that would spell /īz/ in each word. Then write the word.

1. econom_____ **2.** advert_____ **3.** critic_____ **4.** dev_____

5. paral_____ **6.** comprom_____ **7.** apolog_____ **8.** rev_____

9. sympath_____ **10.** special_____ **11.** improv_____ **12.** anal_____

13. steril_____ **14.** emphas_____ **15.** organ_____ **16.** desp_____

17. superv_____ **18.** recogn_____ **19.** hypnot_____ **20.** pasteur_____

MASTERY WORDS

Write the Mastery word for each of these meanings.

1. give advice to   **2.** hide or conceal

3. shock or confuse   **4.** broadcast by television

5. understand or appreciate fully   **6.** make your muscles work

Three of the Mastery words may be used as verbs or nouns. Complete each pair of sentences with a form of a Mastery word. Then write *noun* or *verb* above each word you wrote to show its use.

7. Alicia wore a _____ to the party.

She _____ herself as a Martian.

8. We _____ Maria with a birthday party.

Everyone kept the secret, so our _____ worked.

9. Mrs. Kelly showed us a new _____ in gym.

She _____ every day to keep in shape.

exercise
televise
disguise
surprise
realize
advise

BONUS WORDS

1. Write each Bonus word. Then, next to each word, write a noun or adjective that is related to the word. Use a dictionary if you need help.

2. Write eight sentences using the Bonus words.

3. The sound /e/ is spelled **eo** in *leopard*. Write the Bonus word in which /e/ is spelled the same way.

legalize
familiarize
authorize
utilize
jeopardize
surmise
merchandise
subsidize

27 Science Words

UNIT WORDS

1. anatomy
2. intestine
3. genetics
4. chromosome
5. artery
6. digestive
7. algae
8. spinal
9. capillaries
10. plasma
11. protoplasm
12. traits
13. circulation
14. nucleus
15. organism
16. ligament
17. lungs
18. bacteria
19. recessive
20. dominant

The Unit Words

Of all the scientific words on the Unit word list, only one, *lungs,* has native English origins. The rest of the words are of Latin or Greek origin.

During the Middle Ages Latin was the language of the scholars, while English was used by the common people in everyday speech. That is why certain parts of the body, such as the lungs, heart, nose, ears, eyes, feet, teeth, and head, have native English names. Latin was used by scholars for scientific studies.

Some of these specialized terms, such as *nucleus, algae, bacteria,* and *plasma,* are actually Latin or Greek words, although their original meanings are slightly different. Other terms, such as *chromosome,* were created by scientists out of Greek or Latin roots to name new discoveries.

REMEMBER THIS

The word *anatomical* gives you clues for spelling both schwa sounds in *anatomy.* Compare the pronunciations.

/ə·nat′ə·mē/
/an′·ə·tom′i·kəl/

Which letters spell /ə/ in *anatomy?*

a·NAT·o·my
an·a·TOM·i·cal

Spelling Practice

A. The letter *c* can be used to spell /k/ or /s/. In words that come from Greek, *ch* is often used to spell /k/. Use the Unit words to complete these exercises.

1. Write the word in which *ch* spells the sound /k/.

2. Write the five words in which the sound /k/ is spelled with *c*.

3. Write the two words in which the sound /s/ is spelled with *c*.

B. Complete each of the exercises below using Unit words.

4. The sound /ē/ is spelled with *y* in *artery*. Write the Unit words in which /ē/ is spelled a different way.

5. Write the only Unit word that does not have a Greek or Latin root.

C. Write the Unit word that comes from each of these Greek or Latin words.

6. *G. anatome,* "dissection"

7. *G.* and *L. arteria,* "windpipe"

8. *L. spina,* "backbone"

9. *L. ligamentum,* "a band, tie"

10. *L. intestinus,* "internal"

11. *L. capillus,* "hair"

12. *L. tractus,* "personal characteristic"

13. *G. plasma* "something molded or formed" (two words)

Fig. 296.—Muscles of the back of the leg. Superficial layer.

D. Write the Unit word that is related to each of these groups of words.

14. digest, digestion

15. organic, organization

16. dominate, domineering

17. generation, genesis

18. recession, recess

19. anatomical, anatomize

Spelling and Language • Plurals

UNIT WORDS

anatomy
intestine
genetics
chromosome
artery
digestive
algae
spinal
capillaries
plasma
protoplasm
traits
circulation
nucleus
organism
ligament
lungs
bacteria
recessive
dominant

To form the plural of most nouns, you add the inflectional ending *s.* To form the plural of nouns that end in *s, ss, sh, ch,* or *x,* add *es.*

A. Write the plural form of each of these nouns.

1. lung   2. intestine   3. trait   4. chromosome

5. organism   6. ligament   7. index   8. canvas

9. excess   10. opponent

To form the plural of nouns that end in a consonant and *y,* change the *y* to *i* and add *es,* as in *remedies.* To form the plural of nouns that end in a vowel and *y,* add *s,* as in *essays.*

B. Write the plural form of each of these nouns.

11. anatomy   12. artery   13. capillary   14. controversy

15. attorney   16. primary   17. laboratory   18. survey

19. minority   20. fantasy

The original plural forms of some Latin and Greek words are used in English: *alumnus, alumni; alumna, alumnae; datum, data; crisis, crises.*

C. Write the plural form of each of these nouns. Use the **Spelling Dictionary** if you need help.

21. bacterium   22. alga   23. nucleus   24. diagnosis

Generally, a verb must agree with its subject in number: "The toys *are* in the box." However, some plural nouns take a singular verb: "Gymnastics *is* my favorite sport."

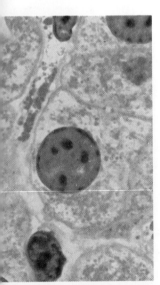

The nucleus of an animal cell

Writing on Your Own

Write a paragraph for your science class that describes two related scientific fields, anatomy and genetics. You can find out about them in science books or an encyclopedia. Tell what scientists study in each field and how the fields are similar and how they are different. Use as many of the Unit words and plurals as you can.

WRITER'S GUIDE For help revising your paragraph, use the checklist on page 256.

118

Spelling on Your Own

UNIT WORDS

Write the Unit words in the order in which they would appear in the index of a science book.

MASTERY WORDS

Write the Mastery word that rhymes with each of these words.

1. curves   **2.** smart

3. Write the two Mastery words that rhyme.

Finish these sentences.

4. After I ate a big lunch, my _____ was full.

5. When the nurse came in, he took my _____.

Can you change a Mastery word into the word *a*? Here's how to do it. Write the Mastery word. Then, taking away one letter at a time, write a list of new and shorter words. You may change the order of letters, but you may not add new letters. Here's an example.

atlas → last → sat → at → a

6. Now you try it. In five steps, change *brain* into the word *a*.

7. In five steps, change *heart* into the word *a*.

nerves
stomach
vein
brain
pulse
heart

BONUS WORDS

Write the Bonus words that are related to these Greek or Latin words.

1. *G. neuron,* "sinew"   **2.** *L. corpusculum,* "little body"
3. *L. ventriculus,* "little belly"   **4.** *L. auricula,* "little ear"

Write the Bonus words that are related to these words.

5. aortic   **6.** invertebrate   **7.** skeleton   **8.** embryonic

Use each Bonus word in a sentence.

corpuscle
auricle
embryo
skeletal
ventricle
vertebra
neural
aorta

28 Syllable Patterns

UNIT WORDS

1. *pivot*
2. *frantic*
3. *focus*
4. *crevice*
5. *rascal*
6. *dishonor*
7. *dislocate*
8. *immodest*
9. *immobile*
10. *rotate*
11. *brilliant*
12. *discover*
13. *misdirect*
14. *nomad*
15. *disrespectful*
16. *ballot*
17. *silence*
18. *sliver*
19. *pageant*
20. *token*

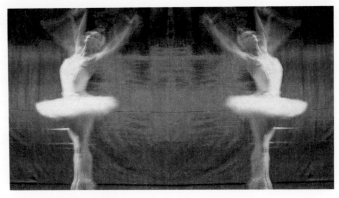

The Unit Words

Often when you are writing or typing, you need to divide a word at the end of a line. You should always check the dictionary if you are not sure how to divide a word. Keep in mind that you never divide a one-syllable word or separate a one-letter syllable from the rest of the word.

Use these rules to divide the Unit words.

1. When a word has two consonant letters between two vowel sounds, divide the word between the consonants. But remember that you should never divide a consonant digraph.

   bal·lot   fran·tic   broth·er

2. When a word has one consonant letter between two vowel sounds:

   a. divide *before* the consonant if the first vowel sound is long or if the second syllable is accented.

   fo·cus

   b. divide *after* the consonant if the first vowel sound is short and the first syllable is accented.

   crev·ice

3. When a word has a prefix or a suffix, separate the prefix or suffix from the base word before dividing the base word.

   dis·hon·or·able

120

Spelling Practice

A. Complete these exercises using the Unit words that do not have prefixes.

1. The word *pattern* has two consonant letters between two vowel sounds. It is divided into syllables this way: **pat·tern.** Write the four two-syllable words that follow this pattern.

2. The word *basis* has a long vowel sound in the first syllable. It is divided into syllables this way: **ba·sis.** Write the five words that follow this pattern.

3. The word *logic* has a short vowel sound in the first syllable. It is divided into syllables this way: **log·ic.** Write the four words that follow this pattern.

4. Now draw a line between the syllables in each word you wrote for **1–3.**

B. Use the Unit words that have prefixes to complete these exercises.

5. Write the word *disrespectful.*

6. Draw lines to separate the prefix and suffix from the base word.

7. Write the two-syllable word that remains. Note that the base word also has a prefix. Now draw a line between the syllables in this word.

8. Write the six other words that have prefixes. Then cross out the prefix in each word.

9. Write the six two-syllable words that remain in **8.**

10. Look carefully at the six words for **9.** Decide which rule you will use to divide each of these words. Then draw a line between the syllables in each word.

C. An anagram is a word formed by changing the order of the letters in another word. For example, *late* is an anagram for *tale.* Write the Unit word that is an anagram for each word.

11. license   **12.** silver

Using the Dictionary to Spell and Write •
Finding Synonyms

A dictionary offers more than the spelling, pronunciation, and meaning of a word. Many dictionaries also have the history of a word and its correct usage.

When you would like to substitute a synonym for a word, check a dictionary. Frequently you will find a synonym listed at the end of a main entry.

A. Read the sentences below. Look up each of the underlined words in the **Spelling Dictionary.** Then write a synonym from the list of Unit words that could replace the underlined word in each sentence.

1. Mei tried to <u>concentrate</u> on her book in spite of the noise.
2. The farmer plans to <u>alternate</u> the crops in the west field.
3. The <u>quiet</u> of the forest signaled an approaching storm.
4. Doug found a <u>fragment</u> of glass in the sink.
5. Take this ring as a <u>symbol</u> of our friendship.
6. The herd remained <u>stationary</u> until the danger passed.

B. Look up each of these Unit words in the **Spelling Dictionary.** Find the six words for which a synonym is listed in the entry. Write the six words in a column and then write their synonyms next to them.

7. dislocate	**8.** disrespectful	**9.** frantic	**10.** misdirect
11. nomad	**12.** pageant	**13.** pivot	**14.** rascal

UNIT WORDS

- pivot
- frantic
- focus
- crevice
- rascal
- dishonor
- dislocate
- immodest
- immobile
- rotate
- brilliant
- discover
- misdirect
- nomad
- disrespectful
- ballot
- silence
- sliver
- pageant
- token

ROGUE?
SCOUNDREL?
SCAMP?
RAPSCALLION?
SCALAWAG?
KNAVE?

RASCAL

Writing on Your Own

Imagine that an explorer has discovered an unknown island. A newspaper reporter is interviewing the explorer about the discovery. Write conversation for the explorer and the newspaper reporter. Use as many Unit words as you can.

 WRITER'S GUIDE For sample conversation, turn to page 265.

Spelling on Your Own

UNIT WORDS

Write the Unit words in columns according to the number of syllables they contain. You will make one column for two-syllable words (13 words) and one column for three-syllable words (6 words). Write the single four-syllable word in a column by itself. Then, using the rules on page 120, divide each Unit word into syllables. Draw vertical lines to separate the syllables.

MASTERY WORDS

The pronunciations of the first syllables of four Mastery words are listed below. Write the four words. Then draw a line to show how each word is divided into syllables.

1. /res/   **2.** /chap/   **3.** /guv/   **4.** /spir/

Write the words that have these long vowel sounds in the first syllables. Draw lines to show how the words are divided into syllables.

5. /ī/   **6.** /ō/

The word *private* has several meanings. Look up *private* in the **Spelling Dictionary.** Then do these exercises.

7. Write a sentence using the first definition of *private*.

8. Write a sentence using the second definition.

9. Now write a sentence using the third definition of *private* and one other Mastery word.

chapter
govern
rescue
private
spirit
chosen

BONUS WORDS

1. Two Bonus words each have a verb-forming suffix. Write these words.

2. Three Bonus words each have a noun-forming suffix. Write these words.

3. One Bonus word has the adjective-forming suffix *-able*. Write this word.

4. Write the Bonus words. Separate the prefix, suffix, or both from each of the Bonus words. Then divide the remaining word if it has more than one syllable.

5. Write sentences using the Bonus words.

disenchantment
reorganize
unprofitable
impersonate
contraption
demerit
treasury
disbelief

29 Double-Letter Spellings

UNIT WORDS

1. apparatus
2. immediately
3. accumulate
4. cooperate
5. exceed
6. aggravate
7. appropriate
8. assistant
9. aggressive
10. exaggerate
11. approximate
12. accelerate
13. satellite
14. interruption
15. accomplish
16. accessory
17. miscellaneous
18. accommodate
19. accuracy
20. occurrence

Accelerate that apparatus!

The Unit Words

Most of the words in this unit have double consonant letters that spell a single sound. Say the word *satellite* to yourself. You hear only one /l/ in *satellite*, but it is spelled with two *l*'s.

satellite   /sat'ə•līt/

Sometimes double consonant letters are the result of assimilation. **Assimilation** is the changing of a sound in a word in order to make the word easier to pronounce. Assimilation frequently occurs when a prefix that ends with a consonant is added to a base word that begins with a consonant. The final consonant of the prefix is changed so that it is the same as the first consonant of the base word. Say *adsistant* and *assistant* to yourself. Which word is easier to say?

☐ The double consonant **c** in *accelerate* and *accessory* spells two sounds, /k/ and /s/.

ac + com + mod
accommodate

REMEMBER THIS

Knowing the principle of assimilation can help you spell *accommodate*. Two prefixes, *ad* and *com*, are added to the Latin root *mod* to give *accommodate* two pairs of double consonant letters.

Spelling Practice

A. Complete these exercises using the Unit words.

1. Write the six words that begin with the letters *acc.*

2. Write the three words that begin with the letters *app.*

3. Write three more words that begin with *a* followed by double consonant letters.

4. Write the two words that begin with other vowel letters followed by double consonant letters.

5. Write the two words that have double vowel letters. Circle the word in which the double letters stand for two different vowel sounds.

6. Write the four words that have two sets of double consonant letters.

B. Write the words that have these double letters between the second and third syllables.

7. ll (two words)   **8.** gg   **9.** rr (two words)

C. Write the Unit word that is a synonym for each of these words.

10. stockpile   **11.** a break   **12.** achieve

13. incident   **14.** annoy   **15.** estimated

D. Replace the underlined words with a synonym from the Unit words.

16. <u>Various kinds of</u> items were on sale.

17. There were so many that I could only give a number that was <u>close but not exact</u>.

18. I saw a lamp that I wanted <u>at that instant</u>.

19. It's a good thing for my budget that a garage sale in my neighborhood is not an everyday <u>thing that happens</u>.

Proofreading • A News Story

Kenji applied for a summer job on a local newspaper. As part of his interview, Kenji was asked to proofread this news story. Kenji found that twelve words had been misspelled. He also noticed that the reporter had omitted four commas. Read the story carefully.

1. Find the twelve spelling mistakes.

2. Find the four places in the story where commas were left out.

> Laura Burrill, Assisstant Director of Miscellaneous Products announced today that the company will apropriate additional funds for the development of satelite materials to accompany its line of exercise equipment sports clothes, and accessories. "We intend to accellerate our production so that our new gym aparratus can be on the market by next fall" Ms. Burrill said. "The demand for our product has far exceded our projections. We believe we can accomodate this growing demand and increase our line with no interuption in service." In addition, Ms. Burrill noted "An aggresive sales campaign will help Miscellaneous acomplish its long-term goals."
>
> Miscelaneous will create 150 new jobs immediately to increase its production capacity by an aproximate 25 percent.

3. Write the twelve misspelled words correctly.

4. Write the news story correctly on a separate sheet of paper.

Writing on Your Own

Write a story for a community newspaper about an event in your school. Be sure to tell who, what, when, where, and why in your first paragraph. Use these and perhaps some other Unit words in the story: *immediately, appropriate, approximate, accuracy, occurrence.*

WRITER'S GUIDE For a sample paragraph from a news story, turn to page 266.

Spelling on Your Own

UNIT WORDS

Imagine that you have been chosen to lead a space expedition. Write a report, log, or adventure story about your experiences. Use as many Unit words in your composition as you can.

MASTERY WORDS

additional
unnecessary
accept
approval
recommend
occasion

Write the Mastery word that has each pair of letters. Then circle the word that also has *ss*.

1. dd　**2.** mm　**3.** nn　**4.** pp　**5.** cc (two words)

Write the Mastery word that is a synonym for each word.

6. permission　**7.** suggest　**8.** event　**9.** extra

The prefixes *un-* and *dis-* both mean "not." They change a word into its antonym. Add *un-* or *dis-* to the word in dark print to form a word that completes the sentence.

10. necessary　Sweaters are ＿＿＿ on a hot day.

11. approval　Iris's frown showed her ＿＿＿ of my plan.

12. acceptable　Ricardo's plan was ＿＿＿ to her also.

Find the misspelled word in each sentence and write it correctly.

13. A birthday is always a special occassion.

14. Can you reccomend a good book?

15. The additional supplies were unneccesary.

BONUS WORDS

inoculate
esteem
apprehensive
dilemma
accusation
annihilate
appalling
allotment

Write the Bonus word that comes from each of these prefixes and words.

1. *ad + prehendere*　**2.** *ad + causa*　**3.** *ad + nihil*
4. *ad + pallere*　**5.** *in + oculus*　**6.** *a(d) + lot*

Complete these exercises using the Bonus words.

7. Now write the word you wrote for **1–6** that does not have an assimilated prefix.

8. Write definitions for *dilemma* and *esteem*. Then use both words in one sentence.

30 Review

Follow these steps when you are unsure of how to spell a word.

- **Say** the word. Recall when you have heard the word used. Think about what it means.
- **Look** at the word. Find any prefixes, suffixes, or other word parts you know. Think about other words that are related in meaning and spelling. Try to picture the word in your mind.
- **Spell** the word to yourself. Think about the way each sound is spelled. Notice any unusual spelling.
- **Write** the word while looking at it. Check the way you have formed your letters. If you have not written the word clearly or correctly, write it again.
- **Check** your learning. Cover the word and write it. If you did not spell the word correctly, practice these steps until the word becomes your own.

UNIT 25

vacant
abundant
frequent
incident
confident
competent
urgent
opponent
efficient
magnificent

UNIT 25 Follow the directions using words from Unit 25. Write the word that is related to each of these words.

1. confidence
2. vacancy
3. competence
4. urgency
5. efficiency
6. oppose
7. incidence
8. abundance

Write an antonym for each word.

9. scarce
10. friend
11. plain
12. seldom

Replace each underlined word with a synonym.

13. We were <u>sure</u> that they would meet us at home.
14. However, the house was <u>empty</u> when we got there.
15. On the table they had left a <u>beautiful</u> package.

WORDS IN TIME

The Latin word for *magnificence* once meant "spending money freely and with good taste." *Magnificent* later came to be added to the titles of certain officials. Today, you are more likely to hear a particularly beautiful sunset or a gorgeous red rose described as "magnificent."

128

Finish these sentences.

16. I must ____ for not saying hello to you at the game.

17. I did not ____ you with your new haircut.

18. No one will ____ you for having hair that is too long!

19. We will ____ our fair in the local newspaper.

20. Let's ask Chris to ____ the games at the fair.

21. The meeting to ____ the fair will be held today.

22. The detective asked the laboratory to ____ the stain.

23. When the laboratory report came back, the detective had to ____ one theory about the crime.

24. I play several instruments, but I ____ in the viola.

25. If you already have a viola player in the group, I will ____ and play the cello.

Write the verb from which each of these nouns was formed.

26. recognition   27. revision

28. supervision   29. criticism

UNIT 26
compromise
analyze
revise
specialize
recognize
criticize
advertise
apologize
supervise
organize

UNIT 27 Finish these sentences using words from Unit 27.

30. The ____ of a cell is very small.

31. You breathe air into your ____.

32. The genes for brown eyes are often ____.

33. Your hands get cold if your ____ is poor.

34. Red hair is one of the ____ in my family.

35. Your ____ cord carries messages to your brain.

36. Diseases can be caused by ____.

37. I had to draw my foot for ____ class.

38. Without ____, life would not exist.

39. An ____ carries blood away from the heart.

40. Write the four words from Unit 27 that have /ē/.

UNIT 27
nucleus
bacteria
circulation
artery
protoplasm
anatomy
spinal
traits
lungs
dominant

brilliant
discover
silence
sliver
rotate
frantic
dislocate
misdirect
ballot
immobile

UNIT 28 Follow the directions using words from Unit 28. Replace the underlined word in each sentence with an antonym.

41. We were happy to <u>lose</u> the treasure.

42. I had a <u>block</u> of wood in my finger.

43. I was <u>calm</u> when I found that my wallet was missing.

44. The silver cup was polished to a <u>dull</u> shine.

45. The <u>noise</u> in the woods was very peaceful.

46. I have to keep my sprained ankle <u>moving</u>.

Divide each of these words into syllables.

47. rotate   **48.** immobile

49. misdirect   **50.** dislocate

51. ballot   **52.** sliver

assistant
appropriate
immediately
accuracy
approximate
cooperate
exceed
interruption
accomplish
miscellaneous

UNIT 29 Follow the directions using words from Unit 29. Finish each sentence.

53. If I set my mind to it, I can _____ a lot in one afternoon.

54. Please let me finish the yard work without _____.

55. You can _____ with me by playing ball at the playground instead of in the yard.

56. You'll have to get your baseball equipment out of the yard _____.

57. The typing test was graded for speed and _____.

58. Several students were able to _____ their previous top typing speeds.

59. The _____ average typing speed in the class was 45 words per minute.

Write the word that is related to each word below.

60. assist

61. miscellany

62. inappropriate

Spelling and Reading
A Book Report

Read this book report. What details does the writer use to arouse the reader's interest?

One of my favorite books is *Sherlock Holmes: Selected Stories,* a collection of stories written by Sir Arthur Conan Doyle. Nearly everyone knows about the famous detective of British fiction. He has a magnificent reputation around the world. If you have never read any Sherlock Holmes stories, you should discover what you've been missing.

The stories of how Holmes can analyze clues to solve crimes are told by his friend and assistant, Dr. Watson. Watson gives an inside look at each incident in the career of Sherlock Holmes. While you read about Holmes's powers of deduction and about each opponent he meets, you also can enjoy a sliver of London life in the 1890's. On every page you can fill your lungs with foggy London air as your carriage bumps over the cobblestones.

A number of interesting characters go in and out of Holmes's rooms on Baker Street. One of my favorites is Helen Stoner. She is a frantic young woman with an urgent problem. She wants Holmes to save her life in the story called "The Speckled Band." Shivers go down your spinal column and ice water flows through every artery as Miss Stoner's tale unfolds. You will be surprised by the outcome of this amazing case. You will be intrigued by how the brilliant Holmes comes to recognize the appropriate clues that lead to the solution.

I recommend Sherlock Holmes's stories to anyone with a taste for adventure. If you enjoy fast-moving stories with as many twists and turns as an old London street, you won't be disappointed.

Write the answers to the questions.
1. Why does the writer of the book report think the reader will be intrigued?
2. Which character is the narrator of the Sherlock Holmes stories?
3. What does the writer mean by saying that a reader of the book will enjoy a sliver of London life in the 1890's?
4. Did the writer's book report make you want to read the book? Tell why or why not.

Underline the review words in your answers. Check to see that you spelled the words correctly.

Spelling and Writing
A Book Report

Words to Help You Write

incident
compromise
traits
discover
appropriate
miscellaneous
emphasize
focus
discover
rascal
occurrence
cooperate
immediately
organize

Think and Discuss

A good book report can make someone want to read the book to see if it is as exciting, funny, frightening, or informative as the writer of the book report says it is. To help a reader decide whether to read a book, a book report should contain some standard information.

The beginning of the report should state the title and the author of the book, then briefly describe the setting (time and place) and the main characters. Who are the two main characters in the book? A report should also summarize the plot without giving away the ending. What is the book described on page 131 about? What details does the writer give in the plot summary? Notice how the writer describes the mood, or feeling, of the book with phrases such as "shivers go down your spinal column" and "ice water flows through every artery." What other phrases does the writer use to describe the mood?

The second part of a book report should include the writer's opinion of the book. Which sentences in the report on page 131 state this opinion? Why is it important to support the opinion in the report?

Apply

What book have you read recently? Write a **book report** about it to share with a friend. Follow the writing guidelines on page 133.

Prewriting

Think about the book you read.

- Make a chart with three sections down the side of your paper. In the first section, write the title, author, characters, and setting.
- In the same section, include some phrases to help you summarize the plot and describe the mood.
- In the second section, jot down a phrase to recommend the book if you liked it.
- In the last section, note some details to support your opinion.

Composing

Use your chart to compose your book report.
- Mention the title, author, main characters, and setting of the book.
- Describe an important incident in the book, without giving away the ending.
- In your plot summary, describe the mood of the book. Use details to support your opinion.

Revising

Read your book report and show it to a classmate. Follow these guidelines to improve your work. Use the editing and proofreading marks on this page to indicate corrections.

 WRITER'S GUIDE For help revising your book report, see the checklist on page 256.

Editing

- Be sure you included all three parts of the report.
- Be sure you have used details from the book to summarize the plot and describe the mood.
- Be sure you supported your opinion of the book with details.

Proofreading

- Check your spelling, capitalization, and punctuation.

Copy your book report onto clean paper. Write carefully and neatly.

Publishing

Have a classmate read your book report. Then ask if your report motivated him or her to read the book.

Editing and Proofreading Marks

≡	capitalize
⊙	make a period
∧	add something
⩘	add a comma
ᵛᵛ ᵛᵛ	add quotation marks
ᵊ	take something away
◯	spell correctly
¶	indent the paragraph
/	make a lowercase letter
∼ tr	transpose

31 Words with /əns/ or /ens/

The Unit Words

There is no easy way to remember whether a word ends in *-ance, -ence,* or *-ense.* Perhaps these generalizations will provide some clues to the correct spellings of the Unit words.

1. Usually, if you can find an English verb in the word, the word will end with *-ance.*

   attend   attendance

2. Usually, if you can think of a related adjective, the noun will end with *-ence.*

   excellent   excellence

3. More words ending in /əns/ or /ens/ are spelled with **ence** than with **ense.** You must memorize the words that end with *ense.*

134

Spelling Practice

A. Add a suffix to each verb to form a related noun. Sometimes it may be necessary to drop or change a letter.

1. attend **2.** resist **3.** acquaint **4.** apply

5. exist **6.** insure **7.** appear **8.** accept

B. Now answer these questions about the words you wrote.

9. What letters spell /əns/ in most of the words?

10. Which word is not spelled with these letters?

C. Write the Unit word that is related to each of these verbs.

11. defend **12.** pretend

13. suspend **14.** expend

D. Write the noun that is related to each of these adjectives.

15. excellent **16.** consequent

17. intelligent **18.** fragrant

19. innocent **20.** evident

21. convenient **22.** abundant

E. Now answer these questions about the words you wrote in part **D.**

23. What letters spell /əns/ in most of the words?

24. Which two words are not spelled with these letters?

25. Which three words have double consonant letters?

26. Which word is spelled with *i* before *e*?

F. Replace the underlined word in each sentence with a Unit word.

27. Someone broke the kitchen <u>machine</u>.

28. All the <u>clues</u> pointed to the visitors.

29. The <u>cost</u> of repairing it will be high.

30. As a <u>result</u>, we will be more careful about who uses our belongings.

135

Spelling and Language • Antonyms

Remember that words that mean the opposite of each other are called **antonyms**. *Frantic* and *calm* are antonyms.

A. Write the Unit word that is an antonym for each of these words.

1. attack   **2.** guilt   **3.** rejection

4. stranger   **5.** scarcity   **6.** submission

7. sincerity   **8.** stench

The Latin prefix *in-* often means "not." The word *innocence*, for example, comes from the Latin word parts *in-*, "not," and *nocens*, "wicked." Adding the prefix *in-* can change a word into its antonym. Remember that prefixes frequently become assimilated when added to a base word. The final consonant changes, often becoming the same as the first consonant of the base word. The prefix *in-* changes to *im-* before *m, b,* or *p,* and to *ir-* before *r.* The negative meaning, however, remains the same.

B. Add the prefix *in-* to the underlined word to write a word that makes the sentence mean the opposite.

9. Staying in a youth hostel is an <u>expensive</u> way to travel.

10. On this sunny Friday afternoon, the class was <u>attentive</u>.

11. The player's injury proved <u>consequential</u> to the outcome of the game.

12. I had a(n) <u>resistible</u> desire for a cool glass of apple juice.

13. The principal considered their prank <u>defensible</u>.

14. Our club meets at a(n) <u>convenient</u> time for Sue.

Writing on Your Own

Write a story about a florist who discovers something strange about the flowers in his or her shop. Have the character of the florist tell the story from the first-person point of view using the words *I, me,* and *my*. Use as many Unit words as you can. You might also wish to add the prefix *in-* to some words to form antonyms.

WRITER'S GUIDE For a sample paragraph from a story in the first-person point of view, turn to page 265.

UNIT WORDS

fragrance
resistance
appliance
appearance
acceptance
insurance
acquaintance
attendance
abundance
excellence
convenience
innocence
evidence
consequence
intelligence
existence
expense
defense
pretense
suspense

HOSTEL

Spelling on Your Own

UNIT WORDS

Each of the Unit words is incomplete. Think of the letters that are missing in each word. Then write the word.

1. abund____
2. accept____
3. acquaint____
4. appear____
5. appli____
6. attend____
7. consequ____
8. conveni____
9. def____
10. evid____
11. excell____
12. exist____
13. exp____
14. fragr____
15. innoc____
16. insur____
17. intellig____
18. pret____
19. resist____
20. susp____

MASTERY WORDS

sense
balance
patience
conference
distance
license

Write the two Mastery words that end with these letters.

1. ance
2. ence
3. ense

Each of these words has a prefix that means "not." Write the Mastery word that is an antonym for each word.

4. nonsense
5. impatience
6. imbalance

Look up the words *balance* and *license* in the **Spelling Dictionary.** Finish these sentences using one of these two words. Before each sentence, write *N* if you used the noun meaning of the word or *V* if you used its verb meaning.

7. The seal can ____ a ball on its nose.

8. Did you get a ____ for your new dog?

BONUS WORDS

endurance
resemblance
persistence
elegance
guidance
offense
vengeance
recurrence

Complete each of these sentences using the Bonus words.

1. There is a ____ between the members of that family.

2. I meant no ____ when I spoke to you in an angry voice.

3. The doctor feared a ____ of malaria in the patient.

4. ____ and ____ are essential for a cross-country runner.

5. The knight swore to seek ____ for the death of his lord.

6. With the expert ____ of Annie Sullivan, Helen Keller learned to speak.

7. The mansion was decorated with ____ and style.

Write a paragraph about a time in your life when persistence was essential.

32 Adjective Suffixes

UNIT WORDS

1. edible
2. digestible
3. eligible
4. divisible
5. accessible
6. reversible
7. predictable
8. likable
9. traceable
10. reliable
11. advisable
12. changeable
13. available
14. persuasive
15. imaginative
16. sensitive
17. impressive
18. explosive
19. instinctive
20. inventive

That may be digestible, sir, but it does not look edible.

The Unit Words

Edible and *digestible* are adjectives with the suffix *-ible,* another spelling for *-able.* This suffix adds the meaning "able to" to verbs and to some root words. Although a greater number of English words end with *-able,* as in *predictable,* there are many words with *-ible* that you must learn to recognize and spell.

Another adjective suffix, *-ive,* adds the meaning "tending to, or having the quality of" to verbs and root words, as in *impressive* and *instinctive.*

Here are some rules for adding *-able, -ible,* and *-ive* to form adjectives.

1. If a word ends with e, drop the final e before adding a suffix beginning with a vowel letter. However, if a word ends with ce or ge, and the suffix begins with a, keep the final e to spell the sounds /s/ and /j/.

   like   likable   trace   traceable

2. When a word ends with a consonant and y, change the y to i before adding the suffix.

   rely   reliable

138

Spelling Practice

A. Add *-able* or *-ible* to each verb to form a Unit word. Remember to drop or change letters when necessary.

1. avail
2. digest
3. change
4. rely
5. trace
6. like
7. advise
8. reverse

B. Write the Unit word that is formed by adding an adjective suffix to each verb. Notice that final e is dropped and d changes to s or ss when the suffix is added.

9. divide
10. explode
11. persuade
12. accede

C. Write the Unit words that are related to each word.

13. imagine
14. impress
15. sense
16. invent
17. instinct

D. Write a Unit word for each of these meanings.

18. able to be traced
19. able to be eaten
20. able to be reached
21. able to qualify for
22. able to be divided
23. able to be predicted
24. able to be digested

E. Complete each of these sentences using a Unit word.

25. Newspaper editors try to be sure that each news item printed in their papers comes from a _____ source.

26. If your eyes are _____ to the sun's rays, you should protect them with sunglasses.

27. All students are _____ to compete in future intramural games.

28. His argument is _____.

29. Some sizes will not be _____ during the semiannual clothing sale.

Proofreading • A Book Report

Paul handed in this book report. When it was returned, Paul saw that he needed to make several corrections. Paul's teacher used these proofreading marks.

/	small letter needed	⋀̧	comma needed
⊤⊢	begin new paragraph	⋀	insert word
⊙	period needed	◯	spelling mistake

1. Read Paul's book report carefully.

I read Stalking The Wild Asparagus by Euell Gibbons for my book report. Mr. Gibbons writes about the abundence of edable wild plants and animals that are easily acessible to everyone. He tells the reader about the existance of many kinds of wild plants that are availabel for the taking. These plants grow in fields, swampy areas, along roadsides and even in vacent city lots. If you use some of the imagineative and inventiv cooking methods that Mr. Gibbons has developed, these foods become not only digestable but pleasurable to eat as well.

You could easily survive at little or no expence by eating nothing but wild foods. How does a breakfast of Elderberry Blow Fritters filled with wild blueberries or Cattail Pollen Muffins and crab apple jelly sound to you? Try some candied acorns; a salad of watercress, chicory, dandelions, and slivors of wild onion; or a bowl of Wild Leek Soup. It is adviseable, however, to follow Mr. Gibbons's instructions carefully when you forage for food.

2. Write the twelve misspelled words correctly.

3. Rewrite Paul's first paragraph on a separate sheet of paper. Make all the necessary corrections.

Writing on Your Own

Imagine that you belong to your school's Library Club. Choose a book that you've read recently and write a book report for the next club meeting. Use as many Unit words as you can.

WRITER'S GUIDE For a sample book report, turn to page 263.

Asparagus

Spelling on Your Own

UNIT WORDS

Write the Unit words. Then add *un-* or *in-* to as many of the words as you can to create their antonyms. Check a dictionary if you need help.

MASTERY WORDS

Finish these exercises using the Mastery words.

1. Write the two words that end with *-able.*
2. Write the two words that end with *-ible.*
3. Write the two words that end with *-ive.*
4. Write the word that means "a member of your family."
5. Write the word that is an antonym for the word *worthless.*
6. Two Mastery words are antonyms for *foolish.* Write these words.
7. The words *valuable* and *invaluable* are not antonyms. *Invaluable* means "priceless." Write a sentence using the word *valuable.* Then write a second sentence using the word *invaluable.*

responsible
sensible
valuable
reasonable
positive
relative

Take away the prefix in each word below and write a Mastery word that has the opposite meaning.

8. unreasonable   9. irresponsible

BONUS WORDS

Write the Bonus word that is related to each of these words.

1. admire   2. collapse   3. auditorium
4. construct   5. combustion   6. alternate
7. conceive   8. inevitably

9. Use each of the Bonus words and its related word in a sentence. Here's an example: "Her voice was not audible in the noisy auditorium."

collapsible
combustible
audible
alternative
constructive
inconceivable
inevitable
admirable

33 /shəl/ and /shəs/ Endings

UNIT WORDS

1. residential
2. potential
3. confidential
4. racial
5. artificial
6. nutritious
7. suspicious
8. beneficial
9. controversial
10. ambitious
11. malicious
12. commercial
13. precious
14. spacious
15. crucial
16. infectious
17. vicious
18. superficial
19. substantial
20. superstitious

The Unit Words

Is the word ending /shəl/ spelled *tial, cial,* or *sial*? Since only a few English words end with *sial,* you must usually decide between *tial* and *cial.* Here are some clues to help you.

1. If you hear the sound /n/ before /shəl/, the spelling is most often *tial.*

   confidential   substantial

2. If the base word ends with *ce* as in *race,* but not *nce* as in *confidence,* the spelling is usually *cial.*

   race   racial

3. All words that end with the sounds /fishəl/ are spelled with *cial.*

   artificial   beneficial   superficial

The second clue for spelling /shəl/ can also help you spell /shəs/. If the base word ends with *ce* (not *nce*), /shəs/ is spelled *cious.*

   malice   malicious
   space   spacious

142

Spelling Practice

A. Write the Unit words that have these base words.

1. malice
2. substance
3. vice
4. commerce
5. race
6. confidence
7. space
8. residence

B. Complete these exercises using the Unit words.

9. Write the three words that end with /fishəl/.

10. Write the word that ends with the letters *sial*.

C. Write the Unit words that are related to these nouns.

11. nutrition
12. ambition
13. infection
14. superstition
15. suspicion

D. Write the Unit word that is a synonym for each word.

16. valuable
17. essential
18. possible
19. debatable

E. Substitute Unit words for the underlined words in the paragraph below.

    The Food and Drug Administration is the agency that enforces the federal laws regulating the profit-making (**20**) food, drug, and cosmetics industries. The FDA requires that all new drugs be investigated for possible (**21**) risks before being sold to the public. Drugs or man-made (**22**) ingredients such as sweeteners or dyes that are considered questionable (**23**) are taken off the market until a full investigation is made. Products must be labeled truthfully. Claims that a new packaged cereal, for example, is nourishing (**24**) or advantageous (**25**) to your health must be proved.

F. Finish each sentence with a Unit word.

26. The _____ person wanted to be company president.

27. The envelope was marked _____ in large red letters.

28. People who are _____ believe fantastic things.

29. Her _____ laugh made everyone chuckle.

30. We live on a quiet _____ street.

Spelling and Language • Adding *-ly*

An **adverb** is used to modify a verb, an adjective, or another adverb. You can often form an adverb by adding *-ly* to an adjective.

UNIT WORDS

residential
potential
confidential
racial
artificial
nutritious
suspicious
beneficial
controversial
ambitious
malicious
commercial
precious
spacious
crucial
infectious
vicious
superficial
substantial
superstitious

A. When you add *-ly* to a word, you usually do not change the spelling of the word. Add *-ly* to each of these adjectives.

1. vicious
2. confidential
3. ambitious
4. superficial
5. controversial
6. imaginative

B. When a word ends with *ble, ly* takes the place of *le.* Add *-ly* to each of these adjectives.

7. reliable
8. predictable
9. comparable

C. When a word ends with *ic,* you usually add *-ally* to form an adverb. Write the adverb form of each adjective.

10. frantic
11. sympathetic
12. synthetic
13. enthusiastic
14. authentic
15. geometric

When you wish to add variety to your writing, try using an adverb in place of an adjective occasionally. Look at these sentences. Which one is the stronger of the two?

The cat gave the food a suspicious sniff.

The cat sniffed the food suspiciously.

Writing on Your Own

In a letter to a friend, describe planning a relative's surprise birthday dinner and shopping for the food. You may wish to use these Unit words in your friendly letter: *confidential, artificial, nutritious, suspicious, spacious, crucial,* and *substantial.* Include some adverbs to add variety to your description.

WRITER'S GUIDE For a sample friendly letter, turn to page 261.

Spelling on Your Own

UNIT WORDS

Write the Unit word that is related to each of these words.

1. controversy	**2.** benefit	**3.** confident	**4.** nutrient
5. potent	**6.** reside	**7.** artifice	**8.** infect
9. suspect	**10.** ambition	**11.** spatial	**12.** superstition
13. malice	**14.** viciously	**15.** crucially	**16.** commercialize
17. racist	**18.** substantiate	**19.** preciousness	**20.** superficiality

MASTERY WORDS

official
special
essential
initial
gracious
cautious

1. Write the two words that have /shəl/ spelled *tial*.

2. Write the two words that have /shəl/ spelled *cial*.

Write the words that are related to these words.

3. office **4.** grace

5. caution **6.** essence

Write the words that are antonyms for these words.

7. ordinary **8.** reckless

9. impolite **10.** unauthorized

A Rhyme Styme is a riddle with two rhyming words for the answer. Complete the answer to the Rhyme Styme with the plural form of a Mastery word.

11. What is a governor's monogram? An official's _____!

BONUS WORDS

atrocious
conscientious
obnoxious
impartial
credentials
judicial
influential
fictitious

Write the Bonus word that comes from each Latin word.

1. *noxius,* "hurtful"

2. *credere,* "to believe"

3. *judicium,* "judgment"

4. *fictus,* "made up"

5. *atrocitas,* "cruelty"

6. *partialis,* "of a part"

7. *conscire,* "to be aware of"

8. *influere,* "to flow into"

Write a short Words in Time report about one of the Bonus words. Explain how the meaning of the Latin word given above relates to the Bonus word's current meaning. You might also list some related words. Think about how the root in related words carries a similar meaning. Look back at the Words in Time features in this book if you need help in writing your paragraph.

34 Words from Greek

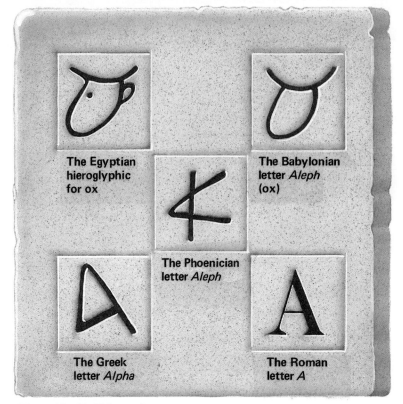

The Egyptian hieroglyphic for ox

The Babylonian letter *Aleph* (ox)

The Phoenician letter *Aleph*

The Greek letter *Alpha*

The Roman letter *A*

The Unit Words

The Greeks were one of the first peoples to use a system of writing in which one symbol represents one specific sound. Our word *alphabet* comes from the names of the first two letters in the Greek system: *alpha* and *beta*.

The Romans, using the Greek alphabet as a base, created the alphabet we use today. There are several letters in the Greek alphabet, however, that have no single-letter equivalents in our alphabet.

Here are some of those Greek letters and their spellings and pronunciations in English.

X is spelled **ch** and pronounced /k/, as in *chaos*.

Φ is spelled **ph** and pronounced /f/, as in *prophet*.

Ψ is spelled **ps** and pronounced /s/, as in *psalm*.

P at the beginning of a word is spelled **rh** and pronounced /r/, as in *rhythm*.

Θ is spelled **th** and pronounced /th/, as in *marathon*.

Spelling Practice

A. Complete these exercises using the Unit words.

1. Write the three words in which the sound /k/ is spelled with *ch*.

2. Write the five words in which /f/ is spelled with *ph*.

3. Write the two words in which /s/ is spelled with *ps*.

4. Write the two words in which /r/ is spelled with *rh*.

B. Write the Unit word that comes from each of these Greek words.

5. *planetes,* "a wanderer"

6. *stadion,* "a length of 600 feet"

7. *gymnastes,* "a trainer of athletes"

8. *automatos,* "self-moving"

9. *akrobatos,* "walking on high"

10. *pneumon,* "a lung"

11. *kaktos,* "a thistle"

C. Write the Unit word for each of these meanings.

12. a pleasing smell

13. a twenty-six mile race

14. a confused state

15. a tragic event

D. Finish each sentence with a Unit word.

16. The game was played in the _____ at the university.

17. I hurt my arm and had to miss _____ class.

18. We worked at one of the water stations during the _____.

19. Our science class saw the star show at the _____.

20. Out in the desert, the _____ was in bloom.

Using the Dictionary to Spell and Write •
Locating Unfamiliar Words

UNIT WORDS

prophet
psalm
rhythm
pneumonia
architecture
psychology
stadium
aroma
pharmacy
chaos
gymnastics
automation
phenomenon
marathon
cactus
physician
catastrophe
planetarium
acrobat
rhinoceros

If you do not know how a word is spelled, you can find it in the dictionary. Suppose that you wish to look up the word *cylinder.* Start by thinking of the spellings you know for initial /s/: *s, c, sc,* and *ps.* Since *s* is the most frequent spelling for /s/, you might begin by looking in the *S* section of the dictionary. The *C* section of the dictionary should be your next choice. The next sound in *cylinder* is /i/. The sound /i/ also may be spelled in several ways: *i, e, y,* and *ui.* Check these letters. You will soon find *cylinder.*

Words borrowed from other languages often keep their original spellings. *Cylinder* comes from ancient Greek. Many words borrowed from Greek have /i/ spelled with *y.* Knowing the common foreign spellings can help you pick the most likely spelling for a word. Then you can find it quickly in the dictionary.

A. Think of the spellings you know for /k/. Then write the spelling for each pronunciation below. In each exercise, the answer will be a Unit word or a word from an earlier unit.

1. /kā′os/   2. /krev′is/
3. /kak′ē/   4. /ik•stingkt′/

B. Think of the spellings you know for /f/. Then write the spellings for each of the pronunciations.

5. /fär′mə•sē/   6. /sfir/
7. /fē′chər/   8. /fi•nom′ə•non/

C. Think of the spellings for the sounds /âr/ heard in *care.* Then write the spelling for each of these pronunciations.

9. /âr/   10. /âr′ē•əl/

act, āte, câre, ärt;   egg, ēven;   if, īce;   on, ōver, ôr;   bŏŏk, fōōd;   up, tûrn;
ə=a in *ago,* e in *listen,* i in *giraffe,* o in *pilot,* u in *circus;*   yōō=u in *music;*   oil;   out;
chair; sing; shop; thank; that; zh in *treasure.*

Writing on Your Own

Write a humorous how-to article for a magazine for young children. Make up your own topic or choose one of these: "How to Make a Cactus Pie," "How to Build the First Planetarium on Your Block," or "How to Train a Rhinoceros." You may wish to use some of these Unit words in your article: *aroma, catastrophe, architecture, stadium, phenomenon,* and *chaos.*

 WRITER'S GUIDE For help editing and proofreading your article, use the marks on page 257.

Spelling on Your Own

UNIT WORDS

Write sentences using all of the Unit words. Use as many of the words as you can in each sentence and underline each Unit word. See how few sentences you can write.

MASTERY WORDS

chorus
alphabet
physical
arithmetic
hero
panic

Write the Mastery words that have these sounds spelled with these letters.

1. /k/ch
2. /i/y
3. /f/ph (two words)
4. final /k/c (two words)

Write the Mastery word that is related to each word.

5. alphabetical
6. heroic
7. panicky
8. choral
9. arithmetical
10. physically

ABCDE

АБВГД

Look at the Greek letters on page 146, and their pronunciations in English. Write the Mastery words that have sounds like these Greek letters.

11. θ
12. Χ
13. Φ (two words)

Complete each sentence with the plural form of the word in dark type. Check the **Spelling Dictionary** if you are not sure how to form the plural of *hero*.

14. **hero**   Who are your favorite movie ____?

15. **alphabet**   English and Russian have different ____.

16. **chorus**   The audience joined in on all the ____.

BONUS WORDS

labyrinth
sophomore
podium
hypocrite
ammonia
episode
melancholy
philosophy

1. The Greek word *hypokrites* means "actor." Explain how a hypocrite is similar to an actor.
2. In Greek mythology, Daedalus built the Labyrinth to confine the Minotaur, a monster. Explain the modern meaning of *labyrinth*.
3. *Sophos* means "wise" in Greek. *Moros* means "foolish." How might a sophomore be considered wise and foolish at the same time? Which other Bonus word has the root *soph*? What does that word mean?
4. Use each word in a sentence that demonstrates its meaning.

35 Multisyllabic Words

UNIT WORDS

1. precipitation
2. companionship
3. irresponsible
4. bewilderment
5. commitment
6. conspiracy
7. extravagant
8. unusually
9. nomination
10. captivity
11. miniature
12. delicatessen
13. intermission
14. exquisite
15. insignificant
16. legislature
17. inheritance
18. semifinalist
19. conspicuous
20. exposure

Precipitation, precipitation,
Exit instantaneously.
Reappear occasionally
Upon future dates.

The Unit Words

Does the message sound unfamiliar? It is this well-known children's rhyme rewritten with multisyllabic words.

Rain, rain, go away.
Come again some other day.

All the words in the original rhyme have Old English origins. In the multisyllabic version, all the words except *upon* have Latin roots.

If you look at pairs of synonyms in the English language, you will often discover that one is a short word from Old English and the other is a longer word with a Latin root. Compare the words *friend* and *companion,* or *careless* and *irresponsible.* The second word in each pair comes from Latin.

Most of the new words you are adding to your vocabulary are multisyllabic. When you encounter an unfamiliar multisyllabic word, divide it into its smaller word parts. Think of the meaning of the root and prefix or suffix. Remember the spelling and pronunciation of each smaller part. This can help you recall the word and use it correctly in your speech and writing.

Spelling Practice

A. Complete these exercises using the Unit words.

1. Write the three words that have a prefix that means "not."

2. Write the four words that have the prefix *com-/con-*, meaning "together; thoroughly."

3. Write the three words that have the prefix *ex-*, "out; from."

4. Write the word that comes from the Italian word *miniatura*, "a small painting."

B. Many multisyllabic words contain very simple base words. Write the Unit words that have these base words.

5. wild   **6.** sign
7. final   **8.** captive

C. Write the Unit words that have these Latin roots.

9. *mit/mis,* "send" (two words)

10. *leg,* "law"

11. *nomin,* "name"

12. *her,* "heir"

13. *capt,* "take"

14. *usus,* "use"

15. *spect,* "look"

D. A malapropism is a misuse or confusion of words that is often humorous. There are some malapropisms in this paragraph. Write the Unit words that should have been used.

    The weather forecast was for heavy <u>participation</u> (**16**), but my <u>committee</u> (**17**) to having a picnic did not change. I had already gotten the picnic supplies from the <u>delectation</u> (**18**) for an <u>extravaganza</u> (**19**) lunch. What difference could a little rain make when you have good food and the <u>championship</u> (**20**) of good friends? You can imagine my <u>belligerence</u> (**21**) when no one showed up at the park!

Spelling and Language •
Avoiding Slang and Informal Writing

UNIT WORDS

precipitation
companionship
irresponsible
bewilderment
commitment
conspiracy
extravagant
unusually
nomination
captivity
miniature
delicatessen
intermission
exquisite
insignificant
legislature
inheritance
semifinalist
conspicuous
exposure

A skillful writer uses a vocabulary that is appropriate to the tone of the composition being written. Slang and informal English should be used only in informal writing.

A. Rewrite each of these sentences substituting a Unit word for the underlined slang or informal expression.

1. This gold bracelet is part of the <u>stuff</u> Grandma left Rosa.

2. Every <u>guy who had made it to the next-to-last round of the tournament</u> posed for the photographers.

3. We bought a carton of Greek salad at the corner <u>deli</u>.

4. Abby has a collection of <u>teensy-weensy</u> glass animals.

5. That is quite a <u>sharp</u> dress you are wearing.

6. Hugh is really <u>a big spender</u> when he buys gifts.

A good writer avoids wordiness. A well-written sentence is clear and contains no unnecessary words.

B. Rewrite each of these sentences substituting a Unit word for the underlined group of words.

7. We met in the lobby during the <u>break you get between acts</u>.

8. After his <u>selection as a candidate</u>, Mr. Lee thanked the delegates.

Writing on Your Own

Your friend Ellen has just moved to a new city. She is lonely and writes asking for your advice. Write a friendly letter to Ellen suggesting two things: (1) get a pet and (2) become involved in some neighborhood activities. Describe how each would help Ellen. Then try to convince Ellen to do what you think is the better idea. Use some Unit words in your letter.

WRITER'S GUIDE For a sample friendly letter, turn to page 261.

Spelling on Your Own

UNIT WORDS

Write each Unit word. Then rewrite each word showing where it can be divided at the end of a line. Use a hyphen to mark each syllable division. For example, you will write *companionship* com-pan-ion-ship. Use the **Spelling Dictionary** if you need help.

MASTERY WORDS

naturally
population
material
independent
vegetable
evaporate

Finish this paragraph using the Mastery words.

     The mayor called upon the town's entire __1__ to save water during the severe water shortage. He asked the people to water their lawns and __2__ gardens in the early morning or the evening when the heat of the sun would not __3__ the water so quickly. He also suggested that they cover their plant beds with wood chips or similar __4__ to help keep the moisture in the ground.

Finish these exercises using the Mastery words.

5. Look up the word *naturally* in the **Spelling Dictionary**. Notice that it has two very different meanings. Write sentences to show both meanings of *naturally*.

6. The word *independent* has a prefix that means "not." Write a definition for *independent*.

7. Look up each Mastery word in the **Spelling Dictionary**. Then write the word using hyphens to show where it can be divided into syllables.

BONUS WORDS

individualize
silhouette
equivalent
utilitarian
predominantly
restoration
simultaneous
inclination

1. Write the Bonus words. Then write a synonym each for as many of the Bonus words as you can.
2. Write the headings *Noun, Verb, Adjective,* and *Adverb.* Write each Bonus word under the correct heading. Some of the words will appear under more than one heading.
3. Use each Bonus word in a sentence.

36 Review

Follow these steps when you are unsure of how to spell a word.

- **Say** the word. Recall when you have heard the word used. Think about what it means.
- **Look** at the word. Find any prefixes, suffixes, or other word parts you know. Think about other words that are related in meaning and spelling. Try to picture the word in your mind.
- **Spell** the word to yourself. Think about the way each sound is spelled. Notice any unusual spelling.
- **Write** the word while looking at it. Check the way you have formed your letters. If you have not written the word clearly or correctly, write it again.
- **Check** your learning. Cover the word and write it. If you did not spell the word correctly, practice these steps until the word becomes your own.

UNIT 31 Follow the directions using words from Unit 31. Complete each sentence.

UNIT 31
evidence
appearance
resistance
existence
defense
appliance
acceptance
convenience
innocence
intelligence

1. The attorney for the _____ summed up her case.

2. She emphasized the _____ of her client.

3. The _____ was not strong enough to convict him.

4. The jury showed their _____ of her case.

5. You may not know how to use this kitchen _____.

6. Use your _____ to figure it out.

7. Directions are on the side of the machine for your _____.

8. It is perhaps one of the handiest machines in _____.

Write the word that is related to each word below.

9. defend   10. exist

11. accept   12. apply

13. appear   14. evident

15. innocent   16. resist

UNIT 32 Follow the directions using words from Unit 32.
Write the word that is related to each word below. Circle the words that do not change their spelling when a suffix is added.

17. eat   **18.** impress   **19.** trace   **20.** like

Replace the underlined phrase in each sentence with a Unit 32 word.

21. The number was <u>able to be divided</u> by five.

22. The jacket was <u>able to be reversed</u>.

23. The outcome was <u>able to be predicted</u>.

24. The argument was <u>able to persuade</u>.

Write the words that fit the definitions.

25. readily used or obtained   **26.** easily upset or angered

UNIT 32

divisible
available
impressive
edible
traceable
reversible
predictable
likable
sensitive
persuasive

UNIT 33 Follow the directions using words from Unit 33.
The final syllable of each of these words is missing. Think of the letters that are needed to complete each word. Then write the word.

27. poten___   **28.** pre___   **29.** commer___   **30.** controver___

31. supersti___   **32.** artifi___   **33.** suspi___   **34.** cru___

35. ambi___   **36.** residen___

Write the word that is related to each word below.

37. commerce   **38.** residence   **39.** suspect

40. potent   **41.** controversy   **42.** ambition

UNIT 33

commercial
potential
controversial
superstitious
precious
residential
artificial
suspicious
ambitious
crucial

WORDS IN TIME

The word *artificial* comes from the Latin roots *ars*, which means "art," and *facere*, which means "to make." Originally *artificium* meant "a skill or trade." Today, *artificial* means "made by human work or art." Sometimes the word can mean "forced or affected," as in the expression "an artificial smile."

stadium
rhythm
gymnastics
physician
architecture
pharmacy
automation
planetarium
chaos
aroma

UNIT 34 Write the word from Unit 34 that fits each definition below.

43. place to fill prescriptions

44. complete disorder

45. pleasant smell

46. doctor of medicine

47. place to watch sporting events

48. the beat of music

49. style of a building

50. tumbling and jumping exercises

51. place to study the movement of stars

52. machines doing the work of people

UNIT 35

miniature
companionship
unusually
legislature
conspicuous
precipitation
commitment
nomination
insignificant
exposure

UNIT 35 Follow the directions using words from Unit 35. Add a word to finish each sentence.

53. The elderly man needed his dog for _____.

54. Because of its _____ reddish coat, the dog was named Rusty.

55. The dog and its master seemed to have a _____ to one another.

56. They went out for walks together even on days when _____ was forecast.

57. The picture would have been good if it had not been a double _____.

58. It showed a _____ pony about the size of a large dog.

59. The _____ debated the issue all week.

60. Opposition to the proposed bill was _____ strong.

61. I accepted the _____ for the student council.

62. I know I'll win because my opponent is concentrating on _____ issues instead of important ones.

Write the word that is a synonym for each word below.

63. rainfall   **64.** tiny   **65.** friendship

66. uncommonly   **67.** promise   **68.** lawmakers

69. unimportant

Spelling and Reading
A Persuasive Composition

Read this persuasive composition. Notice the order in which the persuasive reasons are written.

Now that Star City Junior College and Star City High School have competed in regional academic bowl games, it is time for our own junior high to compete as well. Why should we allow precious school time to be used for such an ambitious project? Here are three of the most persuasive reasons for doing so.

First of all, we compete with other schools in sports, so we should also have the chance to compete in the area of academic achievement. Where else besides high school and college entrance exams will we have such an opportunity to show others how much we have learned?

Second, competing in the regional Junior High School Bowl will help us learn to express ourselves verbally in a competitive atmosphere. In this way we will be working toward an impressive goal: training our minds to recall what we know and to express ourselves clearly and correctly.

Most important, participating in the Bowl will help us develop some crucial skills we will need in our later careers. Learning to work as a team, to share ideas, and to strive toward a common goal are all skills that will help us perform well in the adult world. Without this small commitment to our future needs, we may never reach the heights of our potential!

In conclusion, the entrance of Star City Junior High in the regional Junior High School Bowl offers us students impressive benefits. I hope that at the next school board meeting both parents and teachers will consider the evidence, strike down the insignificant objections, and vote favorably on our participation in this worthwhile activity.

Write your answers to the questions.

1. What is the writer's main reason for writing this persuasive composition?

2. How many reasons does the writer give in support of the issue? What are they?

3. What words does the writer use in the first paragraph to show that the subject of the composition is an important one?

4. What additional reason might be given to support the writer's position on the issue?

Underline the review words in your answers. Check to see that you spelled the words correctly.

Spelling and Writing
A Persuasive Composition

Star City Junior High School

Think and Discuss

A good persuasive composition tries to convince the reader to share the writer's opinion about an issue. What is the issue in this persuasive composition? What stand does the writer take on it?

The first paragraph of a persuasive composition should do two things. First, it should state the argument, or issue, that the writer supports. This first paragraph should also include a statement that the composition will present several reasons for the writer's opinion.

The body of a persuasive composition presents the writer's reasons for his or her opinion. What is the first reason the writer presents in the persuasive composition on page 157? Each reason in an effective persuasive composition is developed in a separate paragraph with supporting details and examples. What details does the writer provide as support for the first reason to allow the junior high school to compete?

In a persuasive composition, the reasons for the writer's opinion are usually arranged in order from least important to most important. This is because the last reason the audience reads is the one most likely to be remembered. Often it is also the reason by which the entire composition is judged. In which paragraph on page 157 did the writer present and support the most important reason for his or her opinion? The last paragraph may summarize the reasons given in the body, and it must always ask the audience to act on what has been read. Why do you think this is important?

As with all other forms of writing, the writer of a persuasive composition must consider who will be reading his or her work. Who is probably the audience for the persuasive composition on page 157? Why might the reasons presented be convincing to the audience?

Apply

Now it is your turn to write a persuasive composition for your classmates. Write a five-paragraph composition on an issue that affects your school or community. Follow the writing guidelines on page 159.

Words to Help You Write

evidence
appearance
existence
defense
intelligence
available
sensitive
persuasive
potential
controversial
crucial
unusually
conspicuous
insignificant
exposure

Prewriting

Think about the issue you have chosen. Decide which side you support.
- Decide who your audience will be.
- Make a list of all the possible reasons your audience might have for agreeing with you. Narrow your list to the three most persuasive.
- List your reasons in order. Decide which reason is least important. List this reason first. List the more important reason next, and save the most important reason for last.
- List details and examples that support each reason.

 THESAURUS For help with words that will make a strong impact on your audience, turn to page 205.

Composing

Use your list to write your persuasive composition.
- State the issue and the position you support in the first paragraph. Explain that you will give three convincing reasons for your stand.
- Write the second, third, and fourth paragraphs of your composition. Follow the order on your list. Give convincing facts to support each reason.
- Write the concluding paragraph. Ask the audience to act on the issue.

Revising

Read your persuasive composition and show it to a classmate. Follow these guidelines to improve your work. Use the editing and proofreading marks on this page to indicate corrections.

Editing

- Be sure your composition clearly expresses the issue and your opinion.
- Be sure your reasons are given in order from least to most important.
- Be sure each reason is supported by details or examples.
- Be sure you have asked your audience to act on the issue.

Proofreading

Check your spelling, capitalization, and punctuation.

Copy your composition onto clean paper. Write carefully and neatly.

Publishing

Read your composition aloud to the class. Even if your classmates do not agree with your stand, have them tell you if your opinion was supported with effective examples.

Editing and Proofreading Marks

≡	capitalize
⊙	make a period
∧	add something
⋏	add a comma
ⱽ ⱽ	add quotation marks
ℛ	take something away
◯	spell correctly
¶	indent the paragraph
/	make a lowercase letter
∼ tr	transpose

SPELLING DICTIONARY

PRONUNCIATION KEY

Remember these things when you read pronunciations:

- Parentheses around a sound symbol show that the sound is not always pronounced. /streng(k)th/
- A primary accent mark ′ follows the syllable that is said with the most force. A secondary accent mark ′ follows the syllable that is said with slightly less force. /ə·rij′ə·nal′ə·tē/

/a/	act, cat	/m/	mother, room	/u/	up, come
/ā/	ate, rain	/n/	new, can	/û/	early, hurt
/â/	care, bear	/ng/	sing, hang	/yo͞o/	mule, few
/ä/	car, father	/o/	on, stop	/v/	very, five
/b/	bed, rub	/ō/	over, go	/w/	will
/ch/	chair, watch	/ô/	or, saw	/y/	yes
/d/	duck, red	/oi/	oil, toy	/z/	zoo, buzz
/e/	egg, hen	/ou/	out, cow	/zh/	treasure
/ē/	even, see	/o͞o/	food, too	/ə/	The schwa
/f/	fish, off	/o͝o/	book, pull		is the sound
/g/	go, big	/p/	pig, hop		represented by
/h/	hat, hit	/r/	ran, car		these letters:
/i/	if, sit	/s/	see, miss		a in ago
/ī/	ice, time	/sh/	show, wish		e in listen
/j/	jump, bridge	/t/	take, feet		i in giraffe
/k/	cat, look	/th/	thing, tooth		o in pilot
/l/	lost, ball	/t͟h/	that, weather		u in circus

Symbols in the Spelling Dictionary

This symbol ► marks a word history.
This symbol ● indicates a note about the correct use of a word.

---

abbreviate

abound

A

ab·bre·vi·ate /ə·brē′vē·āt/ *v.* **ab·bre·vi·at·ed, ab·bre·vi·at·ing** **1** To reduce a word or phrase to a shortened form. **2** To shorten or condense: *abbreviate* the speech.

ab·do·men /ab′də·mən *or* ab·dō′mən/ *n.* **1** In mammals, the part of the body between the thorax and the pelvis; belly. **2** In insects, the hindmost section of the body. *Syn.:* stomach.

ab·duct /ab·dukt′/ *v.* To carry off or lead a person away unlawfully; to kidnap.

ab·nor·mal /ab·nôr′məl/ *adj.* Not normal; unusual; irregular: an *abnormal* reaction.

a·bol·ish /ə·bol′ish/ *v.* To do away with.

ab·o·li·tion /ab′ə·lish′ən/ *n.* **1** The act or state of being abolished or done away with. **2** The ending of slavery in the United States.

a·bound /ə·bound′/ *v.* **1** To be plentiful or abundant. **2** To be filled with: These streams *abound* with trout.

abrupt　　　　　　　　　　　　　　　　　　　　　　　　**admire**

a·brupt /ə·brupt′/ *adj.* **1** Sudden. **2** Steep: an *abrupt* climb. **3** Hasty; quick: an *abrupt* exit. **4** In speech, being rude: an *abrupt* reply.

ab·sence /ab′səns/ *n.* The state of or a period of being away; not being present.

ab·sorb /ab·sôrb′ *or* ab·zôrb′/ *v.* **1** To take up or drink in. **2** To be engaged in completely or take the full attention of.

ab·stain /ab·stān′/ *v.* **1** To refrain; to hold oneself back by choice. **2** To choose not to vote. ► *Abstain* comes from Latin *ab,* "from," and *tenere,* "to hold."

ab·surd /ab·sûrd′ *or* ab·zûrd′/ *adj.* Unreasonable; ridiculous; illogical.

a·bun·dance /ə·bun′dəns/ *n.* An extremely plentiful or more than sufficient supply. ► *Abundance* and the verb *abound* both come from the Latin word *abundare,* "to overflow."

a·bun·dant /ə·bun′dənt/ *adj.* Not scarce; plentiful; ample.—**a·bun′dant·ly** *adv.*

ac·cel·er·ate /ak·sel′ə·rāt/ *v.* **ac·cel·er·at·ed, ac·cel·er·at·ing** **1** To increase or cause to increase speed; hasten. **2** *adj. use:* an *accelerated* rate of inflation.

ac·cen·tu·ate /ak·sen′chōō·āt/ *v.* **ac·cen·tu·at·ed, ac·cen·tu·at·ing** **1** To emphasize or stress. **2** To mark or pronounce with stress: *accentuate* the syllable. ► It is believed that *accentuate* comes from Latin *ac- (ad-),* "to," and *cantus,* "song."

ac·cept /ak·sept′/ *v.* **1** To take or receive something offered or given. **2** To agree to. **3** To welcome; to approve of.

ac·cep·tance /ak·sep′təns/ *n.* **1** The act of accepting, taking, or receiving something offered or given. **2** Approval; favorable reception.

ac·cess /ak′ses/ *n.* **1** Permission or ability to approach, enter, or get: *access* to the files. **2** A means of entrance: The tunnel gives *access* to the street.

ac·ces·si·ble /ak·ses′ə·bəl/ *adj.* **1** Capable of being reached; obtainable: Is the highway *accessible* from here? **2** Easily reached. ► *Accessible* comes from Latin *ac- (ad-),* "to," and *cedere,* "to come."

ac·ces·so·ry /ak·ses′ə·rē/ *n., pl.* **ac·ces·so·ries** **1** Something extra added for decoration or convenience. **2** A person who encourages or aids someone in committing a crime or helps a criminal after the crime.

ac·ci·dent /ak′sə·dənt/ *n.* **1** Something that happens unexpectedly. **2** An event that causes harm or injury, as a collision, etc.

ac·com·mo·date /ə·kom′ə·dāt/ *v.* **ac·com·mo·dat·ed, ac·com·mo·dat·ing** **1** To hold or be suitable for. **2** To provide for. **3** To help or do a favor for.

ac·com·plish /ə·kom′plish/ *v.* To achieve or bring to a successful conclusion.

ac·com·plished /ə·kom′plisht/ *adj.* **1** Completed. **2** Skillful or well-trained.

ac·count·ant /ə·koun′tənt/ *n.* A person whose work involves recording and summarizing amounts of money received or paid out.

ac·cu·mu·late /ə·kyōōm′yə·lāt/ *v.* **ac·cu·mu·lat·ed, ac·cu·mu·lat·ing** To collect or gather: to *accumulate* wealth.

ac·cu·ra·cy /ak′yər·ə·sē/ *n.* Lack of errors; exactness; precision.

ac·cu·sa·tion /ak′yōō·zā′shən/ *n.* A charge of wrongdoing or of having done something illegal.

ac·quain·tance /ə·kwān′təns/ *n.* A person one knows but who is not a close friend.

ac·ro·bat /ak′rə·bat/ *n.* Someone skilled in gymnastic stunts, such as tumbling, etc. ► *Acrobat* comes from the Greek word *akrobatos,* "walking on high."

a·cute /ə·kyōōt′/ *adj.* **1** An angle measuring less than 90°. **2** Severe; sharp: an *acute* pain. **3** Quick to perceive or grasp; keen: an *acute* mind.

a·dapt /ə·dapt′/ *v.* **1** To change for a new use. **2** To adjust to new conditions or circumstances: The children *adapted* quickly to their new home.

ad·dic·tive /ə·dik′tiv/ *adj.* Causing a powerful physical or mental dependence.

ad·di·tion·al /ə·dish′ən·əl/ *adj.* Added to; extra: *additional* help.

ad·he·sive /ad·hē′siv/ **1** *adj.* Designed to stick tight: *adhesive* tape. **2** *n.* Something that is adhesive, such as glue.

ad·ja·cent /ə·jā′sənt/ *adj.* Close by or near; next to; adjoining: *adjacent* seats.

ad·mi·ra·ble /ad′mər·ə·bəl/ *adj.* Worthy of being admired or regarded with wonder, pleasure, or approval.

ad·mi·ra·tion /ad′mə·rā′shən/ *n.* A feeling of wonder, approval, or satisfaction.

ad·mire /ad·mīr′/ *v.* **ad·mired, ad·mir·ing** To regard with wonder, pleasure, or approval.

Abbreviations

n. = noun;　　　*v.* = verb;　　　*adj.* = adjective;　　　*adv.* = adverb;　　　*prep.* = preposition;
conj. = conjunction

ad·mit /ad·mit′/ *v.* **ad·mit·ted, ad·mit·ting**
1 To allow or permit to enter or join.   **2** To
confess.

ad·o·les·cent /ad′ə·les′ənt/   **1** *n.* A person in
the transitional period between childhood
and adulthood: The *adolescent* looked forward to becoming an adult.   **2** *adj.* Having
the characteristics of adolescence.

a·dopt /ə·dopt′/ *v.*   **1** To become the legal par-
ent of another person's child.   **2** *adj. use:* an
adopted daughter.   **3** To take on, accept, or
use as one's own: to *adopt* a new name.
4 To vote to accept: to *adopt* a law.

a·drift /ə·drift′/ *adj., adv.* Drifting in which-
ever way the current or wind moves.

ad·van·tage /ad·van′tij/ *n.*   **1** Anything that
is of benefit or gain: The home team had the
advantage.   **2** Benefit or gain; profit.

ad·ver·sar·y /ad′vər·ser′ē/ *n., pl.* **ad·ver·sar·**
ies An enemy or opponent: My *adversary*
won the game.

ad·ver·tise /ad′vər·tīz/ *v.* **ad·ver·tised, ad·**
ver·tis·ing   **1** To present a product, organization, idea, etc., in order to persuade people to buy, support, or approve of it: to
advertise on TV.   **2** To call public attention
to: to *advertise* for a lost dog.

ad·vice /ad·vīs′/ *n.* A suggestion made or an
opinion given: good *advice.*

ad·vis·a·ble /ad·vī′zə·bəl/ *adj.* Worth doing;
sensible to do; wise.

ad·vise /ad·vīz′/ *v.* **ad·vised, ad·vis·ing**   **1** To
make suggestions; to give advice: My friend
advised me to be careful.   **2** To inform; to
communicate information.

aer·i·al /âr′ē·əl/   **1** *adj.* Of, from, or in the air.
2 *adj.* Of, by, or for aircraft: an *aerial* attack.
3 *n.* An antenna used for radio or television
reception.

a·gainst /ə·genst′/ *prep.*   **1** In the opposite
direction of: walking *against* the wind.
2 In contact or in collision with: The cat
brushed *against* my leg.   **3** In opposition to;
contrary to: *against* his parents' wishes.

a·gent /ā′jənt/ *n.*   **1** A person or group that
has the power to act on behalf of another: a
publicity *agent.*   **2** A person or thing that
causes a certain result or effect: a cleaning
agent.   **3** A spy: secret *agent.*

ag·gra·vate /ag′rə·vāt/ *v.* **ag·gra·vat·ed, ag·**
gra·vat·ing   **1** To make worse or more
severe. **2** To provoke to anger. **3** *adj. use:* an
aggravating noise: The drilling made an *ag-*
gravating sound.

ag·gres·sive /ə·gres′iv/ *adj.*   **1** Quick to attack.   **2** Eager; forceful.

aisle /īl/ *n.* A passageway between sections of
seats, as in a theater or church, or between
rows, as in a supermarket.

al·gae /al′jē/ *n. pl.* A large group of simple
plants that grow in water and damp places
and lack true roots, stems, or leaves.
● *Algae* is the plural form of the Latin word
alga, "seaweed."

al·ge·bra /al′jə·brə/ *n.* A branch of mathematics that deals with the relations between
numbers and uses letters and other symbols
to represent specific numbers.

al·ien /āl′yən *or* ā′lē·ən/   **1** *adj.* Foreign. **2** *adj.*
Very unusual; strange.   **3** *n.* A person who is
not a citizen of the country in which he or
she is living: Before I became a citizen I was
an *alien.*

al·ler·gy /al′ər·jē/ *n., pl.* **al·ler·gies** A condition of sensitivity to certain substances,
such as foods, pollen, etc.

al·lot·ment /ə·lot′mənt/ *n.*   **1** The act of giving out a share or portion.   **2** A share or
portion: an *allotment* of food.

a·loft /ə·lôft′/ *adv.*   **1** In or to a high place;
high up: climbed *aloft.*   **2** In the air; in
flight: soared *aloft.*

a·loof /ə·lo͞of′/ *adj.*   **1** Reserved or distant in
manner.   **2** *adv.* At a distance, especially in
feeling or manner.

al·pha·bet /al′fə·bet/ *n.*   **1** The letters that
form the separate parts of a written language: My niece knows all the letters of the
alphabet.   **2** Any system of letters or characters representing the sounds of a language:
manual alphabet.

al·ter·nate /*v.* ôl′tər·nāt, *adj., n.* ôl′tər·nət/ *v.*
al·ter·nat·ed, al·ter·nat·ing, *adj., n.*   **1** *v.*
To interchange repeatedly and regularly
with one another: Day *alternates* with night.
2 *adj.* Existing, occurring, or following by
turns: *alternate* stripes of red and blue.
3 *adj.* Every other: *alternate* days.   **4** *n.* A
substitute or stand-in. *Syn.:* rotate.

al·ter·na·tive /ôl·tûr′nə·tiv/   **1** *n.* A choice offered between two or more things: You leave
me no *alternative.*   **2** *n.* Either of the two or
more things to be chosen.   **3** *adj.* Able to be
used instead of something else: When the
well went dry, we began searching for an
alternative source of water.

a·lum·na /ə·lum′nə/ *n., pl.* **a·lum·nae**
/ə·lum′nē/ A female graduate of a specific
school, college, or university.

a·lum·nus /ə·lum′nəs/ *n., pl.* **a·lum·ni**
/ə·lum′nī/ A male graduate of a specific
school, college, or university.

amateur

aorta

am·a·teur /am'ə·cho͞or *or* am'ə·t(y)o͞or/ *n.*
1 A person who engages in any art, study, or sport for enjoyment rather than for financial benefit. 2 A person inexperienced or unskilled in a particular activity.

am·bas·sa·dor /am·bas'ə·dər *or* am·bas'ə·dôr/ *n.* A diplomatic official of the highest rank sent to represent his or her government in another country.

am·bi·tious /am·bish'əs/ *adj.* 1 Eager to succeed; aspiring. 2 Requiring great effort or ability; challenging: an *ambitious* plan.— **am·bi'tious·ly** *adv.*

am·mo·nia /ə·mōn'yə/ *n.* 1 A colorless, suffocating, gaseous compound of nitrogen and hydrogen. 2 A cleaning product manufactured by dissolving this gaseous compound in water.

am·ple /am'pəl/ *adj.* **am·pler, am·plest** 1 Generous or more than adequate in size or capacity. 2 Plentiful: *ample* food. 3 Sufficient to satisfy a need: *ample* money for the trip. *Syn.*: plentiful.

am·pli·fy /am'plə·fī/ *v.* **am·pli·fied, am·pli·fy·ing** 1 To enlarge or increase in power, amount, etc.: to *amplify* sound. 2 To enlarge or expand through the addition of details: He *amplified* his original statement.

an·a·lyze /an'ə·līz/ *v.* **an·a·lyzed, an·a·lyz·ing** 1 To separate into smaller parts or elements in order to examine closely: to *analyze* a chemical. 2 To study or examine critically.—**an'a·lyst** *n.*

a·nat·o·my /ə·nat'ə·mē/ *n., pl.* **a·nat·o·mies** 1 The structure of an animal or plant. 2 The human body; skeleton. 3 The science dealing with the structure of organisms.

an·gle /ang'gəl/ *n., v.* **an·gled, an·gling** 1 *n.* A geometric shape formed by two lines that share a common end point. 2 *v.* To move or turn at an angle.

an·ni·hi·late /ə·nī'ə·lāt/ *v.* **an·ni·hi·lat·ed, an·ni·hi·lat·ing** To destroy utterly and completely.

an·nul /ə·nul'/ *v.* **an·nulled, an·nul·ling** To do away with or cancel; to put an end to.

a·non·y·mous /ə·non'ə·məs/ *adj.* 1 By or from a person whose name is not known or given: The Red Cross received an *anonymous* gift. 2 One whose name is not known: an *anonymous* face in the crowd.

an·ten·na /an·ten'ə/ *n.* 1 *pl.* **an·ten·nas** A system of wires, rods, or reflecting surfaces by which electromagnetic waves are sent out and received. 2 *pl.* **an·ten·nae** /an·ten'nē/ One of the jointed, sensitive, movable feelers occurring in pairs on the heads of various insects and shellfish.

an·thro·pol·o·gy /an'thrə·pol'ə·jē/ *n.* The study of the origins, physical and cultural development, and social customs and beliefs of human societies.

an·ti·bi·ot·ic /an'ti·bī·ot'ik/ *n.* A substance, such as penicillin, produced by a microorganism, that kills or weakens other microorganisms harmful to people. ► *Antibiotic* comes from Greek *anti-*, "against," and *biotik*, "pertaining to life."

an·ti·dote /an'ti·dōt/ *n.* Something that prevents, counteracts, or removes the effects of poison, evil, etc.; a remedy: He was given an *antidote* for his snake bite. ► *Antidote* comes from Greek *anti-*, "against," and *didonai*, "to give."

an·ti·pol·lu·tion /an'tē·pə·lo͞o'shən/ *adj.* Designed to reduce or eliminate pollution: *antipollution* devices.

an·ti·sep·tic /an'ti·sep'tik/ 1 *adj.* Preventing infection or disease by killing or stopping the growth of germs; sterile. 2 *n.* A substance, such as alcohol, that checks the growth of germs. ► *Antiseptic* comes from Greek *anti-*, "against," and *septikos*, "rotting."

an·to·nym /an'tə·nim/ *n.* A word that has the opposite meaning from another.

a·or·ta /ā·ôr'tə/ *n., pl.* **a·or·tas** The large artery extending from the left side of the heart, through which blood passes to all parts of the body except the lungs. *Alternate plural:* **aortae.**

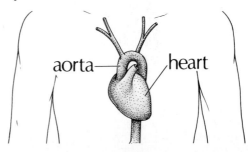

aorta   heart

---

act, āte, câre, ärt;   egg, ēven;   if, īce;   on, ōver, ôr;   bo͞ok, fo͞od;   up, tûrn;
ə=a in *ago*, e in *listen*, i in *giraffe*, o in *pilot*, u in *circus*;   yo͞o=u in *music*;   oil;   out;
chair; sing; shop; thank; that; zh in *treasure*.

165

apologize   **ashamed**

a·pol·o·gize /ə·pol′ə·jīz/ *v.* **a·pol·o·gized, a·pol·o·giz·ing** To ask pardon or say one is sorry for a fault, offense, or mistake.

ap·pall /ə·pôl′/ *v.* **ap·palled, ap·pall·ing** To fill with dismay, horror, or shock. *Alternate spelling:* **appal.**

ap·pall·ing /ə·pôl′ing/ *adj.* Causing dismay; shocking; frightful: an *appalling* mistake.

ap·pa·ra·tus /ap′ə·rat′əs *or* ap′ə·rā′təs/ *n., pl.* **ap·pa·ra·tus** A device or the equipment needed for a particular purpose. *Alternate plural:* **apparatuses.**

ap·par·el /ə·par′əl/ *n.* Clothes; garments.

ap·par·ent /ə·par′ənt/ *adj.* **1** Obvious. **2** Seeming; only appearing to be. *Syn.:* evident.—**ap·par′ent·ly** *adv.*

ap·peal /ə·pēl′/ **1** *v.* To make an earnest plea or request: to *appeal* for help. **2** *n.* A plea or request. **3** *v.* To ask someone for a decision in one's favor. **4** *v.* To be attractive or pleasing.

ap·pear·ance /ə·pir′əns/ *n.* **1** The act of appearing or becoming visible: His sudden *appearance* surprised us. **2** The outward style or manner of a person or thing.

ap·pen·dix /ə·pen′diks/ *n., pl.* **ap·pen·dix·es** **1** A section at the end of a book. **2** A narrow, closed tube in the human body, extending from the large intestine. *Alternate plural:* **appendices.** ► *Appendix* comes from Latin *ap- (ad-),* "to," and *pendere,* "to hang."

ap·pli·ance /ə·plī′əns/ *n.* A machine that does a specific task, as a refrigerator, iron, dryer, etc.

ap·pli·cant /ap′li·kənt/ *n.* A person who applies for something or requests something, such as a job.

ap·pli·ca·tion /ap′li·kā′shən/ *n.* **1** The act of applying or putting on. **2** Something applied: an *application* to relieve itching. **3** A particular or specific way of being applied or used: The word *manual* has many different *applications.* **4** A formal, written request, as for a job or acceptance into a school.

ap·pre·ci·ate /ə·prē′shē·āt/ *v.* **ap·pre·ci·at·ed, ap·pre·ci·at·ing** **1** To recognize the value or quality of something: to *appreciate* music. **2** To be thankful or grateful: I *appreciate* your help.

ap·pre·hend /ap′rə·hend′/ *v.* **1** To capture or arrest. **2** To understand or comprehend: to *apprehend* a theorem. ► *Apprehend* comes from Latin *ap- (ad-),* "to, at," and *prehendere,* "to grasp."

ap·pre·hen·sive /ap′rə·hen′siv/ *adj.* Uneasy or fearful about something that might occur; worried.

ap·pro·pri·ate /*adj.* ə·prō′prē·it, *v.* ə·prō′prē·āt/ *adj., v.* **ap·pro·pri·at·ed, ap·pro·pri·at·ing** **1** *adj.* Proper or suitable. **2** *v.* To put aside for a specific purpose: to *appropriate* funds.

ap·prov·al /ə·proo′vəl/ *n.* **1** Formal permission. **2** A favorable or positive feeling or opinion: the *approval* of your peers.

ap·prox·i·mate /*adj.* ə·prok′sə·mit, *v.* ə·prok′sə·māt/ *adj., v.* **ap·prox·i·mat·ed, ap·prox·i·mat·ing** **1** *adj.* Nearly or almost exact. **2** *v.* To estimate roughly: to *approximate* the number attending.

ar·bi·trar·y /är′bə·trer′ē/ *adj.* **1** Based on one's own will, beliefs, ideas, etc.: an *arbitrary* decision. **2** Not restricted by law; random: an *arbitrary* rule.

arch·er·y /är′chər·ē/ *n.* The art or sport of shooting with a bow and arrow.

ar·chi·tec·ture /är′kə·tek′chər/ *n.* **1** The science or profession of designing and erecting buildings and other structures. **2** The style of a building design: Gothic *architecture.*

a·rith·me·tic /ə·rith′mə·tik/ *n.* The study of numbers in terms of addition, subtraction, multiplication, and division.

a·ro·ma /ə·rō′mə/ *n.* A pleasant smell or fragrance.

ar·ter·y /är′tər·ē/ *n., pl.* **ar·ter·ies** **1** Any of the blood vessels that carry blood away from the heart to any part of the body. **2** A main highway or channel.

ar·tic·u·late /*adj.* är·tik′yə·lit, *v.* är·tik′yə·lāt/ *adj., v.* **ar·tic·u·lat·ed, ar·tic·u·lat·ing** **1** *adj.* Uttered clearly in distinct syllables or words: *articulate* speech. **2** *adj.* Able to express one's thoughts clearly in words. **3** *v.* To speak clearly and distinctly: Please *articulate* so I can understand you.

ar·ti·fi·cial /är′tə·fish′əl/ *adj.* **1** Made synthetically rather than by nature. **2** Not natural or genuine; false; affected.

a·shamed /ə·shāmd′/ *adj.* Feeling shame; upset or embarrassed because of a mistake or an improper action.

a·shore /ə·shôr´/ *adv., adj.* **1** To or on the shore: Row the boat *ashore.* **2** On land.

as·pect /as´pekt/ *n.* **1** A way in which something may be looked at, regarded, or approached: one *aspect* of the problem. **2** Look; appearance: The castle had a gloomy *aspect.*

as·sis·tant /ə·sis´tənt/ **1** *n.* A person who assists, aids, or helps. **2** *adj.* Assisting, aiding, or helping another worker.

as·so·ci·ate /*v.* ə·sō´shē·āt *or* ə·sō´sē·āt, *n.* ə·sō´shē·ət *or* ə·sō´sē·ət/ *v.* **as·so·ci·at·ed, as·so·ci·at·ing,** *n.* **1** *v.* To make or see a connection between; to bring into relation, as thought, feeling, experience, etc.: We *associate* red hearts with Valentine's Day. **2** *n.* A person who works with, spends time with, or has dealings with another: She introduced me to her *associate.* **3** *v.* To spend time with: to *associate* with the neighbors.

as·sure /ə·shoor´/ *v.* **as·sured, as·sur·ing** To convince or promise.

a·stride /ə·strīd´/ **1** *adv.* With one leg on each side: to sit *astride.* **2** *prep.* With one leg on each side of: *astride* the horse.

as·trol·o·gy /ə·strol´ə·jē/ *n.* The study of the stars and planets and their supposed influence on a person's life.

as·tro·naut /as´trə·nôt/ *n.* A person who travels in space.

as·tro·nom·i·cal /as´trə·nom´i·kəl/ *adj.* **1** Pertaining to astronomy. **2** Almost too large to imagine; enormous.

as·tron·o·my /ə·stron´ə·mē/ *n.* The scientific study of the stars, planets, and other heavenly bodies. ● *Astronomy* is the scientific study of the material universe beyond the earth's atmosphere. *Astrology* is the nonscientific study of the heavenly bodies and their supposed influence on human affairs.

as·tro·phys·ics /as´trō·fiz´iks/ *n.* A branch of astronomy that deals with the physical properties of heavenly bodies.

at·mos·phere /at´məs·fir/ *n.* **1** The mass of air surrounding the earth. **2** Mood; feeling of a situation: The *atmosphere* at the meeting was tense.

at·om /at´əm/ *n.* **1** The smallest particle of an element that can exist independently. Atoms are made up of protons and neutrons in nuclei that are surrounded by electrons. **2** A tiny amount; a bit.

a·tom·ic /ə·tom´ik/ *adj.* **1** Pertaining to atoms: *atomic* energy. **2** Tiny; minute.

a·tro·cious /ə·trō´shəs/ *adj.* **1** Horribly wicked. **2** Very bad in any way.

at·tach·ment /ə·tach´mənt/ *n.* **1** Affection; fondness: an *attachment* to a friend. **2** A part that connects, fastens, or joins to something: a vacuum cleaner *attachment.*

at·tempt /ə·tempt´/ **1** *v.* To try. **2** *n.* A try; an act of effort.

at·ten·dance /ə·ten´dəns/ *n.* **1** The act of attending or being present. **2** The number of people attending or present.

at·ten·tive /ə·ten´tiv/ *adj.* Giving or showing attention, interest, or notice.

at·tor·ney /ə·tûr´nē/ *n., pl.* **at·tor·neys** A lawyer.

at·trac·tion /ə·trak´shən/ *n.* **1** The act or power of attracting, causing interest, or drawing someone or something near. **2** Something that attracts or interests.

au·di·ble /ô´də·bəl/ *adj.* Able to be heard.

au·ri·cle /ôr´i·kəl/ *n.* One of the two upper chambers or sections of the heart.

au·then·tic /ô·then´tik/ *adj.* **1** Trustworthy; reliable: an *authentic* document. **2** Genuine; real: an *authentic* Navajo blanket.— **au·then´ti·cal·ly** *adv.*

au·thor·i·ty /ə·thôr´ə·tē/ *n., pl.* **au·thor·i·ties 1** The power to command, make decisions, judge, etc. **2** *(usually pl.)* Persons having the legal right to enforce the law: local *authorities.* **3** A person with special knowledge; an expert.

au·thor·ize /ô´thə·rīz/ *v.* **au·thor·ized, au·thor·iz·ing 1** To give authority or official power to. **2** To give permission for.

au·to·bi·og·ra·phy /ô´tə·bī·og´rə·fē/ *n., pl.* **au·to·bi·og·ra·phies** The story of someone's life written by that person.

au·to·graph /ô´tə·graf/ **1** *n.* A person's signature. **2** *v.* To write one's own name.

au·to·ma·tion /ô´tə·mā´shən/ *n.* The operation or control of a process, machine, etc., by electronic or mechanical means instead of by human beings.

aux·il·ia·ry /ôg·zil´yər·ē/ *adj., n., pl.* **aux·il·ia·ries 1** *adj.* Serving as an aid; helpful: *auxiliary* police. **2** *n.* A person or thing that gives help or aid; helper.

a·vail·a·ble /ə·vā´lə·bəl/ *adj.* Readily used or obtained.

---

act, āte, câre, ärt;   egg, ēven;   if, īce;   on, ōver, ôr;   bŏŏk, fŏŏd;   up, tûrn;
ə=**a** in *ago,* **e** in *listen,* **i** in *giraffe,* **o** in *pilot,* **u** in *circus;*   yŏŏ=**u** in *music;*   oil;   out;
chair; si**ng**; **sh**op; **th**ank; **th**at; **zh** in *treasure.*

av·er·age /av′rij/ *adj., n., v.* **av·er·aged, av·er·ag·ing** **1** *adj.* Typical; common; ordinary: *average* height. **2** *n.* The sum of the elements in a set of numbers divided by the number of elements in the set. **3** *v.* To calculate an average.

a·vert /ə·vûrt′/ *v.* **1** To turn away. **2** To prevent or ward off: to *avert* a crash. ▶ *Avert* comes from Latin *a- (ab-)*, "off, away," and *vertere*, "to turn."

ax·is /ak′sis/ *n., pl.* **ax·es** /ak′sēz/ **1** The line, real or imaginary, around which something turns. **2** A line on a graph used as a fixed reference for determining the position of a point or a series of points forming a curve or a surface.

B

back·ward /bak′wərd/ **1** *adv.* Toward the back: to move *backward*. **2** *adv.* With the back facing to the front. **3** *adj.* Directed toward the back: a *backward* glance.

bac·te·ri·a /bak·tir′ē·ə/ *n., pl.* Microscopic organisms that can be helpful or harmful to people. ● *Bacterium* is the singular form of *bacteria*.

bal·ance /bal′əns/ *v.* **bal·anced, bal·anc·ing,** *n.* **1** *v.* To keep something in position without letting it fall. **2** *n.* The ability to keep one's body in a certain position without falling: It takes *balance* to ride a bike. **3** *n.* The amount of money one has in a bank account. **4** *n.* The remainder or amount left over.

bal·lot /bal′ət/ *n.* **1** A piece of paper on which a voter marks his or her choice in private: After filling out her *ballot,* the voter slipped it into the box. **2** The total number of votes in an election.

bank·rupt·cy /bangk′rupt·sē/ *n., pl.* **bank·rupt·cies** The condition of having been declared unable to pay one's debts by a court and having all property removed and distributed among one's creditors: Since she could not pay her bills, she was forced to declare *bankruptcy.*

be·friend /bi·frend′/ *v.* To act as a friend to; to help; to aid.

be·lat·ed /bi·lā′tid/ *adj.* Coming after the expected or usual time; late.

be·lit·tle /bi·lit′(ə)l/ *v.* **be·lit·tled, be·lit·tling** To cause a person or thing to seem less or unimportant.

bel·lig·er·en·cy /bə·lij′ər·ən·sē/ *n.* The state or condition of being engaged in war or conflict.

bel·lig·er·ent /bə·lij′ər·ənt/ **1** *adj.* Tending to fight; warlike; hostile: a *belligerent* feeling. **2** *adj.* Waging or engaged in war. **3** *n.* A person or nation engaged in a war or fighting.

ben·e·fi·cial /ben′ə·fish′əl/ *adj.* Useful; helpful; worthwhile.

be·queath /bi·kwēth′ *or* bi·kwēth′/ *v.* To leave your possessions to another when you die, by means of a will.

be·sides /bi·sīdz′/ **1** *adv.* Also; as well. **2** *prep.* In addition to. **3** *adv.* Moreover; furthermore.

bev·er·age /bev′ər·ij *or* bev′rij/ *n.* Any liquid intended for drinking.

be·wil·der /bi·wil′dər/ *v.* To baffle or confuse; to puzzle.—**be·wil′der·ment** *n.*

bib·li·og·ra·phy /bib′lē·og′rə·fē/ *n., pl.* **bib·li·og·ra·phies** A list of books, frequently by one author or about one subject.

bi·og·ra·phy /bī·og′rə·fē/ *n., pl.* **bi·og·ra·phies** The story of someone's life.

bi·ol·o·gy /bī·ol′ə·jē/ *n.* The science that studies life and the ways in which living organisms grow, develop, and reproduce.

bloc /blok/ *n.* A united group that supports and promotes certain interests: a labor *bloc.*

bough /bou/ *n.* A large branch of a tree.

bound·a·ry /boun′də·rē *or* boun′drē/ *n., pl.* **bound·a·ries** Something that indicates an outer limit or edge.

brain /brān/ *n.* **1** The part of the central nervous system, located in the skull of humans and other vertebrate animals, that controls and coordinates mental and physical actions. **2** *(pl.)* Intelligence.

breadth /bredth/ *n.* The distance from side to side; width.

brib·er·y /brī′bər·ē/ *n.* The giving, offering, or taking of a gift meant to persuade someone to do something wrong; graft: *bribery* of an official.

bril·liant /bril′yənt/ *adj.* **1** Shining brightly; glowing; sparkling. **2** Demonstrating great intelligence, skill, or talent: a *brilliant* lawyer. **3** Distinguished; splendid: a *brilliant* performance. *Syn.:* glowing.

buoy /boi *or* boo′ē/ *n.* An anchored, floating object used to mark a channel or a dangerous area in the water.

buoy·an·cy /boi′ən·sē *or* boo′yən·sē/ *n.* **1** The ability or power to keep afloat. **2** Cheerfulness.

buoy·ant /boi′ənt *or* boo′yənt/ *adj.* **1** Able or tending to float or rise in liquid or air. **2** Cheerful; lighthearted.

c

cac·tus /kak′təs/ *n., pl.* **cac·tus·es** Any of the leafless, spiny plants that grow in hot desert regions and often produce large, colorful flowers: The *cactus* I got for my birthday needs water only once every two weeks. *Alternate plural:* **cacti.**

cal·lous /kal′əs/ *adj.* Unfeeling; coldhearted: a *callous* comment.

can·cel /kan′səl/ *v.* **can·celed, can·cel·ing** **1** To call off or do away with: The noon lecture was *canceled.* **2** To mark or cross out something to show it has been noted or used: to *cancel* a check. **3** To compensate or make up for: His kindness *canceled* out his previous rudeness. *Alternate spellings:* **cancelled, cancelling.**

can·vas /kan′vəs/ *n.* **1** A closely woven, heavy cloth made of cotton, hemp, or flax, used for sails, tents, etc.: The sail was made of *canvas.* **2** *adj. use:* a *canvas* tent. **3** A piece of canvas on which an artist paints. **4** Any painting on canvas.

can·vass /kan′vəs/ *v.* To go about seeking votes, sales, opinions, etc., from a district, group of people, etc.: Please *canvass* the neighborhood for volunteers.

cap·il·lar·y /kap′ə·ler′ē/ *n., pl.* **cap·il·lar·ies** One of the minute blood vessels that connect the arteries with the veins.

cap·tiv·i·ty /kap·tiv′ə·tē/ *n., pl.* **cap·tiv·i·ties** Imprisonment or confinement.

ca·tas·tro·phe /kə·tas′trə·fē/ *n.* A sudden tragic event; disaster.

cau·tious /kô′shəs/ *adj.* Very careful or watchful: a *cautious* driver.

ce·leb·ri·ty /sə·leb′rə·tē/ *n., pl.* **ce·leb·ri·ties** A famous or well-known person.

cem·e·ter·y /sem′ə·ter′ē/ *n., pl.* **cem·e·ter·ies** A graveyard.

change·a·ble /chān′jə·bəl/ *adj.* **1** Capable of change; varying. **2** Fickle.

chan·nel /chan′əl/ *n., v.* **chan·neled, chan·nel·ing** **1** *n.* A body of water connecting two larger bodies of water. **2** *v.* To cut a channel in or through. **3** *n.* A system for transmitting and receiving something by electronic means, as a television or radio frequency. *Alternate spellings:* **channelled, channelling.**

cha·os /kā′os/ *n.* Complete disorder and confusion.

chap·ter /chap′tər/ *n.* **1** A main division of a book, usually numbered and often having a title. **2** An important portion or division of anything: a *chapter* in your life. **3** A branch or division of a society, club, etc.

chim·ney /chim′nē/ *n., pl.* **chim·neys** A vertical structure containing a hollow passage through which smoke, gases, etc., are carried off from a fireplace, furnace, or stove.

choose /chooz/ *v.* **chose, cho·sen, choos·ing** **1** To select or pick from a group. **2** To prefer or decide to do something.

cho·re·og·ra·pher /kôr′ē·og′rə·fər/ *n.* A person who creates and composes steps or movements for a dance.

chor·us /kôr′əs/ *n.* **1** A group of singers or dancers who perform together. **2** The part of a song that is repeated after every verse.

chro·mo·some /krō′mə·sōm/ *n.* One of the threadlike bodies found in a cell that carry the genes which determine the passage of hereditary traits.

cir·cu·la·tion /sûr′kyə·lā′shən/ *n.* **1** A moving around or through something back to where it started: the *circulation* of water in a fish tank. **2** The continuous movement of the blood through the body. **3** The passage of anything from one person or place to another. **4** The number of copies a newspaper, magazine, etc., distributes.

---

act, āte, câre, ärt;　　egg, ēven;　　if, īce;　　on, ōver, ôr;　　book, food;　　up, tûrn;
ə=a in *ago,* e in *listen,* i in *giraffe,* o in *pilot,* u in *circus;*　　yoo=u in *music;*　　oil;　　out;
　　chair;　sing;　shop;　thank;　that;　zh in *treasure.*

cite

cite /sīt/ *v.* **cit·ed, cit·ing**   **1** To quote or mention, especially as an authority; to refer to as an example: She *cited* Shakespeare to support her point.   **2** To call upon officially; to summon to appear in court.

civ·i·li·za·tion /siv′ə·lə·zā′shən/ *n.*   **1** The condition of human society in which culture and science are highly developed.   **2** The society and culture of a people, place, or time: modern *civilization*.

civ·i·lize /siv′ə·līz/ *v.* **civ·i·lized, civ·i·liz·ing**   **1** To order or change so as to make fit for society.   **2** *adj. use:* a *civilized* person.

clar·i·fy /klar′ə·fī/ *v.* **clar·i·fied, clar·i·fy·ing**   **1** To make understandable: The President *clarified* his previous statement.   **2** To make clear or pure, as a liquid: We *clarified* the soup by straining it.

clock·wise /klok′wīz′/ *adv., adj.* In the direction in which the hands of a clock move: We skated *clockwise* around the rink.

coarse /kôrs/ *adj.* **coars·er, coars·est** Rough; not fine or smooth; in large grains: *coarse* salt.

co·in·cide /kō′in·sīd′/ *v.* **co·in·cid·ed, co·in·cid·ing**   **1** To take place at the same time.   **2** To match or agree exactly: His plans *coincided* with mine.

co·in·ci·dence /kō·in′sə·dəns/ *n.* An apparently chance happening or appearance of two things at the same time or in the same place: It was a *coincidence* that we met at the movies.

col·laps·i·ble /kə·laps′ə·bəl/ *adj.* Capable of being folded up.   ► *Collapsible* comes from Latin *col- (con-)*, "together," and *labi*, "to fall or slip."

colo·nel /kûr′nəl/ *n.* A military rank below that of a brigadier general.

complicated

com·bus·ti·ble /kəm·bus′tə·bəl/ *adj.* Able to catch fire or burn easily.

co·me·di·an /kə·mē′dē·ən/ *n.* An entertainer who attempts to make people laugh: We all found the *comedian* very funny.

com·mer·cial /kə·mûr′shəl/   **1** *adj.* Having to do with business or with buying and selling: a *commercial* product.   **2** *n.* An advertisement on radio or television.

com·mit·ment /kə·mit′mənt/ *n.*   **1** The act or state of promising or pledging.   **2** A pledge or promise.

com·mu·ni·cate /kə·myōō′nə·kāt/ *v.* **com·mu·ni·cat·ed, com·mu·ni·cat·ing** To convey, exchange, or express thoughts, ideas, messages, information, etc.

com·pan·ion·ship /kəm·pan′yən·ship/ *n.* Friendship: The *companionship* of friends is always welcome.

com·par·a·ble /kom′pər·ə·bəl *or* kom′prə·bəl/ *adj.* Capable of being or similar enough to be compared.—**com′pa·ra·bly** *adv.*

com·pare /kəm·pâr′/ *v.* **com·pared, com·par·ing**   **1** To describe as similar; to liken.   **2** To look for or show similarities and differences.

com·pel /kəm·pel′/ *v.* **com·pelled, com·pel·ling** To force or pressure into action.

com·pe·tent /kom′pə·tənt/ *adj.* Possessing ability; capable: a *competent* worker.

com·pet·i·tor /kəm·pet′ə·tər/ *n.* A person who competes, as in games or business; a rival. *Syn.:* opponent.

com·ple·men·ta·ry /kom′plə·men′tər·ē/ *adj.*   **1** Serving to fill up, contrast, or complete: All the pieces of a puzzle are *complementary*.   **2** Of two angles that together form a right angle.

com·pli·cate /kom′plə·kāt/ *v.* **com·pli·cat·ed, com·pli·cat·ing** To make difficult, complex, intricate, or entangled: Don't *complicate* matters by changing your mind now.

com·pli·cat·ed /kom′plə·kā′tid/ *adj.* Not simple; intricate; complex: Computers are *complicated* devices.

com·pli·men·ta·ry /kom′plə·men′tər·ē/ *adj.*
1 Paying a compliment; expressing praise or
admiration. **2** Given away free.

com·pose /kəm·pōz′/ *v.* **com·posed, com·**
pos·ing **1** To make up; to form. **2** To create or write. **3** To make calm or relaxed.
4 *adj. use:* a *composed* manner.

com·po·si·tion /kom′pə·zish′ən/ *n.* **1** What
something is made of; the parts of a whole.
2 A thing that is put together or created: a
musical *composition*. **3** A short essay.

com·pro·mise /kom′prə·mīz/ *n., v.* **com·**
pro·mised, com·pro·mis·ing **1** *n.* A set-
tlement of differences in which each side
gives up part of its demands or makes mutual concessions. **2** *v.* To settle a dispute in
this way.

con·ceal /kən·sēl′/ To hide or keep secret.

con·ceive /kən·sēv′/ *v.* **con·ceived, con·**
ceiv·ing **1** To think of or develop, as an
idea. **2** To imagine; to understand.

con·cen·trate /kon′sən·trāt/ *v.* **con·cen·**
trat·ed, con·cen·trat·ing, *n.* **1** *v.* To fix
one's full attention on. **2** *v.* To gather or
bring closely together. **3** *v.* To make
stronger or less diluted: We often buy orange
juice that has been *concentrated* and frozen.
4 *n.* A concentrated solution. *Syn.:* focus.

con·demn /kən·dem′/ *v.* **1** To judge as being
wrong. **2** To convict or sentence to punishment: to *condemn* a criminal to prison.
3 To declare unfit or unsafe for use or service: to *condemn* a building.

con·dem·na·tion /kon′dem·nā′shən/ *n.* The
act or condition of being blamed or con-
demned.

con·duct / *n.* kon′dukt, *v.* kən·dukt′/ **1** *n.*
Personal behavior; way of acting: good *con-*
duct. **2** *v.* To act or behave oneself: to *con-*
duct oneself properly. **3** *v.* To direct or manage an action; to carry on: to *conduct* a
meeting. **4** *v.* To direct, guide, or lead: to
conduct a choir. **5** *v.* To serve as a channel,
especially for electricity, heat, sound, etc.

con·fer·ence /kon′fər·əns *or* kon′frəns/ *n.* A
meeting held for discussion or consultation
of a particular subject.

con·fess /kən·fes′/ *v.* To admit guilt, love,
shame, etc. *Syn.:* admit.

con·fi·dence /kon′fə·dəns/ *n.* **1** Trust or
faith. **2** Self-assurance; faith in oneself.
3 A secret.

con·fi·dent /kon′fə·dənt/ *adj.* Having
confidence; self-reliant; assured.
—con′fi·dent·ly *adv.*

con·fi·den·tial /kon′fə·den′shəl/ *adj.* Given in
trust, faith, or confidence; secret.—
con′fi·den′tial·ly *adv.*

con·geal /kən·jēl′/ *v.* To thicken or become
solid, as by cooling; to harden.

con·grat·u·la·tion /kən·grach′oo·lā′shən *or*
kən·grach′ə·lā′shən/ *n.* **1** The expression of
joy or pleasure. **2** *(pl.)* Good wishes.

con·gru·ent /kong′groo·ənt/ *adj.* Coinciding
exactly when one is placed on another; exactly the same size and shape.

con·sci·en·tious /kon′shē·en′shəs/ *adj.* Careful
and responsible.

con·se·quence /kon′sə·kwens/ *n.* Result or effect: the *consequences* of an action.

con·ser·va·tion /kon′sər·vā′shən/ *n.* The act
of protecting or preserving from loss, injury,
decay, or waste.

con·sis·ten·cy /kən·sis′tən·sē/ *n., pl.* **con·**
sis·ten·cies **1** The degree of firmness, den-
sity, or stiffness: a lumpy *consistency.*
2 Strong adherence to the same principles,
ways of acting, etc.

con·sis·tent /kən·sis′tənt/ *adj.* Constantly
maintaining the same principles, ways of
acting, etc.; not self-contradictory: *consistent*
behavior.

con·so·la·tion /kon′sə·lā′shən/ **1** The act or
condition of consoling or being consoled;
comfort. **2** A person or thing that consoles:
My dog is a *consolation* to me.

con·sole¹ /kən·sōl′/ *v.* **con·soled, con·sol·ing**
To comfort someone who is grieving, un-
happy, or disappointed; to cheer up.

con·sole² /kon′sōl/ *n.* **1** The part of an organ
that contains the keyboards, pedals, etc., by
means of which the instrument is played.
2 A radio, phonograph, or television cabinet
that stands on the floor.

con·spic·u·ous /kən·spik′yoo·əs/ *adj.* Easily
noticed; attracting attention.

con·spir·a·cy /kən·spir′ə·sē/ *n., pl.* **con·**
spir·a·cies A secret plan made by two or
more people to do something unlawful; a
plot: a *conspiracy* against the government.

con·struc·tive /kən·struk′tiv/ *adj.* Helping to
improve or make better. ► *Constructive*
comes from Latin *con-,* "together," and
struere, "to build."

---

act, āte, câre, ärt;   egg, ēven;   if, īce;   on, ōver, ôr;   book, food;   up, tûrn;
ə=a in *ago,* e in *listen,* i in *giraffe,* o in *pilot,* u in *circus;*   yoo=u in *music;*   oil;   out;
chair; sing; shop; thank; that; zh in *treasure.*

contagious

con·ta·gious /kən·tā′jəs/ *adj*. Easily spread from one person to another. *Syn.*: catching, infectious, communicable.

con·tam·i·nate /kən·tam′ə·nāt/ *v*. **con·tam·i·nat·ed, con·tam·i·nat·ing** To make impure.

con·tem·po·rar·y /kən·tem′pə·rer′ē/ *adj., n., pl.* **con·tem·po·rar·ies** **1** *adj*. Living or occurring during the same period of time. **2** *n*. A person living at the same time as another: George Washington and the composer Mozart were *contemporaries*. **3** *adj*. Modern: *contemporary* furniture.

con·tend·er /kən·ten′dər/ *n*. A person who engages in a competition or contest.

con·tes·tant /kən·tes′tənt/ *n*. A person who enters a contest or competition.

con·tin·u·ous /kən·tin′yoo·əs/ *adj*. Continuing or going on without interruption: *continuous* music.

con·trac·tion /kən·trak′shən/ *n*. **1** A tightening, drawing together, or shortening, as of the muscles. **2** A shortened form of a word or word group that uses an apostrophe to indicate letters or sounds left out.

con·tra·dict /kon′trə·dikt′/ *v*. **1** To say the opposite of: to *contradict* someone. **2** To be opposite of or contrary to: His actions *contradict* his words.

con·trap·tion /kən·trap′shən/ *n*. A mechanical gadget or device.

con·tri·bu·tion /kon′trə·byoo′shən/ *n*. **1** The act of giving or contributing. **2** Something offered, as money to a charity, a written piece to a magazine, etc. *Syn.*: donation.

con·trol /kən·trōl′/ *v*. **con·trolled, con·trol·ling,** *n*. **1** *v*. To have power or authority to direct, manage, or command. **2** *n*. Power or authority to direct, manage, or command: She had *control* of the money. **3** *v*. To hold in check; to restrain: *Control* your anger. **4** *n*. *(often pl.)* A device used to operate a machine.

con·tro·ver·sial /kon′trə·vûr′shəl/ *adj*. Tending to cause or arouse controversy, disagreement, conflict, or argument.—**con′tro·ver′sial·ly** *adv*.

con·tro·ver·sy /kon′trə·vûr′sē/ *n., pl.* **con·tro·ver·sies** A dispute or debate.

con·ven·ience /kən·vēn′yəns/ *n*. **1** Comfort; benefit; advantage or accommodation: a rest area for the *convenience* of travelers. **2** Anything that saves time, simplifies work, or adds to a person's comfort. **3** The condition of being suited to one's plans, purpose, or comfort.

cram

con·ver·sa·tion /kon′vər·sā′shən/ *n*. An informal discussion; a talk.

con·vert·i·ble /kən·vûr′tə·bəl/ **1** *adj*. Able to be changed. **2** *n*. Something convertible, such as a car with a top that folds down.

co·op·er·ate /kō·op′ə·rāt/ *v*. **co·op·er·at·ed, co·op·er·at·ing** To work willingly with others for a common purpose.

co·or·di·nate /*v*. kō·ôr′də·nāt, *n*. kō·ôr′də·nit/ *v., n.* **co·or·di·nat·ed, co·or·di·nat·ing** **1** *v*. To bring into the right or proper movement or condition; to fit together smoothly; to harmonize: to *coordinate* a project. **2** *n*. One of a set of numbers used to define the position of a point, line, etc., in space, as on a graph.

cord /kôrd/ *n*. **1** A rope or string made of several strands twisted or braided together. **2** A pair of insulated wires used to connect an appliance, etc., to an electric outlet: a telephone *cord*.

cor·pus·cle /kôr′pəs·əl/ *n*. One of the red or white cells forming part of the blood.

coun·cil /koun′səl/ *n*. **1** A meeting or assembly for discussion. **2** The legislative body of a city or town.

coun·sel /koun′səl/ *n., v.* **coun·seled, coun·sel·ing** **1** *n*. Advice: good *counsel*. **2** *n*. A lawyer or law firm handling a court case. **3** *v*. To give advice. *Alternate spellings:* **counselled, counselling**.

coun·ter·clock·wise /koun′tər·klok′wīz′/ *adj., adv*. In the direction opposite to the direction of a clock's hands.

coun·ter·feit /koun′tər·fit/ **1** *adj*. Copied with the intent to deceive; forged. **2** *n*. Forgery: This dollar bill is a *counterfeit*. **3** *v*. To make an imitation or counterfeit of; to forge.

cour·te·ous /kûr′tē·əs/ *adj*. Considerate; respectful. *Syn.*: polite.

cram /kram/ *v*. **crammed, cram·ming** **1** To pack tightly into a small space; to stuff. **2** To study hard for a short period of time. **3** To fill or stuff quickly, as with food.

credentials

cre·den·tials /kri·den′shəlz/ *n. pl.* Evidence, as a certificate, letter, etc., of authority, rights, status, or trustworthiness: The investigator showed us his *credentials*.

crev·ice /krev′is/ *n.* A narrow opening caused by a crack or split: There were many *crevices* on the old brick wall.

cri·sis /krī′sis/ *n., pl.* **cri·ses** /krī′sēz/ A very important, dangerous, or difficult moment in any series of events, by which the trend of future events is determined.

cri·te·ri·on /krī·tir′ē·ən/ *n., pl.* **cri·te·ri·a** A standard of judgment; a rule or principle for testing anything: What are your *criteria* for selecting the winner? *Alternate plural:* **cri·terions.**

crit·i·cize /krit′ə·sīz/ *v.* **crit·i·cized, crit·i·ciz·ing** **1** To make judgments about the merits and faults of someone or something: to *criticize* a book. **2** To find fault with: to *criticize* a person's sloppiness.

cru·cial /krōō′shəl/ *adj.* Involving a very important decision, result, or effect: Her help was *crucial* to his plan.

cryp·tic /krip′tik/ *adj.* Having a secret or mysterious meaning; hidden.

cum·ber·some /kum′bər·səm/ *adj.* Awkward or hard to move or manage; unwieldy: The package was very *cumbersome* for one person to manage.

cur·i·ous /kyŏŏr′ē·əs/ *adj.* **1** Eager to learn. **2** Unusual or strange: a *curious* story.

cur·rant /kûr′ənt/ *n.* **1** A small sour berry, often used for jelly. **2** A small seedless raisin. ► *Currant* comes from the French words *raisin de Corauntz,* "raisin of Corinth," the name for this food.

cur·rent /kûr′ənt/ **1** *n.* A large body of water or air that moves in a certain direction: a river *current*. **2** *n.* The flow or movement of an electrical charge through a wire or other conductor. **3** *adj.* Belonging to the present time: the *current* style. ► *Current* comes from the Latin word *currere,* "to run."

cus·to·di·an /kus·tō′dē·ən/ *n.* A caretaker, superintendent, or janitor: Ask the *custodian* to clean the room.

cus·to·dy /kus′tə·dē/ *n., pl.* **cus·to·dies** Care and control; charge; guardianship: *custody* of a child.

cus·tom·ar·y /kus′tə·mer′ē/ *adj.* Based on custom or habit; usual: a *customary* route.

deficient

cyl·in·der /sil′in·dər/ *n.* **1** A geometric figure bounded by two circles and the parallel surfaces that connect them: Bring me the jar that is shaped like a *cylinder*. **2** Any object having this shape.

D

da·ta /dā′tə *or* dat′ə/ *n. pl.* Facts; statistics: It took seven people to gather all the available *data*. ● *Data* is the plural form of the Latin word *datum,* "fact."

debt /det/ *n.* **1** Something that is owed by one person to another: a *debt* of kindness. **2** The condition of owing: to be in *debt* to a store.

de·coy /*n.* di·koi′ *or* dē′koi, *v.* di·koi′/ **1** *n.* A person, animal, or object used as a lure to trap prey: a police *decoy*. **2** *v.* To lure or lead into danger or a trap.

de·duc·tion /di·duk′shən/ *n.* **1** A conclusion or inference based on reasoning: Sherlock Holmes solved mysteries by clever *deduction*. **2** An amount that is taken away or subtracted: a tax *deduction*.

de·fense /di·fens′/ *n.* **1** The act of guarding or protecting against: the *defense* of freedom. **2** Something that guards or protects: The fort was their *defense* against the enemy. **3** An argument that defends, justifies, or supports: to give a *defense* of one's actions. **4** The answer to charges brought against someone on trial: to testify in one's own *defense*.

de·fi·cien·cy /di·fish′ən·sē/ *n., pl.* **de·fi·cien·cies** An amount that is lacking; incompleteness; insufficiency: A *deficiency* of vitamins is often the cause of disease.

de·fi·cient /di·fish′ənt/ *adj.* Not complete; insufficient or inadequate; lacking: Potato chips are *deficient* in nutrition.

---

act, āte, câre, ärt; egg, ēven; if, īce; on, ōver, ôr; bŏŏk, fōōd; up, tûrn;
ə=a in *ago,* e in *listen,* i in *giraffe,* o in *pilot,* u in *circus*; yōō=u in *music*; oil; out;
chair; sing; shop; thank; that; zh in *treasure.*

de·hy·drate /dē·hī′drāt/ *v.* **de·hy·drat·ed, de·hy·drat·ing** **1** To take water out of; to dry up. **2** *adj. use: dehydrated* fruit.

del·e·gate /*n.* del′ə·gāt *or* del′ə·gət, *v.* del′ə·gāt/ *n., v.* **del·e·gat·ed, del·e·gat·ing** **1** *n.* A person designated to act for or represent another person or a group; a representative. **2** *v.* To choose, appoint, or send someone as a delegate. **3** *v.* To give or entrust power or duties to others: to *delegate* authority.

de·lib·er·ate /*adj.* di·lib′ər·it, *v.* di·lib′ə·rāt/ *adj., v.* **de·lib·er·at·ed, de·lib·er·at·ing** **1** *adj.* On purpose; intended: a *deliberate* lie. **2** *adj.* Slow and careful in deciding and acting: She was *deliberate* about her choice. **3** *v.* To think over carefully; to consider; to ponder: She *deliberated* before responding.

del·i·ca·tes·sen /del′ə·kə·tes′(ə)n/ *n.* A store that sells prepared foods such as cooked meats, salads, cheese, etc.: I buy my lunch at the *delicatessen* down the street.

de·mer·it /di·mer′it/ *n.* A mark against someone for poor work or misconduct: You'll have to quit the team if you receive another *demerit*.

de·moc·ra·cy /di·mok′rə·sē/ *n., pl.* **de·moc·ra·cies** A system of government in which the people rule by voting directly or by electing representatives to hold government offices and make the laws.

dem·o·crat·ic /dem′ə·krat′ik/ *adj.* **1** Of or relating to a political system in which power is held by the people. **2** Treating all people as equals.

de·pen·dent /di·pen′dənt/ **1** *adj.* Relying on or needing someone or something else for support, aid, etc.: Windmills are *dependent* on moving air currents. **2** *n.* A person who depends on someone or something else for support, aid, etc. **3** *adj.* In grammar, of a clause that cannot stand alone as a sentence and can only be used in connection with other forms. **4** *adj.* Determined by something else: Our trip is *dependent* on the weather.

der·ma·tol·o·gy /dûr′mə·tol′ə·jē/ *n.* The scientific study of the skin and the treatment of skin diseases.

de·scrip·tion /di·skrip′shən/ *n.* The act of telling about something in words, either spoken or written: a short *description* of the story. ▶ *Description* comes from Latin *de-*, "down," and *scribere*, "to write."

des·ert¹ /dez′ərt/ **1** *n.* An extremely dry area where little or no life exists because of the lack of water. **2** *adj.* Of or like a desert; barren.

de·sert² /di·zûrt′/ *v.* To leave or abandon, especially when one has a duty to remain.

de·spise /di·spīz′/ *v.* **de·spised, de·spis·ing** To regard with disdain or scorn; to dislike intensely; to loathe.

des·sert /di·zûrt′/ *n.* A sweet food eaten at the end of a meal.

de·vise /di·vīz′/ *v.* **de·vised, de·vis·ing** To figure out; to invent: to *devise* a scheme.

di·ag·no·sis /dī′əg·nō′sis/ *n., pl.* **di·ag·no·ses** /dī′əg·nō′sēz/ **1** The process of determining the nature of a disease by examining and analyzing its symptoms. **2** The decision reached by such an examination. **3** An analysis of the nature of a problem or a statement of its solution: We listened to her *diagnosis* of the problem. ▶ *Diagnosis* comes from Greek *dia-*, "through," and *gignoskein*, "to know."

di·ag·o·nal /dī·ag′ə·nəl/ *adj.* Extending in a slanting direction from one edge of a solid figure to an opposite edge.

di·a·gram /dī′ə·gram/ *n., v.* **di·a·gramed, di·a·gram·ing** **1** *n.* A line drawing that shows or explains the parts, operation, etc., of something; illustration. **2** *v.* To make such an outline or drawing. *Alternate spellings:* **diagrammed, diagramming.** ▶ *Diagram* comes from Greek *dia-*, "through," and *graphein*, "to write."

di·al /dī′(ə)l/ *n., v.* **di·aled, di·al·ing** **1** *n.* A flat surface with numbers or signs on it, and a movable pointer that indicates time, temperature, etc. **2** *n.* A knob used to control a radio, television, etc. **3** *n.* The movable disk on some telephones. **4** *v.* To place a phone call by registering the numbers. *Alternate spellings:* **dialled, dialling.**

di·a·lect /dī′ə·lekt/ *n.* A variation in a language, characteristic of a particular region or class, that is distinguished from the standard language by grammar, vocabulary, etc.

di·am·e·ter /dī·am′ə·tər/ *n.* **1** A line segment joining two points on a circle and passing through the center of the circle. **2** The measure of this line segment.

di·a·ry /dī′(ə·)rē/ *n., pl.* **di·a·ries** **1** A daily record of one's own experiences, feelings, etc. **2** A book for keeping such a record.

dic·tate /dik′tāt/ *v.* **dic·tat·ed, dic·tat·ing** **1** To say something aloud for a person to write or for a machine to record. **2** To give orders; to command with authority: to *dictate* an order.

dic·tion·ar·y /dik′shən·er′ē/ *n., pl.* **dic·tion·ar·ies** A book that contains a selection of words, arranged in alphabetical order, and gives meanings, pronunciations, spellings, word histories, etc.

di·gest·i·ble /di·jes′tə·bəl *or* dī·jes′tə·bəl/ *adj.* Capable of being digested or absorbed by the body; easily digested.

di·ges·tive /di·jes′tiv *or* dī·jes′tiv/ *adj.* Having to do with digestion, or the process of changing food chemically into a form that can be used by the body.

dig·it /dij′it/ *n.* **1** A finger or toe. **2** Any of the numerals 0 through 9.

di·lem·ma /di·lem′ə/ *n.* **1** A situation requiring a choice between equally unpleasant or bad alternatives. **2** Any difficult situation or problem.

di·plo·ma·cy /di·plō′mə·sē/ *n., pl.* **di·plo·ma·cies** **1** The handling of relations between nations. **2** Skill in handling other people; tact.

dip·lo·mat /dip′lə·mat/ *n.* **1** A person whose job is to work out or handle relations between nations in situations other than war. **2** A person who is tactful in dealing with others.

dis·as·ter /di·zas′tər/ *n.* An event causing great distress or damage.

dis·as·trous /di·zas′trəs/ *adj.* Causing great suffering, destruction, or damage.

dis·be·lief /dis′bi·lēf′/ *n.* A refusal or inability to believe or accept as true.

dis·cov·er /dis·kuv′ər/ *v.* **1** To gain sight or knowledge of something before anyone else: to *discover* an island. **2** To learn or find out, especially for the first time: to *discover* an answer to a math problem. *Syn.*: unearth.

dis·crim·i·nate /dis·krim′ə·nāt/ *v.* **dis·crim·i·nat·ed, dis·crim·i·nat·ing** **1** To make a distinction; to recognize differences between: to *discriminate* between shades of blue. **2** To show prejudice; to exclude.

dis·en·chant /dis′en·chant′/ *v.* To deprive or free from a pleasant but false belief or illusion; disillusion.—**dis′en·chant′ment** *n.*

dis·guise /dis·gīz′/ *v.* **dis·guised, dis·guis·ing,** *n.* **1** *v.* To change the appearance or manner so as not to be recognized. **2** *n.* Something that disguises, as a costume or mask. **3** *v.* To hide or conceal: *disguised* the true facts.

dis·hon·or /dis·on′ər/ **1** *n.* Lack or loss of honor; disgrace or humiliation. **2** *v.* To bring shame to; to disgrace; to insult.

dis·in·fec·tant /dis′in·fek′tənt/ *n.* A chemical substance used to destroy germs.

dis·lo·cate /dis′lō·kāt′/ *v.* **dis·lo·cat·ed, dis·lo·cat·ing** **1** To put or force out of joint or position, as a bone. **2** To put or throw into chaos or disorder. **3** *adj. use:* a *dislocated* shoulder.

dis·pel /dis·pel′/ *v.* **dis·pelled, dis·pel·ling** To drive away; to scatter: Her confidence *dispelled* all our fears.

dis·play /dis·plā′/ **1** *v.* To show or place for viewing; to exhibit. **2** *n.* An exhibit, showing, or arrangement of things to be seen: a window *display*. **3** *n.* The act of revealing; exhibition: a *display* of kindness. **4** *v.* To show or reveal openly: to *display* poor judgment.

dis·pose /dis·pōz′/ *v.* **dis·posed, dis·pos·ing** **1** To give a tendency or inclination to: My nature *disposed* me to be sympathetic to her problems. **2** To arrange or put in a particular order.—**dispose of** To get rid of, as by throwing away, etc.: to *dispose* of garbage.

dis·po·si·tion /dis′pə·zish′ən/ *n.* The way an individual or animal acts; nature; temperament: a friendly *disposition*.

dis·re·spect·ful /dis′ri·spekt′fəl/ *adj.* Showing a lack of respect; lacking courtesy or politeness; rude: a *disrespectful* remark. *Syn.*: discourteous.

dis·tance /dis′təns/ *n.* **1** The amount of space between two points, lines, etc. **2** A place far away: a car in the *distance*.

dis·tract /dis·trakt′/ *v.* To draw attention away: The whispering *distracted* him.

dis·trac·tion /dis·trak′shən/ *n.* The act of distracting or diverting; that which draws away or diverts attention.

dis·trib·ute /dis·trib′yoot/ *v.* **dis·trib·ut·ed, dis·trib·ut·ing** **1** To divide and give out in shares: to *distribute* food. **2** To scatter or spread: Lakes are *distributed* throughout the state.

dis·tri·bu·tion /dis′trə·byoo′shən/ *n.* The act or manner in which something is distributed or given out: equal *distribution*.

di·ver·sion /di·vûr′zhən/ *n.* Distraction from attention to ordinary matters; recreation; relaxation; amusement.

---

act, āte, câre, ärt;   egg, ēven;   if, īce;   on, ōver, ôr;   book, food;   up, tûrn;
ə=a in *ago*, e in *listen*, i in *giraffe*, o in *pilot*, u in *circus*;   yoo=u in *music*;   oil;   out;
chair;   sing;   shop;   thank;   that;   zh in *treasure*.

div·i·dend /div′ə·dend/ *n.* **1** In mathematics, a number that is divided by another number. **2** The portion of a corporation's profit distributed to a shareholder.

di·vis·i·ble /di·viz′ə·bəl/ *adj.* **1** Capable of being divided. **2** Able to be divided by a certain number, leaving no remainder.

doc·u·ment /*n.* dok′yə·mənt, *v.* dok′yə·ment′/ **1** *n.* A written or printed paper that gives information or evidence. **2** *v.* To supply or prove with such a written or printed paper: to *document* an argument with photographs.

doc·u·men·ta·ry /dok′yə·men′tər·ē/ *adj., n., pl.* **doc·u·men·ta·ries** **1** *adj.* Dealing with, consisting of, or based on facts: *documentary* proof. **2** *n.* A movie, novel, etc., that deals with factual information.

dom·i·nant /dom′ə·nənt/ *adj.* **1** Commanding; controlling; most important of all: a *dominant* idea. **2** More active or stronger than an opposing hereditary characteristic or trait: a *dominant* gene.

do·na·tion /dō·nā′shən/ *n.* **1** The act of presenting something as a gift, contribution, etc. **2** A gift of money or goods. *Syn.:* contribution.

dough·nut /dō′nut′/ *n.* A small ring-shaped cake, fried in deep fat.

drag /drag/ *v.* **dragged, drag·ging** **1** To haul or pull. **2** To go or pass with extreme slowness: The meeting *dragged* on for hours.

drought /drout/ *n.* An extended period of little or no rainfall.

drown /droun/ *v.* **1** To die or kill by suffocating with water or another liquid. **2** To cover or wet with a liquid: to *drown* meat in gravy. **3** To keep from being heard: The radio will *drown* out the talking.

drudg·er·y /druj′ər·ē/ *n., pl.* **drudg·er·ies** Distasteful, dull, or hard work: Shoveling snow is often *drudgery*.

du·al /d(y)oo′əl/ *adj.* Of or consisting of two parts; double. *Dual* comes from the Latin word *dualis*, "double."

du·el /d(y)oo′əl/ *n., v.* **du·eled, du·el·ing** **1** *n.* A formal combat with weapons fought between two people in the presence of witnesses. **2** *n.* A conflict or contest: a *duel* of words. **3** *v.* To fight a duel. *Alternate spellings:* **duelled, duelling.** ▶ *Duel* comes from the Latin word *duellum*, "a fight between two people," from *duo*, "two" + *bellum*, "war."

du·pli·cate /*v.* d(y)oo′plə·kāt, *n., adj.,* d(y)oo′plə·kət/ **1** *v.* To copy an original exactly. **2** *n.* An exact copy of an original. **3** *adj.* Made exactly like something else: a *duplicate* picture.

E

e·col·o·gy /i·kol′ə·jē *or* ē·kol′ə·jē/ *n.* The study of the relationships between living things and their environment: Our class took a field trip to the country in order to study *ecology*.

e·con·o·mize /i·kon′ə·mīz/ *v.* **e·con·o·mized, e·con·o·miz·ing** To use sparingly and avoid waste; to be thrifty and frugal: to *economize* on expenses.

e·co·sphere /ē′kō·sfi(ə)r′ *or* ek′ō·sfi(ə)r′/ *n.* The area of the universe in which life exists.

ec·sta·sy /ek′stə·sē/ *n.* Extraordinary happiness, pleasure, or delight.

ed·i·ble /ed′ə·bəl/ *adj.* Suitable to eat: Some mushrooms are *edible*.

ed·u·ca·tion·al /ej′oo·kā′shən·əl/ *adj.* Of or having to do with or providing for education, learning, or teaching: Watching a documentary film is very *educational*.

ef·fi·cient /i·fish′ənt/ *adj.* Producing results with little effort or waste; capable.— **ef·fi′cient·ly** *adv.*

el·e·gance /el′ə·gəns/ *n.* The quality or state of being elegant or beautiful in a graceful and refined way.

el·e·gant /el′ə·gənt/ *adj.* **1** Tastefully fine; luxurious: an *elegant* dress. **2** Refined; dignified; graceful: *elegant* manners.— **el′e·gant·ly** *adv.*

el·e·men·ta·ry /el′ə·men′tər·ē/ *adj.* **1** Having to do with basic principles: an *elementary* math course. **2** Undeveloped; not advanced: Addition and subtraction are *elementary* operations in mathematics.

el·i·gi·ble /el′ə·jə·bəl/ *adj.* Able to qualify for: Since you are eighteen, you are *eligible* to enter the contest.

e·man·ci·pate /i·man′sə·pāt/ *v.* **e·man·ci·pat·ed, e·man·ci·pat·ing** To set free, as from bondage, oppression, etc.: President Lincoln *emancipated* the slaves.

embroidery

evaporate

em·broi·der·y /im·broi′dər·ē/ *n.*, *pl.* **em·broi·der·ies** Decorative stitching, usually in patterns with colored threads; needlework.

em·bry·o /em′brē·ō/ *n.*, *pl.* **em·bry·os** A plant or animal in its earliest stages of development, as a mammal not yet born.

e·merge /i·mûrj′/ *v.* **e·merged, e·merg·ing** To come forth or come out, so as to be visible. ► *Emerge* comes from Latin *e- (ex-)*, "out," and *mergere*, "to dip."

em·i·grate /em′ə·grāt/ *v.* **em·i·grat·ed, em·i·grat·ing** To move out of a country or region in order to settle in another.

e·mit /i·mit′/ *v.* **e·mit·ted, e·mit·ting** To send forth or give off; to discharge: The sun *emits* heat. ► *Emit* comes from Latin *e- (ex-)*, "out," and *mittere*, "to send."

em·pha·size /em′fə·sīz/ *v.* **em·pha·sized, em·pha·siz·ing** To give importance or significance to; to stress.

em·pire /em′pīr′/ *n.* A group of countries or nations, often far away from each other, ruled by one person or government.

en·cour·age /in·kûr′ij/ *v.* **en·cour·aged, en·cour·ag·ing** 1 To give courage or hope to; to coax. 2 To be favorable for: Rain *encourages* plant growth. *Syn.:* urge.

en·dur·ance /in·d(y)oor′əns/ *n.* The ability to withstand hardship, strain, stress, etc.

en·er·get·ic /en′ər·jet′ik/ *adj.* Full of energy; lively. *Syn.:* vigorous.

en·tan·gle /in·tang′gəl/ *v.* **en·tan·gled, en·tan·gling** 1 To tangle, knot up, or snare. 2 To trap or involve in a problem or difficulty: to become *entangled* in a lawsuit.

en·thu·si·as·tic /in·thoo′zē·as′tik/ *adj.* Full of enthusiasm; excited or interested; eager: They were very *enthusiastic* about starting their dance class.—**en·thu′si·as′ti·cal·ly** *adv.*

ep·i·sode /ep′ə·sōd/ *n.* An incident or brief series of related events that form part of a story, a person's life, etc.

e·qui·lat·er·al /ē′kwə·lat′ər·əl/ *adj.* Having the same length on all sides: I can draw an *equilateral* triangle.

e·quiv·a·lent /i·kwiv′ə·lənt/ 1 *adj.* Equal in value, measure, force, importance, etc.: Two dimes are *equivalent* to four nickels. 2 *n.* Something that is equivalent: 100°C is the *equivalent* of 212°F.

er·ror /er′ər/ *n.* 1 A mistake. 2 The condition of being incorrect or mistaken: to be in *error*. 3 In baseball, a misplay that allows a player to reach base safely: The third baseman made another *error*.

es·ca·late /es′kə·lāt/ *v.* **es·ca·lat·ed, es·ca·lat·ing** To increase in intensity, magnitude, etc., especially by stages.

es·say /es′ā/ *n.* A short composition on a particular subject, especially one in which the writer expresses his or her own ideas: The *essay* was about my trip to Spain.

es·sen·tial /ə·sen′shəl/ *adj.* 1 Basic; fundamental. 2 Absolutely necessary: Water is *essential* to life on Earth.

es·teem /ə·stēm′/ 1 *v.* To regard highly or with great respect. 2 *n.* Favorable opinion; respect: to hold a person in high *esteem*.

et·y·mol·o·gy /et′ə·mol′ə·jē/ *n.*, *pl.* **et·y·mol·o·gies** 1 The history or derivation of a word, tracing the development of its present form and meaning. 2 The study of the history of words.

e·vade /i·vād′/ *v.* **e·vad·ed, e·vad·ing** 1 To get or keep away from by cleverness: The fox *evaded* the hunters. 2 To avoid or elude: to *evade* punishment.

e·val·u·ate /i·val′yoo·āt/ *v.* **e·val·u·at·ed, e·val·u·at·ing** To judge value or determine worth: to *evaluate* a person's work.

e·vap·o·rate /i·vap′ə·rāt/ *v.* **e·vap·o·rat·ed, e·vap·o·rat·ing** 1 To turn into vapor: The boiling water *evaporated*. 2 To remove moisture or liquid from. 3 To vanish, fade, or disappear: Her plans *evaporated* when it began to rain.

---

act, āte, câre, ärt;   egg, ēven;   if, īce;   on, ōver, ôr;   bŏŏk, fōōd;   up, tûrn;
ə=a in *ago*, e in *listen*, i in *giraffe*, o in *pilot*, u in *circus*;   yōō=u in *music*;   oil;   out;
chair;   sing;   shop;   thank;   that;   zh in *treasure*.

evidence   **exquisite**

ev·i·dence /ev′ə·dəns/ *n.* **1** That which tends to prove or disprove the truth of something; proof: *evidence* of a crime.

ev·i·dent /ev′ə·dənt/ *adj.* Easily seen or understood; obvious. *Syn.:* apparent.

ex·ag·ger·ate /ig·zaj′ə·rāt/ *v.* **ex·ag·ger·at·ed, ex·ag·ger·at·ing** **1** To say that something is more than it is; to overstate. **2** To make something appear larger than it really is. **3** *adj. use:* an *exaggerated* story.

ex·am·ple /ig·zam′pəl/ *n.* **1** Something used to represent a whole group; a sample: an *example* of a good composition. **2** A pattern or model of something to be imitated or avoided: Set a good *example*. **3** A sample problem that is already worked out.

ex·ceed /ik·sēd′/ *v.* **1** To be greater or better than what is anticipated or expected. **2** To go beyond what is allowed.

ex·cel /ik·sel′/ *v.* **ex·celled, ex·cel·ling** To be exceptionally good at; to surpass: to *excel* in sports.

ex·cel·lence /ek′sə·ləns/ *n.* The state or fact of excelling, being of very high quality, or exceptionally good.

ex·cep·tion /ik·sep′shən/ *n.* **1** An exclusion. **2** Something that does not conform to the general pattern: an *exception* to the rule.

ex·cess /*n.* ek′ses *or* ik·ses′, *adj.* ek′ses/ **1** *n.* An amount, degree, or supply of something beyond what is needed or proper: an *excess* of anger. **2** *adj.* Over what is usual, allowed, or needed: Don't carry *excess* weight while hiking.

ex·clu·sive /iks·kloo′siv/ *adj.* **1** Resisting the admission of outsiders to association, membership, etc.: an *exclusive* circle of friends. **2** Excluding all others from a part or share; belonging to only one: *exclusive* rights. **3** Complete; total; undivided: *exclusive* attention.

ex·er·cise /ek′sər·sīz/ *v.* **ex·er·cised, ex·er·cis·ing,** *n.* **1** *v.* To develop, train, or condition by active use or movement. **2** *n.* Active movement of the body to strengthen it and keep it healthy. **3** *n. (usually pl.)* A series of movements done or performed as a means of practice or training: piano *exercises*.

ex·haust /ig·zôst′/ **1** *v.* To make or become very tired. **2** *v.* To use up or consume completely. **3** *n.* The gases or fumes that escape from an engine.

ex·hib·it /ig·zib′it/ **1** *v.* To display or put on public view. **2** *n.* A public display. **3** *n.* Something put on display. **4** *v.* To show signs of or demonstrate: to *exhibit* fatigue. **5** *n.* Something given as evidence in a court of law.

ex·hi·bi·tion /ek′sə·bish′ən/ *n.* **1** A public showing or display. **2** An open display or expression: an *exhibition* of poor manners.

ex·is·tence /ig·zis′təns/ *n.* **1** The state or fact of being. **2** Life; something that exists. **3** A manner, style, or mode of living: a happy *existence*.

ex·it /eg′zit *or* ek′sit/ **1** *n.* A way out of an enclosed place, as a door: the nearest *exit*. **2** *v.* To go out or leave.

ex·pect /ik·spekt′/ *v.* **1** To look forward to; to regard as likely to happen: to *expect* company. **2** To look for with reason or justification: to *expect* good work.

ex·pec·ta·tion /ek′spek·tā′shən/ *n.* **1** A thing eagerly looked forward to or awaited; anticipation. **2** *(often pl.)* A hope for future success or profit: high *expectations*.

ex·pel /ik·spel′/ *v.* **ex·pelled, ex·pel·ling** **1** To drive or force out: to *expel* air from the lungs. **2** To dismiss or banish.

ex·pense /ik·spens′/ *n.* **1** Cost; price. **2** *(pl.)* Money needed to cover the cost of something. **3** A cause for spending: A new coat is an *expense*.

ex·pla·na·tion /ek′splə·nā′shən/ *n.* **1** The act or process of explaining. **2** A reason or cause: She gave the teacher an *explanation* for her tardiness.

ex·plo·sive /ik·splō′siv/ **1** *adj.* Able to explode or to cause an explosion. **2** *n.* A substance that can explode or blow up.

ex·po·nent /ik·spō′nənt/ *n.* **1** A person or thing that explains, encourages, or represents something: an *exponent* of the democratic system. **2** A number placed above to show how many times another number is to be multiplied by itself. In $5^2 = 5 \times 5 = 25$, ^{2} is the *exponent*.

ex·po·sure /ik·spō′zhər/ *n.* **1** The act or condition of being exposed, uncovered, or unprotected. **2** The position or direction of something with regard to the sun: northern *exposure*. **3** The length of time required for light to produce the desired effect on photographic film. **4** A section of film that makes a single picture: There are 36 *exposures* on this roll.

ex·qui·site /eks′kwi·zit *or* ik·skwiz′it/ *adj.* **1** Very fine or delicate: an *exquisite* necklace. **2** Very beautiful: an *exquisite* dress. **3** Of rare excellence; admirable: *exquisite* taste.

extend   **fluent**

ex·tend /ik·stend′/ *v.* **1** To stretch out. **2** To prolong or increase in time or space: to *extend* a subscription. **3** *adj. use:* an *extended* illness. **4** To stretch, reach, or last: The town *extends* for ten miles.

ex·tinct /ik·stingkt′/ *adj.* **1** No longer living or in existence: Dinosaurs are *extinct*. **2** No longer active: an *extinct* volcano.

ex·tract /*v.* ik·strakt′, *n.* eks′trakt/ **1** *v.* To take, pull, or draw out. **2** *n.* A solid or liquid substance pressed or taken from a plant, drug, etc.

ex·traor·di·nar·y /ik·strôr′də·ner′ē *or* eks′trə·ôr′də·ner′ē/ *adj.* Remarkable; very unusual; *extraordinary* intelligence.

ex·trav·a·gant /ik·strav′ə·gənt/ *adj.* **1** Spending much more than necessary; wasteful. **2** Going beyond or exceeding the limits of reason or necessity.

F

false·hood /fôls′hŏŏd/ *n.* Untruthfulness; dishonesty; a lie.

fa·mil·iar /fə·mil′yər/ *adj.* **1** Well acquainted with something: *familiar* with modern music. **2** Often experienced or encountered: a *familiar* song.

fa·mil·iar·ize /fə·mil′yə·rīz/ *v.* **fa·mil·iar·ized, fa·mil·iar·iz·ing** To make well acquainted, known, or familiar.

fan·tas·tic /fan·tas′tik/ *adj.* **1** Odd; unreal. **2** Amazing; unbelievable.

fan·ta·sy /fan′tə·sē/ *n., pl.* **fan·ta·sies** **1** Imagination: a world of *fantasy*. **2** A creation of the imagination that is very different from the real world: a science fiction *fantasy*.

fas·ci·nate /fas′ə·nāt/ *v.* **fas·ci·nat·ed, fas·ci·nat·ing** To attract, charm, or interest; to hold the attention of.

fas·ci·nat·ing /fas′ə·nā′ting/ *adj.* Enchanting; charming; captivating.

fa·tal /fāt′(ə)l/ *adj.* **1** Causing death: a *fatal* blow. **2** Causing total ruin or disaster: a *fatal* decision.

fa·tal·i·ty /fā·tal′ə·tē/ *n., pl.* **fa·tal·i·ties** A death resulting from disaster or accident: fire *fatalities*.

fa·vor·ite /fā′vər·it *or* fāv′rit/ **1** *n.* A person or thing regarded with special favor or preferred over others. **2** *adj.* Best liked: my *favorite* book.

feint /fānt/ **1** *n.* An action meant to deceive, trick, or mislead; a pretense. **2** *n.* A pretended blow or attack intended to distract an opponent from the real blow or attack. **3** *v.* To trick or deceive with a *feint*.

fic·ti·tious /fik·tish′əs/ *adj.* **1** Not genuine; false; made-up: Sally used the *fictitious* name Melissa in her novel. **2** Pertaining or relating to fiction: Alex is a *fictitious* character in Harold's play.

flair /flâr/ *n.* A natural ability, talent, or skill; knack: a *flair* for acting.

flare /flâr/ *n., v.* **flared, flar·ing** **1** *v.* To blaze with a sudden burst of flame. **2** *n.* A bright light used as a signal: In the distance we could see a red *flare*. **3** *v.* To explode or burst out in sudden anger or violence: to *flare* up in anger. **4** *v.* To open or spread outward, like the shape of a bell: The pants *flared* at the bottom. **5** *n.* A spreading or widening outward: The skirt has a slight *flare*.

flat·ter·y /flat′ər·ē/ *n., pl.* **flat·ter·ies** Excessive compliments; praise that is often not sincere.

flu·ent /flōō′ənt/ *adj.* **1** Capable of speaking or writing with smoothness or ease. **2** Spoken or written with smoothness or ease; effortless: She speaks *fluent* Chinese.—**flu′ent·ly** *adv.* ► *Fluent* comes from the Latin verb *fluere*, "to flow."

---

act, āte, câre, ärt;   egg, ēven;   if, īce;   on, ōver, ôr;   bŏŏk, fōōd;   up, tûrn;
ə=a in *ago*, e in *listen*, i in *giraffe*, o in *pilot*, u in *circus*;   yōō=u in *music*;   oil;   out;
chair; sing; shop; thank; that; zh in *treasure*.

focus   **geometric**

fo·cus /fō′kəs/ *n., pl.* **fo·cus·es,** *v.* **fo·cused, fo·cus·ing** **1** *n.* The point at which a lens brings light rays together to make a sharp image. **2** *v.* To adjust the focus to produce a clear image. **3** *n.* The main or central point of interest or importance. **4** *v.* To concentrate one's energy or attention on something. *Alternate plural:* **foci.** *Alternate spellings:* **focussed, focussing.**

foe /fō/ *n.* An enemy or rival. *Syn.:* rival.

fore·word /fôr′wûrd′/ *n.* An introduction to a book; a preface.

for·mal·ly /fôr′mə·lē/ *adv.* In a formal or strict way; according to rule, ceremony, or custom.

for·mer·ly /fôr′mər·lē/ *adv.* In the past; once; previously: She was *formerly* the mayor.

for·mu·la /fôr′myə·lə/ *n., pl.* **for·mu·las** **1** An established procedure or rule: a *formula* for success. **2** An equation or set of symbols that shows the makeup of a chemical substance or a mathematical relationship. **3** A prescription or the mixture for a prescription prepared according to a formula: an infant's *formula. Alternate plural:* **for·mulae.**

for·ward /fôr′wərd/ **1** *adj.* Toward, at, or near the front: *forward* movement. **2** *adv.* To or toward the front: to walk *forward.* **3** *v.* To send onward: to *forward* mail. **4** *adv.* To the future: to look *forward* to a trip.

frac·tion /frak′shən/ *n.* **1** Part of a whole. **2** A tiny amount. **3** A rational number that is more than zero and less than 1, or the sum of a whole number and such a rational number.

frac·ture /frak′chər/ *n., v.* **frac·tured, frac·tur·ing** **1** *n.* The act of breaking or cracking, especially a bone. **2** *n.* A break or crack, especially in a bone. **3** *v.* To break or crack.

frag·ile /fraj′əl/ *adj.* Easily shattered or damaged; delicate: *fragile* china.

frag·ment /frag′mənt/ *n.* A broken-off part or incomplete piece; a chip. *Syn.:* sliver.

fra·grance /frā′grəns/ *n.* **1** Sweetness of smell. **2** A sweet or delicate smell, as of flowers or perfume.

frail /frā(ə)l/ *adj.* **1** Physically weak; in delicate health: a *frail* child. **2** Slight; weak.

fran·tic /fran′tik/ *adj.* Emotionally out of control; filled with fear and anxiety.—**fran·ti·cal·ly** *adv.*

fre·quent /*adj.* frē′kwent, *v.* fri·kwent′/ **1** *adj.* Happening often. **2** *v.* To go somewhere often: to *frequent* a restaurant.—**fre′quent·ly** *adv.*

fright·en /frīt′(ə)n/ *v.* **fright·ened, fright·en·ing** **1** To fill with fear; to scare. **2** To drive away by scaring.

fru·gal /frōo′gəl/ *adj.* **1** Avoiding waste; thrifty: a *frugal* shopper. **2** Entailing little expense; scanty: a *frugal* meal.—**fru·gal′i·ty** *n.*

fu·tile /fyōo′təl/ *adj.* Done in vain; useless; ineffective: a *futile* attempt.

G

gait /gāt/ *n.* A manner of walking, stepping, or running: an awkward *gait.*

gal·ler·y /gal′ər·ē/ *n., pl.* **gal·ler·ies** **1** A room or building for the display of art works. **2** A balcony in a theater, especially the highest one.

gauge /gāj/ *v.* **gauged, gaug·ing,** *n.* **1** *v.* To appraise, judge, or estimate. **2** *n.* Any of various systems, standards, or instruments for measuring: a gas *gauge.*

gene /jēn/ *n.* In plants and animals, a part within the chromosome that is basic to the development of hereditary characteristics.

gen·er·ous /jen′ər·əs/ *adj.* **1** Sharing; unselfish. **2** Larger: A *generous* portion of meat. ► *Generous* comes from the Latin word *generosus,* "of noble birth."

ge·net·ics /jə·net′iks/ *n., pl.* The science that studies heredity, the resemblances and differences of related organisms, and the causes of variation.

ge·og·ra·phy /jē·og′rə·fē/ *n.* **1** The science that studies the earth's surface and its life. **2** The natural features of an area. *Geography* comes from the Greek word *geographein,* "to describe the earth's surface."

ge·o·log·i·cal /jē′ə·loj′ə·kəl/ *adj.* Of or having to do with geology, the study of the earth's physical history through its rocks and minerals: a *geological* survey.

ge·ol·o·gy /jē·ol′ə·jē/ *n.* The science that studies the earth's physical history through its rocks and minerals.

ge·o·met·ric /jē′ə·met′rik/ *adj.* **1** Pertaining to the principles of geometry. **2** Having straight lines and simple curves; based on simple geometric shapes.—**ge′o·met′ri·cal·ly** *adv.*

ge·om·e·try /jē·om′ə·trē/ *n.* A branch of mathematics that studies the relationships of points, lines, angles, surfaces, and solids. ▶ *Geometry* comes from the Greek word *geometrein,* "to measure the earth."

go·ril·la /gə·ril′ə/ *n.* A large and powerful ape, found in Africa.

gov·ern /guv′ərn/ *v.* To rule or guide.

gra·cious /grā′shəs/ *adj.* **1** Courteous; polite: a *gracious* host. **2** Having good taste; elegant; luxurious: a *gracious* home.

grad·u·ate /*v.* graj′oo·āt, *n.* graj′oo·ət/ *v.* **grad·u·at·ed, grad·u·at·ing,** *n.* **1** *v.* To complete school; to earn a diploma. **2** *n.* A person who is graduating or has graduated.

graph /graf/ *n.* A diagram that shows the relation between two or more things by using dots, lines, bars, etc.

graph·ite /graf′īt/ *n.* A soft form of carbon, used in lead pencils and as a lubricant for machinery.

gro·cer·y /grō′sər·ē *or* grōs′rē/ *n., pl.* **gro·cer·ies** **1** A store that sells food and other goods. **2** *(pl.)* The foods and goods sold in such a store.

grue·some /groo′səm/ *adj.* Horrible, especially in a disgusting way.

guer·ril·la /gə·ril′ə/ *n.* **1** A member of a fighting group that uses surprise and sabotage as battle techniques. **2** *adj. use: guerrilla* warfare. *Alternate spelling:* **guerilla.**

gui·dance /gīd′(ə)ns/ *n.* **1** The act of guiding or leading; direction. **2** Advice or counsel.

gym·nas·tics /jim·nas′tiks/ *n. pl.* **1** Physical exercises that develop muscular strength, control, and agility. **2** The practice or art of such physical exercises.

H

hand·some /han′səm/ *adj.* **hand·som·er, hand·som·est** Attractive, especially in a dignified way.—**hand′some·ly** *adv.*

hatch·er·y /hach′ər·ē/ *n., pl.* **hatch·er·ies** A place for hatching eggs of fish or chickens.

haul /hôl/ **1** *v.* To pull or drag with force. **2** *v.* To move or carry a load, as in a truck. **3** *n.* The distance over which something is moved or carried: a long *haul.* **4** *n.* The amount of something caught, taken, or acquired: a *haul* of fish.

heart /härt/ *n.* **1** The muscular organ that pumps blood throughout the body. **2** The part of a person that reacts emotionally. **3** The ability to be generous, good, etc.: a kind *heart.* **4** Enthusiasm: His *heart* was not in his work. **5** The main, central, or essential part: the *heart* of the town.

heir /âr/ *n.* A person who inherits or is entitled to inherit the position or property of another: *heir* to the throne.

hem·i·sphere /hem′ə·sfir/ *n.* **1** A half of a sphere or ball. **2** *(often written* **Hemisphere)** One half of the world or globe, as Eastern Hemisphere, Southern Hemisphere, etc.

he·red·i·tar·y /hə·red′ə·ter′ē/ *adj.* Passed down from parents to their children or from ancestors to their descendants: Brown eyes are *hereditary* in our family.

he·ro /hir′ō *or* hē′rō/ *n., pl.* **he·roes** **1** A person known for his or her courage, great deeds, etc. **2** The main character in a play, story, etc.

hes·i·tant /hez′ə·tənt/ *adj.* Uncertain; doubtful; undecided.—**hes′i·tant·ly** *adv.*

high·way /hī′wā/ *n.* A main road.

hin·drance /hin′drəns/ *n.* A person or thing that hinders or gets in the way; an obstacle or obstruction. *Syn.:* obstacle.

---

act, āte, câre, ärt; egg, ēven; if, īce; on, ōver, ôr; book, food; up, tûrn;
ə=a in *ago,* e in *listen,* i in *giraffe,* o in *pilot,* u in *circus;* yoo=u in *music;* oil; out;
chair; sing; shop; thank; that; zh in *treasure.*

hoard

immobile

hoard /hôrd/ **1** *v.* To save and store away for preservation or future use, often in a greedy way: to *hoard* treasure. **2** *n.* A pile or stock of something hoarded: a *hoard* of food. ► *Hoard* comes from the Old English word *hordian,* which is related to *hydan,* "to hide or conceal."

hon·or·ar·y /on′ə·rer′ē/ *adj.* **1** Given as an honor: an *honorary* degree. **2** Given as an honor, without powers, pay, etc.: an *honorary* member.

horde /hôrd/ *n.* **1** A large group; a mass or crowd: a *horde* of people. **2** A wandering group, as a tribe or clan. ► *Horde* comes from the Polish word *horda,* "army."

hor·i·zon·tal /hôr′ə·zon′təl/ *adj.* Parallel to the ground or horizon; level: You must place the pieces in a *horizontal* position.

hu·man /(h)yoo′mən/ **1** *n.* A person. **2** *adj.* Relating to or having to do with people: *human* nature. **3** *adj.* Having or showing traits, usually virtues or weaknesses, that are natural to people: It is only *human* to make a mistake.

hu·man·i·ty /(h)yoo·man′ə·tē/ *n., pl.* **hu·man·i·ties** **1** The human race. **2** The condition or quality of being human; kindness. **3** *(pl.)* The area of learning that includes literature, history, philosophy, etc., as distinguished from the sciences.

hy·drant /hī′drənt/ *n.* An upright pipe connected to a water main from which water may be drawn: The fire was put out with water from the *hydrant.*

hy·drau·lic /hī·drô′lik/ *adj.* Operated by water or another liquid in motion or under pressure: *hydraulic* brakes.

hy·dro·e·lec·tric /hī′drō·i·lek′trik/ *adj.* Pertaining to electricity produced by water power: The dam produces enough *hydroelectric* power to light three cities.

hy·dro·foil /hī′drə·foil/ *n.* **1** A device similar to a short airplane wing, attached to a boat below the water line, which lifts the boat slightly out of the water so that it can move at faster speeds. **2** A boat equipped with hydrofoils.

hy·dro·gen /hī′drə·jən/ *n.* A light, colorless, odorless, flammable gas, found mainly in combination with oxygen, as in water.

hyp·no·tize /hip′nə·tīz/ *v.* **hyp·no·tized, hyp·no·tiz·ing** **1** To produce hypnosis, a sleep-like condition in which a person responds to suggestions or instructions made by a hypnotist. **2** To charm; to fascinate.—**hyp′no·tist** *n.*

hyp·o·crite /hip′ə·krit/ *n.* A person who pretends to have admirable or desirable attitudes, beliefs, or qualities he or she does not really possess.

hy·pot·e·nuse /hī·pot′ə·n(y)oos/ *n.* In a right triangle, the side opposite the right angle.

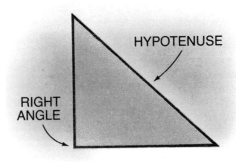
HYPOTENUSE
RIGHT ANGLE

hy·poth·e·sis /hī·poth′ə·sis/ *n., pl.* **hy·poth·e·ses** An idea assumed to be true for the purpose of debate, study, etc.: I proceeded on the *hypothesis* that he was correct.

i·den·ti·fy /ī·den′tə·fī/ *v.* **i·den·ti·fied, i·den·ti·fy·ing** To recognize or show what something is or who someone is.

il·lus·tra·tion /il′ə·strā′shən/ *n.* **1** A picture in a book, magazine, etc., used to explain or decorate. **2** A comparison or an example intended as an explanation.

il·lus·tri·ous /i·lus′trē·əs/ *adj.* Very famous; renowned: an *illustrious* lawyer.

im·ag·i·nar·y /i·maj′ə·ner′ē/ *adj.* Existing only in the mind or imagination; unreal.

im·ag·i·na·tive /i·maj′ə·nə·tiv *or* i·maj′ə·nā′tiv/ *adj.* Full of or demonstrating imagination, or the power to form mental pictures, see things in new ways, or create new ideas.—**im·ag′i·na·tive·ly** *adv.*

im·i·tate /im′ə·tāt/ *v.* **im·i·tat·ed, im·i·tat·ing** **1** To attempt to act or look the same as; to copy; to mimic: to *imitate* an older sister. **2** To have the appearance of: The polyester material *imitates* silk.

im·me·di·ate·ly /i·mē′dē·it·lē/ *adv.* Without delay; at once; instantly.

im·mi·grate /im′ə·grāt/ *v.* **im·mi·grat·ed, im·mi·grat·ing** To come to a new country or region with the intention of living there permanently.

im·mo·bile /i·mō′bəl/ *adj.* **1** Not able to be moved; fixed. **2** Not moving.

im·mod·est /i·mod′ist/ *adj.* **1** Not modest; indecent; shameless: *immodest* clothing. **2** Not humble; bold; forward: *immodest* claims.

im·mor·tal /i·môr′təl/ *adj.* Living or remembered forever: The works of William Shakespeare are *immortal.*

im·mor·tal·i·ty /im′ôr·tal′ə·tē/ *n.* Life or fame that lasts forever.

im·par·tial /im·pär′shəl/ *adj.* Not favoring one person, side, etc.; not biased.

im·pel /im·pel′/ *v.* **im·pelled, im·pel·ling** To force, drive, or urge on; to compel: Don's conscience *impelled* him to admit his guilt.

im·per·son·ate /im·pûr′sən·āt/ *v.* **im·per·son·at·ed, im·per·son·at·ing** **1** To mimic or copy. **2** To pretend to be by assuming the appearance or mannerisms of: He wore a naval uniform to *impersonate* a sailor.

im·pli·cate /im′plə·kāt/ *v.* **im·pli·cat·ed, im·pli·cat·ing** To show to be involved or connected with something, as a scheme or crime.

im·pres·sive /im·pres′iv/ *adj.* Producing strong admiration; awesome; imposing.

im·pro·vise /im′prə·vīz/ *v.* **im·pro·vised, im·pro·vis·ing** **1** To perform or carry out with little or no planning: The actor *improvised* his lines. **2** To make something from whatever materials are available: The children *improvised* a swing from an old tire.

in·ci·dent /in′sə·dənt/ *n.* An event or happening; occurrence.

in·ci·den·tal /in′sə·den′təl/ *adj.* Happening by chance or without intention.

in·ci·den·tal·ly /in′sə·den′təl·ē/ *adv.* **1** As a secondary or chance happening along with something else: The movie mentioned our town *incidentally.* **2** By the way: *Incidentally,* are you going to the party?

in·cli·na·tion /in′klə·nā′shən/ *n.* **1** A personal liking or preference. **2** A tendency toward a certain condition, action, etc.: an *inclination* to worry. **3** A slant; slope.

in·con·ceiv·a·ble /in′kən·sē′və·bəl/ *adj.* Impossible or unimaginable.

in·de·pen·dent /in′di·pen′dənt/ *adj.* **1** Not governed by another country. **2** Not influenced or swayed by others: an *independent* thinker. **3** Not dependent on anyone else for support or money: financially *independent.*

in·dex /in′deks/ *n., pl.* **in·dex·es,** *v.* **1** *n.* An alphabetical list of topics at the end of a book that shows the pages on which each topic is discussed. **2** *v.* To put information in an index. *Alternate plural:* **indices.**

in·dif·fer·ent /in·dif′rənt *or* in·dif′ər·ənt/ *adj.* **1** Not caring one way or another; without enthusiasm: He was *indifferent* to math. **2** Neither good nor bad: an *indifferent* artist.

in·di·vid·u·al·ize /in′də·vij′o͞o·ə·līz/ *v.* **in·di·vid·u·al·ized, in·di·vid·u·al·iz·ing** **1** To adapt to individual needs. **2** *adj.* use: *individualized* instruction.

in·duc·tion /in·duk′shən/ *n.* **1** The act of inducting or officially bringing into military service, an office, etc. **2** The process of arriving at a conclusion by observing particular facts: Newton discovered the law of gravity through his powers of *induction.*

in·dus·try /in′dəs·trē/ *n., pl.* **in·dus·tries** **1** Any division of manufacturing or business activity: the automobile *industry.* **2** Manufacturing as a whole.

in·ev·i·ta·ble /in·ev′ə·tə·bəl/ *adj.* Certain to occur; unavoidable.

in·ex·act /in′ig·zakt′/ *adj.* Not exact; not totally accurate or true.

in·fant /in′fənt/ **1** *n.* A child during the earliest period of its life; a baby. **2** *adj.* Pertaining to an infant or child of this age: *infant* clothes. ► *Infant* comes from Latin *in-* "not," and *fans,* "speaking."

in·fec·tious /in·fek′shəs/ *adj.* **1** Spread by or producing infection; contagious. **2** Likely to spread from one person to another; contagious: *infectious* enthusiasm.

in·flu·en·tial /in′flo͞o·en′shəl/ *adj.* Having or exerting influence; having the power to affect others.

in·for·ma·tion /in′fər·mā′shən/ *n.* **1** The act or fact of informing. **2** Knowledge or facts about a particular subject.

in·her·i·tance /in·her′ə·təns/ *n.* **1** The act, fact, or right of inheriting or being left something upon the owner's death. **2** Something inherited.

in·i·tial /in·ish′əl/ *adj., n., v.* **in·i·tialed, in·i·tial·ing** **1** *adj.* Earliest; first: an *initial* reaction. **2** *n. (often pl.)* The first letter of a proper name. **3** *v.* To sign one's initials. *Alternate spellings:* **initialled, initialling.**

---

act, āte, câre, ärt; egg, ēven; if, īce; on, ōver, ôr; bo͝ok, fo͞od; up, tûrn;
ə=a in *ago,* e in *listen,* i in *giraffe,* o in *pilot,* u in *circus;* yo͞o=u in *music;* oil; out;
chair; sing; shop; thank; *th*at; zh in *treasure.*

in·no·cence /in′ə·səns/ *n.* **1** Freedom from guilt, blame, or moral wrong. **2** Purity of mind; simplicity: the *innocence* of a child.

in·oc·u·late /in·ok′yə·lāt/ *v.* **in·oc·u·lat·ed, in·oc·u·lat·ing** To give a person or animal immunity or resistance to a disease by injecting vaccines, serums, or other prepared substances into the body.

in·scrip·tion /in·skrip′shən/ *n.* Words, letters, etc., written or engraved to preserve an important fact or idea in memory.

in·sig·nif·i·cant /in′sig·nif′ə·kənt/ *adj.* Unimportant: an *insignificant* reason.

in·spec·tor /in·spek′tər/ *n.* **1** A person who inspects or examines something carefully. **2** A police officer, usually ranking next below a superintendent.

in·spi·ra·tion /in′spə·rā′shən/ *n.* **1** A good idea or impulse that usually comes to someone suddenly; a bright idea. **2** The power to arouse a good feeling or idea: We found *inspiration* in her words. **3** A person or thing that inspires or arouses a good feeling or idea: Her words were an *inspiration*.

in·spire /in·spīr′/ *v.* **in·spired, in·spir·ing** To arouse or influence a certain thought, feeling, or desire to do something.

in·stinc·tive /in·stingk′tiv/ *adj.* Of, having to do with, or coming from instinct or natural impulse.

in·su·late /in′sə·lāt/ *v.* **in·su·lat·ed, in·su·lat·ing** To cover, surround, or separate with material that prevents or reduces the loss of electricity, heat, sound, etc.

in·sur·ance /in·shŏŏr′əns/ *n.* **1** The act of protecting someone or something against damage, injury, or loss. **2** Coverage by a policy or contract that guarantees that if payments are made on a regular basis, money will be reimbursed if damage, injury, or loss occurs.

in·sure /in·shŏŏr′/ *v.* **in·sured, in·sur·ing** **1** To buy, give, or get protection against damage, injury, or loss: to *insure* a car. **2** To guarantee: to *insure* success. **3** To guard or to protect: to *insure* against error.

in·tel·li·gence /in·tel′ə·jəns/ *n.* **1** The capacity to reason and understand. **2** *adj. use:* an *intelligence* test.

in·tent /in·tent′/ **1** *n.* Purpose or aim. **2** *adj.* Having one's efforts or attention firmly fixed on something: an *intent* stare.— **in·tent′ly** *adv.*

in·ten·tion /in·ten′shən/ *n.* Plan, purpose, or intent: Diane has no *intention* of attending the party.

in·ter·mis·sion /in′tər·mish′ən/ *n.* A pause or break between periods of activity, especially a break between the acts of a play; recess.

in·ter·rup·tion /in′tə·rup′shən/ *n.* **1** The act of interrupting or breaking in. **2** Something that interrupts or breaks in.

in·tes·tine /in·tes′tin/ *n. (often pl.)* A long coiled tube in the abdomen that helps in the digestion of food and the elimination of waste from the body.

in·tro·duc·to·ry /in′trə·duk′tər·ē or in′trə·duk′trē/ *adj.* Serving to introduce, present, or begin: *introductory* remarks.

in·trud·er /in·trōōd′ər/ *n.* A person who trespasses or enters without permission. *Syn.:* trespasser, invader, meddler.

in·vade /in·vād′/ *v.* **in·vad·ed, in·vad·ing** **1** To enter by force with the purpose of conquering or plundering: The army *invaded* the region. **2** To intrude upon; to infringe: to *invade* one's privacy. **3** To spread over or into, as if invading: *invaded* by ants.

in·ven·tive /in·ven′tiv/ *adj.* Skillful at or showing imagination or originality.

in·vert /in·vûrt′/ *v.* **1** To turn upside down. **2** To reverse the order or arrangement of something: to *invert* a fraction.

in·ves·ti·gate /in·ves′tə·gāt/ *v.* **in·ves·ti·gat·ed, in·ves·ti·gat·ing** To examine thoroughly in order to discover the facts.

in·vi·ta·tion /in′və·tā′shən/ *n.* A spoken or written request asking someone to come to a place or to do something.

ir·re·spon·si·ble /ir′i·spon′sə·bəl/ *adj.* Not responsible or reliable.

ir·ri·tate /ir′ə·tāt/ *v.* **ir·ri·tat·ed, ir·ri·tat·ing** **1** To annoy or make angry; to bother. **2** To make sore or raw; to inflame.

i·sos·ce·les /ī·sos′ə·lēz/ *adj.* Pertaining to a triangle that has two equal sides.

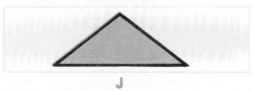

J

jar·gon /jär′gən/ *n.* **1** Confused or meaningless talk or writing; gibberish. **2** The special vocabulary shared by members of a particular group or profession.

jeop·ard·ize /jep′ər·dīz/ *v.* **jeop·ard·ized, jeop·ard·iz·ing** To endanger; to risk.

jew·el·ry /jōō′əl·rē/ *n.* Objects worn for decoration, such as necklaces, rings, etc.

judicial

ju·di·cial /jŏŏ·dish′əl/ *adj.* Of or having to do with the administration of justice, judges, or courts of law.

jus·ti·fy /jus′tə·fī/ *v.* **jus·ti·fied, jus·ti·fy·ing** **1** To show something to be just, correct, or reasonable: to *justify* an expense. **2** To give good reason for: to *justify* actions.

K

khak·i /kak′ē/ *adj., n., pl.* **khak·is** **1** *adj.* Light brown in color. **2** *n.* A heavy, light-brown cotton fabric, often used for military uniforms, work clothes, etc.

kin·der·gar·ten /kin′dər·gär′tən/ *n.* A class or school for young children between the ages of four and six.

knoll /nōl/ *n.* A mound or small, round hill.

L

la·bel /lā′bəl/ *n., v.* **la·beled, la·bel·ing** **1** *n.* A slip of paper or other material bearing information, instructions, etc., fastened to something. **2** *v.* To fasten or attach a label to something. *Alternate spellings:* **labelled, labelling.**

lab·o·ra·to·ry /lab′ə·rə·tôr′ē *or* lab′rə·tôr′ē/ *n., pl.* **lab·o·ra·to·ries** A place that is equipped for scientific work or other types of testing and experiments.

lab·y·rinth /lab′ə·rinth/ *n.* A confusing arrangement of paths; a maze. ► *Labyrinth* comes from the Greek word *labyrinthos,* a maze in Greek mythology, located on the island of Crete.

late /lāt/ *adj.* **lat·er, la·test, last,** *adv.* **1** *adj.* Happening after or past a certain time; tardy: a *late* arrival. **2** *adv.* At or until an advanced time of the day, month, etc.: to sleep *late.* **3** *adj.* Toward the end or close of something: *late* summer.

lightning

lat·ter /lat′ər/ *adj.* **1** Later or nearer the end: the *latter* part of the book. **2** Being the second of two things mentioned: The *latter* suggestion is better than the former. **3** *n. use:* The second of two things referred to: She prefers the *latter* to the former.

le·gal /lē′gəl/ *adj.* **1** Pertaining to the law: *legal* documents. **2** Allowed by or based on law: the *legal* speed limit.

le·gal·i·ty /li·gal′ə·tē/ *n.* The condition of being lawful or allowed by the law.

le·gal·ize /lē′gəl·īz/ *v.* **le·gal·ized, le·gal·iz·ing** To make legal.

leg·is·la·ture /lej′is·lā′chər/ *n.* A body of people that has the power to make, change, or repeal the laws of a country or state.

length·wise /leng(k)th′wīz′/ *adj., adv.* In the direction of the length; parallel to the longest side: to cut bread *lengthwise.*

le·vel /lev′əl/ *adj., n., v.* **lev·eled, lev·el·ing** **1** *adj.* Having a flat surface: a *level* floor. **2** *adj.* Of even height: The two piles of books were *level* with each other. **3** *n.* Height; depth: a water *level* of eight feet. **4** *v.* To make flat, even, or smooth. *Alternate spellings:* **levelled, levelling.**

li·a·ble /lī′ə·bəl/ *adj.* **1** Likely; apt: It is *liable* to snow. **2** Legally responsible: *liable* for damages.

li·bel /lī′bəl/ *n., v.* **li·beled, li·bel·ing** **1** *n.* A false or misleading written statement or picture that damages a person's reputation; slander. **2** *v.* To make or publish a damaging statement. *Alternate spellings:* **libelled, libelling.**

li·brar·y /lī′brer′ē *or* lī′brə·rē/ *n., pl.* **li·brar·ies** **1** A place where books, magazines, etc., are kept. **2** A collection of books.

li·cense /lī′sens/ *n., v.* **li·censed, li·cens·ing** **1** *n.* Legal or formal permission to do, be, or own something: a *license* to fish. **2** *n.* A certificate, tag, or plate showing such permission. **3** *v.* To issue a license or legal permission: She is *licensed* to drive a car.

lieu·ten·ant /lŏŏ·ten′ənt/ *n.* A military rank in the army or navy.

lig·a·ment /lig′ə·mənt/ *n.* A band of tissue that connects bones or helps to hold organs in place in the body.

light·ning /līt′ning/ *n.* A sudden flash of light caused by an electric discharge in the atmosphere.

---

act, āte, câre, ärt; egg, ēven; if, īce; on, ōver, ôr; bŏŏk, fŏŏd; up, tûrn;
ə=a in *ago,* e in *listen,* i in *giraffe,* o in *pilot,* u in *circus;* yŏŏ=u in *music;* oil; out;
chair; sing; shop; thank; ŧħat; zh in *treasure.*

likable

lik·a·ble /līʹkə·bəl/ *adj.* Pleasing; enjoyable. *Alternate spelling:* likeable.

like·li·hood /līkʹlē·hŏŏd/ *n.* The possibility or probability that something will take place.

like·wise /līkʹwīzʹ/ *adv.* **1** The same; in a like manner: Since she did you a favor, you can do *likewise.* **2** In addition; also: He plays the piano and *likewise* the violin.

liq·ue·fy /likʹwə·fī/ *v.* **liq·ue·fied, liq·ue·fy·ing** To make or become liquid or fluid.

lit·er·a·ture /litʹər·ə·chər *or* litʹrə·chər/ *n.* **1** Written works in general. **2** Written material that deals with a particular subject: scientific *literature.*

live·li·hood /līvʹlē·hŏŏd/ *n.* An income; a means of earning a living.

lo·cal /lōʹkəl/ *adj.* **1** Of or having to do with an area, neighborhood, or region. **2** Stopping at all or almost all points or stations along its run (of a train, plane, etc.).

lo·cal·i·ty /lō·kalʹə·tē/ *n., pl.* **lo·cal·i·ties** A specific place, area, or region.

loi·ter /loiʹtər/ *v.* To linger or pass time idly: The boys *loitered* by the doorway.

lone·some /lōnʹsəm/ *adj.* Sad because of a lack of companionship; lonely.

lung /lung/ *n.* Either of the two saclike respiratory organs found in the chest of a human being and other vertebrate animals that breathe air.

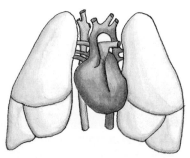

M

ma·chin·er·y /mə·shēnʹ(ə·)rē/ *n.* **1** A collection of mechanical devices or machines. **2** The working parts of a machine.

mag·nif·i·cent /mag·nifʹə·sənt/ *adj.* **1** Grand; splendid: a *magnificent* castle. **2** Superb; excellent: a *magnificent* book.

mag·ni·fy /magʹnə·fī/ *v.* **mag·ni·fied, mag·ni·fy·ing** **1** To make something look bigger than its real size; to enlarge. **2** To make something more important than it really is; to exaggerate.

martial

main·te·nance /mānʹtə·nəns/ *n.* The act of maintaining, carrying on, or giving financial support.

ma·li·cious /mə·lishʹəs/ *adj.* Showing or having malice or the desire to harm or injure; spiteful.—**ma·liʹcious·ly** *adv.*

man·age·ment /manʹij·mənt/ *n.* **1** The act or practice of managing or directing. **2** The person or people as a group who manage a business or institution.

ma·neu·ver /mə·n(y)ōōʹvər/ **1** *n.* Any skillful movement or action: a *maneuver* to gain control of a company. **2** *v.* To act out a skillful movement or action, especially around obstacles: to *maneuver* a car through heavy traffic.

man·i·cure /manʹə·kyōōr/ *n., v.* **man·i·cured, man·i·cur·ing** **1** *n.* The grooming of the hands and fingernails; hand care. **2** *v.* To groom the hands and fingernails: My friend *manicured* my nails.

ma·nip·u·late /mə·nipʹyə·lāt/ *v.* **ma·nip·u·lat·ed, ma·nip·u·lat·ing** **1** To handle, manage, operate, or work a machine: to *manipulate* a car. **2** To control, manage, or influence in a dishonest or shrewd way: to *manipulate* a person.

man·u·al /manʹyōō·əl/ **1** *adj.* Of or having to do with the hands: *manual* skill; *manual* alphabet. **2** *adj.* Worked or done by hand and not by machine: *manual* computation. **3** *adj.* Requiring or utilizing physical skill and energy: a *manual* laborer. **4** *n.* A small book, especially one giving instructions or information; handbook: a travel *manual.*—**manʹu·al·ly** *adv.*

man·u·fac·ture /manʹyə·fakʹchər/ *v.* **man·u·fac·tured, man·u·fac·tur·ing,** *n.* **1** *v.* To make or produce a product, especially on a large scale. **2** *v.* To produce as if by manufacturing: Spiders *manufacture* webs. **3** *n.* The act or process of manufacturing: the *manufacture* of automobiles.

man·u·script /manʹyə·skript/ *n.* A book, article, poem, etc., handwritten or typed: I delivered the *manuscript* to the publisher.

mar·a·thon /marʹə·thon/ *n.* **1** A foot race on a course measuring 26 miles 385 yards, or 42.2 kilometers. **2** Any long-distance race. **3** Any contest of endurance: The *marathon* lasted five hours.

mar·i·tal /marʹə·təl/ *adj.* Pertaining to marriage or the married state.

mar·tial /märʹshəl/ *adj.* **1** Pertaining to war or military life. **2** Having to do with self-defense techniques: *martial* arts.

ma·te·ri·al /mə·tir′ē·əl/ **1** *n.* The substance of which something is composed. **2** *adj.* Having to do with matter; physical. **3** *n.* Cloth.

math·e·mat·ics /math′ə·mat′iks/ *n.* The science that deals with size, form, and relationships in terms of numbers and symbols.

meas·ure·ment /mezh′ər·mənt/ *n.* **1** The act of measuring. **2** Extent, size, quantity, etc., found by measuring. **3** A system of measuring or measures: liquid *measurement*.

me·di·an /mē′dē·ən/ *n.* **1** The middle number in a series or sequence of numbers. **2** The dividing strip on a highway.

med·i·cine /med′ə·sən/ *n.* **1** Any substance used in treating a disease or illness. **2** The science of treating disease and illness and preserving health.

med·i·tate /med′ə·tāt/ *v.* **med·i·tat·ed, med·i·tat·ing** To think quietly and deeply over a period of time; to reflect: She *meditated* on the origins of the universe.

mel·an·chol·y /mel′ən·kol′ē/ **1** *adj.* Gloomy; sad; depressed: a *melancholy* mood. **2** *n.* Depression; sadness. **3** *adj.* Causing sadness: a *melancholy* song.

mel·on /mel′ən/ *n.* A large, juicy fruit that grows on a vine, as a watermelon.

mem·o·ra·ble /mem′ər·ə·bəl *or* mem·rə·bəl/ *adj.* Worthy of being remembered; hard to forget.—**mem′o·ra·bly** *adv.*

mer·chan·dise /*n.* mûr′chən·dīz *or* mûr′chən·dīs, *v.* mûr′chən·dīz/ **1** *n.* Goods bought and sold for profit. **2** *v.* To buy and sell goods for profit. **3** *v.* To promote the sale of goods: to *merchandise* sportswear.

me·te·or·ol·o·gy /mē′tē·ə·rol′ə·jē/ *n.* The science that deals with the atmosphere, winds, and weather.

min·i·a·ture /min′(ē·)ə·chər/ **1** *n.* A small model or copy of something. **2** *adj.* Very small; tiny: *miniature* pony.

mi·nor /mī′nər/ **1** *adj.* Of less importance or not important: a *minor* problem. **2** *n.* A person under the legal age: *Minors* must be accompanied by an adult. **3** *n.* A subject or course of study second in importance to a major: Her *minor* is philosophy. **4** *v.* To study such a subject or course of study: to *minor* in biology. **5** *adj.* In music, a scale with a semitone between the second and third tones and whole tones between the first and second, third and fourth, and fourth and fifth tones.

mi·nor·i·ty /mə·nôr′ə·tē/ *n., pl.* **mi·nor·i·ties 1** Less than half of the whole: Only a *minority* of the people voted for the law. **2** *adj. use:* a *minority* party. **3** A group different in some way, as in race, religion, or ethnic background, from the majority of the population: French-speaking people are a *minority* in Canada.

mis·cel·la·ne·ous /mis′ə·lā′nē·əs/ *adj.* Various; made up of many different things or elements: *miscellaneous* papers.

mis·chie·vous /mis′chi·vəs/ *adj.* **1** Full of mischief: The children were very *mischievous* today. **2** Slightly annoying. **3** Tending to cause harm, trouble, or injury: *Mischievous* gossip can hurt people.

mis·di·rect /mis′di·rekt′/ *v.* To direct, guide, or lead wrongly. *Syn.*: mislead.

mis·sile /mis′əl/ *n.* Something, especially a weapon, thrown or shot, as a bullet, stone, rocket, etc.: a guided *missile*.

mock·er·y /mok′ər·ē/ *n., pl.* **mock·er·ies 1** Ridicule: *Mockery* of others is cruel. **2** Something which is or is worthy of being mocked, ridiculed, or made fun of: The contest was a *mockery*.

mod·el /mod′əl/ *n., v.* **mod·eled, mod·el·ing 1** *n.* A miniature copy of something: a *model* of a ship. **2** *adj. use:* a *model* airplane. **3** *v.* To form material into a model: to *model* clay. **4** *v.* To plan, form, or design after something: He *modeled* himself after his brother. **5** *n.* A specific style or design: the latest *model*. **6** *n.* A person who poses for an artist, photographer, etc.: The *model* had on a beautiful outfit. **7** *v.* To pose for an artist, photographer, etc. *Alternate spellings:* **mod·elled, modelling.**

act, āte, câre, ärt;   egg, ēven;   if, īce;   on, ōver, ôr;   bŏŏk, fōōd;   up, tûrn;
ə=a in *ago*, e in *listen*, i in *giraffe*, o in *pilot*, u in *circus*;   yōō=u in *music*;   oil;   out;
chair; sing; shop; thank; that; zh in *treasure*.

moderate

nomination

mod·er·ate /*adj.* mod′ər·ət, *v.* mod′ə·rāt/ *adj.,
v.* **mod·er·at·ed, mod·er·at·ing** **1** *adj.* Not
extreme or excessive; keeping within proper
limits: *moderate* speed. **2** *adj.* Not extreme
or radical in beliefs, actions, etc.: a *moderate*
politician. **3** *v.* To act as moderator or
chairperson of a debate, meeting, or other
program: to *moderate* a discussion.

mod·er·a·tion /mod′ə·rā′shən/ *n.* The condition or quality of being moderate; avoidance
of extremes.

mod·i·fy /mod′ə·fī/ *v.* **mod·i·fied, mod·i·
fy·ing** To change somewhat or make less
extreme: *modify* one's opinion.

mor·al¹ /môr′əl/ **1** *adj.* Good or decent in
character. **2** *adj.* Relating to standards or
principles of right and wrong: a *moral* decision. **3** *n.* (*pl.*) Conduct, standards, or
principles relating to right and wrong.

mor·al² /môr′əl/ *n.* A lesson demonstrated by
a story.

mo·ral·i·ty /mə·ral′ə·tē/ *n., pl.* **mo·ral·i·ties**
1 A system of rules, standards, or principles
of good or honorable conduct. **2** Moral or
virtuous conduct.

mort·gage /môr′gij/ *n., v.* **mort·gaged, mort·
gag·ing** **1** *n.* A claim or the contract that
establishes a claim on property, given as
security or insurance for a loan. **2** *v.* To
arrange a loan, using property as insurance.

mov·ie /mōō′vē/ *n.* **1** A motion picture; film.
2 A theater where a motion picture or film
is shown.

mul·ti·pli·ca·tion /mul′tə·plə·kā′shən/ *n.*
1 The act or state of increasing in number
or degree. **2** A mathematical process of
adding one or more of the same number together, as 3 × 2 = 2 + 2 + 2 = 6.

mus·cle /mus′əl/ *n.* **1** One of the bundles of
stringy tissue in the body that contract and
stretch to produce the body's movements.
2 Physical strength or hard work: Chopping
wood requires a lot of *muscle.*

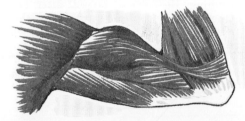

mus·cu·lar /mus′kyə·lər/ *adj.* **1** Made of
muscle or using muscle: *muscular* tissue.
2 Having well-developed muscles.

mys·ter·y /mis′tər·ē/ *n., pl.* **mys·ter·ies**
1 Something that is or seems impossible to
know or understand. **2** An action that
arouses curiosity because it seems impossible to know or understand. **3** A story about
an event that has this quality.

mys·ti·fy /mis′tə·fī/ *v.* **mys·ti·fied, mys·
ti·fy·ing** To puzzle, bewilder, or baffle.

my·thol·o·gy /mi·thol′ə·jē/ *n., pl.* **my·
thol·o·gies** **1** A collection of stories or
myths, especially about gods, heroes, etc., of
the past. **2** The study of stories or myths
dealing with gods, heroes, etc., of the past.

N

na·ive /nä·ēv′/ *adj.* **1** Unaffected; innocent:
a *naive* child. **2** Inexperienced: *naive* in the
world of business.

na·tion·al /nash′ən·əl/ *adj.* Having to do with
a nation as a whole.

nat·u·ral·ly /nach′ər·əl·ē/ *adv.* **1** In a natural
way; by nature: *naturally* curly hair. **2** Certainly; of course.

neigh·bor·hood /nā′bər·hŏŏd/ *n.* A small section of a city or town, sometimes with a
"personality" somewhat different from that
of the surrounding area.

nerve /nûrv/ *n.* **1** One or more bundles of
fibers that carry impulses between the brain
or spinal cord and all other parts of the body.
2 Courage; firmness, especially in a difficult
situation. **3** Offensive boldness: The
stranger had some *nerve* to say that.

neu·ral /n(y)ŏŏ·rəl/ *adj.* Having to do with
nerves: a *neural* disorder.

neu·tral /n(y)ŏŏ′trəl/ *adj.* **1** Not on either
side in a combat, contest, argument, etc.: a
neutral observer. **2** Not belonging to either
of the opposing sides: *neutral* territory.
3 Neither acid nor alkaline. **4** Not strongly
one thing or another; middling: a *neutral*
color.

neu·tral·i·ty /n(y)ŏŏ·tral′ə·tē/ *n.* A neutral
condition, attitude, or policy, especially the
decision of a nation not to take sides in a
war.

no·mad /nō′mad/ *n.* **1** A member of a group
or tribe that has no fixed home and moves
from place to place. **2** Any person who
moves from place to place aimlessly. *Syn.*:
wanderer.

nom·i·nate /nom′ə·nāt/ *v.* **nom·i·nat·ed, nom·
i·nat·ing** To name or select someone for an
appointment or as a candidate.

nom·i·na·tion /nom′ə·nā′shən/ *n.* **1** The act
of nominating or naming as a candidate or

of appointing to an office.   **2** The state, condition, or fact of being nominated.

no·ti·fy /nō′tə·fī/ *v.* **no·ti·fied, no·ti·fy·ing** To give notice of something.

nu·cle·ar /n(y)ōō′klē·ər/ *adj.* **1** Of, having to do with, or like a nucleus or nuclei.   **2** Of, having to do with, or using atomic energy.

nu·cle·us /n(y)ōō′klē·əs/ *n., pl.* **nu·cle·i** **1** The small central mass, surrounded by a membrane, in an animal or plant cell.   **2** The central core of an atom.   **3** A point around which other things are gathered. *Alternate plural:* **nucleuses.**

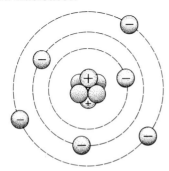

nui·sance /n(y)ōō′səns/ *n.* A bothersome or annoying person or situation.

nurs·er·y /nûr′sər·ē/ *n., pl.* **nurs·er·ies** **1** A baby's or children's room.   **2** A place where trees and plants are raised.   **3** A place where children are cared for.

nu·tri·tious /n(y)ōō·trish′əs/ *adj.* Providing the proper nourishment; nourishing: The school provides a *nutritious* lunch.

O

ob·liv·i·on /ə·bliv′ē·ən/ *n.*   **1** The state or fact of being totally forgotten: A fad often fades into *oblivion.*   **2** Forgetfulness.

ob·nox·ious /əb·nok′shəs/ *adj.* Causing strong dislike; hateful; offensive.

ob·ser·vant /əb·zûr′vənt/ *adj.* Quick to observe or notice; alert; attentive.

ob·sta·cle /ob′stə·kəl/ *n.* Something that prevents or hinders; obstruction.

ob·tuse /əb·t(y)ōōs′/ *adj.*   **1** Of an angle measuring more than 90° but less than 180°.   **2** Slow to comprehend; insensitive: too *obtuse* to understand.   **3** Blunt; dull.

oc·ca·sion /ə·kā′zhən/ *n.*   **1** A particular time that something happened.   **2** An important

event.   **3** An opportunity or a good time to do something: an *occasion* to return the favor.   **4** Cause or reason: I have never had *occasion* to complain.

oc·cu·pant /ok′yə·pənt/ *n.* A person who occupies or lives in a certain place: the former *occupant* of the house.

oc·cur·rence /ə·kûr′əns/ *n.* The act or fact of taking place or occurring; something that happens; incident: Snowfall is a rare *occurrence* in south Florida.

of·fense /ə·fens′/ *n.* **1** A violation or breaking of a law.   **2** The act of offending or displeasing: She meant no *offense.*   **3** Something that offends, causes displeasure, or angers: The discussion was an *offense* to his beliefs.   **4** /*also* ô′fens/ Attack or assault: weapons of *offense.*   **5** /*also* ô′fens/ In sports, as football, hockey, etc., the team in possession of the ball, puck, etc.

of·fi·cial /ə·fish′əl/   **1** *n.* A person who holds an office or position and has certain duties or powers, as in the government, an organization, etc.   **2** *adj.* Of or pertaining to an office of authority: an *official* act.   **3** *adj.* Authorized; approved: an *official* order.   **4** *adj.* Given the authority to carry out a special duty: an *official* umpire.

om·i·nous /om′ə·nəs/ *adj.* Threatening or foreboding, like a bad omen: The clouds looked very *ominous. Syn.:* threatening.
► *Ominous* comes from the Latin word *ominosus,* "threatening."

op·po·nent /ə·pō′nənt/ *n.* A person who opposes or competes with another, as in sports, a contest, etc.; a rival: Who is your *opponent* in the contest?

or·gan·ism /ôr′gən·iz′əm/ *n.* A form of life, as an animal or plant, composed of mutually dependent organs or parts that support vital processes.

or·gan·ize /ôr′gən·īz/ *v.* **or·gan·ized, or·gan·iz·ing** **1** To form, bring together, or gather as a whole, usually for a particular purpose.   **2** To arrange or put into a system or order: Organize your notes before you begin to write the paper.

o·rig·i·nal /ə·rij′ə·nəl/ *adj.*   **1** Part of the early beginnings of something; first: The *original* settlers of New York were Dutch.   **2** Created totally by one's own mind and work: an *original* idea.

act, āte, câre, ärt;   egg, ēven;   if, īce;   on, ōver, ôr;   bŏŏk, fōōd;   up, tûrn;
ə=**a** in *ago,* **e** in *listen,* **i** in *giraffe,* **o** in *pilot,* **u** in *circus;*   y**ōō**=**u** in *music;*   oil;   out;
chair; si**ng**; **sh**op; **th**ank; **th**at; **zh** in *treasure.*

originality

personal

o·rig·i·nal·i·ty /ə·rij′ə·nal′ə·tē/ *n*. The quality of being creative and new in what you think or do.

o·rig·i·nate /ə·rij′ə·nāt/ *v*. **o·rig·i·nat·ed, o·rig·i·nat·ing** To begin or come into existence; to initiate: to *originate* a plan.

oth·er·wise /uth′ər·wīz′/ *adv*. **1** In other circumstances; if it were not this way: The rain delayed us; *otherwise*, we would have been on time. **2** In a different way: She can't behave *otherwise*. **3** If not: I'll write this down; *otherwise*, I'll forget it.

out·ra·geous /out·rā′jəs/ *adj*. **1** Shockingly cruel: an *outrageous* action. **2** Insulting; rude: an *outrageous* remark. **3** Unbelievable: an *outrageous* statement. *Syn*.: unbelievable, shocking, fantastic.

P

pag·eant /paj′ənt/ *n*. **1** An elaborate public spectacle, usually held in celebration of a historical event. **2** A colorful and spectacular show or parade: a school *pageant*. *Syn*.: spectacle.

pan·el /pan′əl/ *n., v*. **pan·eled, pan·el·ing** **1** *n*. A section of a wall, ceiling, or window that is set off in some way from the rest of the surface. **2** *v*. To put up panels. *Alternate spellings:* **panelled, panelling.**

pan·ic /pan′ik/ *n., v*. **pan·icked, pan·ick·ing** **1** *n*. Sudden fear and terror. **2** *v*. To be filled with fear and terror.

par·al·lel·o·gram /par′ə·lel′ə·gram/ *n*. A four-sided geometric figure with opposite sides that are parallel and equal.

par·a·lyze /par′ə·līz/ *v*. **par·a·lyzed, par·a·lyz·ing** **1** To bring about a loss of the power of movement or feeling. **2** To make powerless or helpless: A power failure can *paralyze* an entire city.

pa·ren·the·sis /pə·ren′thə·sis/ *n., pl*. **pa·ren·the·ses** One of a pair of punctuation marks ( ) used to set off words, phrases, etc.

par·tic·i·pant /pär·tis′ə·pənt/ *n*. A person who takes part in something.

par·tic·u·lar /pər·tik′yə·lər *or* pə·tik′yə·lər/ *adj*. **1** Relating to a specific person, place, or thing. **2** Unusual; exceptional; special: a meeting of *particular* importance. **3** Precise; hard to please: *particular* about one's clothes.

par·ti·tion /pär·tish′ən/ **1** *n*. A division or separation. **2** *v*. To divide or separate. **3** *n*. Something that divides or separates, as a wall, etc. **4** *v*. To divide or separate by such a partition.

pas·teur·ize /pas′chə·rīz/ *v*. **pas·teur·ized, pas·teur·iz·ing** To heat a liquid, as milk, wine, etc., to a very high temperature in order to kill harmful bacteria.

pas·try /pās′trē/ *n., pl*. **pas·tries** A sweet, baked food, especially one with a crust made with flour and shortening, as a pie or tart.

pa·tience /pā′shəns/ *n*. **1** The ability to wait or experience difficulties without complaining. **2** Calmness and understanding.

pa·trol /pə·trōl′/ *v*. **pa·trolled, pa·trol·ling**, *n*. **1** *v*. To go through or around an area for the purpose of guarding it. **2** *n*. The act of patrolling. **3** *n*. The person or group that patrols.

pause /pôz/ *v*. **paused, paus·ing**, *n*. **1** *v*. To stop briefly. **2** *n*. A brief or short stop.

pe·cul·iar /pi·kyo͞ol′yər/ *adj*. **1** Odd or strange: a *peculiar* odor. **2** Belonging to one group, person, or place; distinctive: Igloos are *peculiar* to the North.

ped·es·tal /ped′is·təl/ *n*. The base that supports a column, statue, vase, etc.

peer[1] /pir/ *v*. To look at hard and closely, especially at something difficult to see.

peer[2] /pir/ **1** *n*. One that is of equal standing with another. **2** *adj*. Of or belonging to the same group in society, especially based on age, grade, or status: *peer* pressure.

pen·ta·gon /pen′tə·gon/ *n*. **1** A closed plane figure having five straight sides and five angles. **2** (*written* **Pentagon**) The five-sided building in Washington, D.C., that houses the Department of Defense.

pe·rim·e·ter /pə·rim′ə·tər/ *n*. **1** The circumference, border, or outer boundary of any plane figure, or the length of such a boundary. **2** The outer limits of anything: beyond the *perimeter* of understanding.

per·ma·nent /pûr′mə·nənt/ *adj*. Intended to go on without change; lasting.

per·pen·dic·u·lar /pûr′pən·dik′yə·lər/ **1** *adj*. Upright. **2** *n*. In math, a line that forms a right angle with another line.

per·plex /pər·pleks/ *v*. **1** To confuse or bewilder: The strange noise *perplexed* her. **2** *adj. use*: a *perplexed* expression.

per·se·cute /pûr′sə·kyo͞ot/ *v*. **per·se·cut·ed, per·se·cut·ing** To mistreat or oppress.

per·sis·tence /pər·sis′təns/ *n*. Determination; endurance.

per·son·al /pûr′sən·əl/ *adj*. **1** Having to do with a certain person or persons; private: *personal* hygiene. **2** Done in person: a *personal* appearance. **3** In grammar, representing person: *personal* pronouns.

per·son·al·i·ty /pûr′sən·al′ə·tē/ *n., pl.* **per·son·al·i·ties** **1** The manner or expressed qualities of a person that make him or her different from other people. **2** Attractive personal qualities, such as charm, enthusiasm, a sense of humor, etc.

per·son·nel /pûr′sə·nel′/ *n.* **1** The people employed by a business, military group, etc.; employees. **2** A division of an organization concerned with matters relating to employees. **3** *adj. use: personnel* office.

per·spi·ra·tion /pûr′spə·rā′shən/ *n.* **1** Moisture given off through pores in the skin; sweat. **2** The act of sweating.

per·sua·sive /pər·swā′siv/ *adj.* Able to or tending to persuade or convince someone to do something: a *persuasive* argument.

pe·ti·tion /pə·tish′ən/ **1** *n.* A formal, written request made to a person or a group in authority. **2** *v.* To submit a petition.

pet·ri·fy /pet′rə·fī/ *v.* **pet·ri·fied, pet·ri·fy·ing** **1** To become stone or like stone. **2** *adj. use: petrified* forest. **3** To make rigid or motionless with fear or surprise.

phar·ma·cy /fär′mə·sē/ *n., pl.* **phar·ma·cies** **1** The science or business of preparing and selling medicines. **2** A drugstore.

phe·nom·e·non /fi·nom′ə·non/ *n., pl.* **phe·nom·e·na** **1** An event that can be observed. **2** An extraordinary person or thing: Mozart was a musical *phenomenon.*

phi·los·o·phy /fi·los′ə·fē/ *n., pl.* **phi·los·o·phies** **1** The study of the truths or principles of knowledge, being, or conduct. **2** The study of the basic principles of a branch of knowledge: the *philosophy* of science. **3** The guiding principles in practical affairs: a *philosophy* of life.

pho·to /fō′tō/ *n., pl.* **pho·tos** A photograph.

pho·to·cop·y /fō′tō·kop′ē/ *n., pl.* **pho·to·cop·ies,** *v.* **pho·to·cop·ied, pho·to·cop·y·ing** **1** *n.* A photographic copy of printed or written matter. **2** *v.* To make such a copy.

pho·to·gen·ic /fō′tō·jen′ik/ *adj.* Being an attractive subject for photography or possessing features that photograph well.

pho·tog·ra·phy /fə·tog′rə·fē/ *n.* **1** The process or art of producing images through the chemical action of light on film, usually by means of a camera. **2** The hobby or business of producing photographs.

pho·to·syn·the·sis /fō′tō·sin′thə·sis/ *n.* The process by which plants, using chlorophyll and sunlight as energy, form carbohydrates from carbon dioxide and water.

phys·i·cal /fiz′i·kəl/ *adj.* **1** Having to do with the body. **2** Having to do with matter or the laws of nature. **3** Having to do with matter and energy, but not chemical composition: a *physical* science.

phy·si·cian /fi·zish′ən/ *n.* A medical doctor. ► *Physician* comes from the Greek word *physikos,* "physical."

pier /pir/ *n.* **1** A structure extending out over water. **2** A massive structural support, as for the arch of a bridge.

piv·ot /piv′ət/ **1** *n.* A pin or shaft on which a part turns. **2** *v.* To turn on, or as on, a pivot or point. *Syn.:* turn.

plan·e·tar·i·um /plan′ə·târ′ē·əm/ *n., pl.* **plan·e·tar·i·ums** A room or building with an apparatus that can project images of the stars and other celestial bodies on a domed ceiling. *Alternate plural:* **planetaria.** ► *Planetarium* is made up of the base word *planet* and the Latin suffix *-arium,* "a place connected with." *Planet* comes from a Greek word that means "wanderer."

plas·ma /plaz′mə/ *n.* The liquid part of blood, without the blood corpuscles.

pleas·ant /plez′ənt/ *adj.* **1** Enjoyable; pleasing. **2** Agreeable or friendly in disposition, manner, etc.

pli·a·ble /plī′ə·bəl/ *adj.* **1** Easily twisted, folded, or molded; flexible. **2** Easily directed or persuaded.

plu·ral /ploor′əl/ **1** *adj.* Pertaining to more than one. **2** *n.* The form that a word takes when it indicates more than one.

plu·ral·i·ty /ploo·ral′ə·tē/ *n., pl.* **plu·ral·i·ties** The number of votes by which a winning candidate defeats his nearest rival.

pneu·mo·nia /n(y)oo·mōn′yə/ *n.* A disease that inflames the lungs, caused by bacterial or viral infection.

---

act, āte, câre, ärt;   egg, ēven;   if, īce;   on, ōver, ôr;   bŏŏk, fōŏd;   up, tûrn;
ə=a in *ago,* e in *listen,* i in *giraffe,* o in *pilot,* u in *circus;*   yōŏ=u in *music;*   oil;   out;
chair;   sing;   shop;   thank;   that;   zh in *treasure.*

podium   **private**

po·di·um /pō′dē·əm/ *n., pl.* **po·di·ums** A small platform on which the conductor of an orchestra, a public speaker, etc., stands. *Alternate plural:* **podia.** ▶ *Podium* is a Latin spelling of Greek *podion,* "little foot."

po·et /pō′it/ *n.* A person who writes poetry.

pol·i·tics /pol′ə·tiks/ *n. pl.* The way government operates; the art or science of government.

pol·y·gon /pol′i·gon/ *n.* A closed plane figure having three or more straight sides.

pop·u·la·tion /pop′yə·lā′shən/ *n.* **1** The total number of people living in a country, city, town, etc. **2** The total number of people of a specific group, class, etc.: the school-age *population.*

por·ous /pôr′əs/ *adj.* Full of tiny pores, holes, or openings that air or liquid can pass through: Wood is a *porous* substance.

pos·i·tive /poz′ə·tiv/ *adj.* **1** Admitting no doubt or denial: *positive* evidence. **2** Certain; affirmative; definite. **3** Very sure of oneself; confident: a *positive* attitude. **4** Useful: *positive* criticism. **5** Consisting of the kind of electricity that attracts and is counteracted by electrons.

po·ten·tial /pə·ten′chəl/ **1** *adj.* Possible but not yet actual. **2** *n.* An ability, such as a talent, that may or may not be developed: Her painting has *potential.*

pot·ter·y /pot′ər·ē/ *n., pl.* **pot·ter·ies** **1** Bowls, pots, vases, etc., made from clay and hardened by baking or firing. **2** The art or craft of making pottery. **3** The place where pottery is made.

prac·ti·cal /prak′ti·kəl/ *adj.* **1** Having to do with actual use rather than theory: a *practical* knowledge of farming. **2** Useful; functional: a *practical* gadget. **3** Realistic; sensible: a *practical* individual.—**prac′ti·cal′i·ty** *n.*

pre·cious /presh′əs/ *adj.* **1** Highly prized or valuable: a *precious* stone. **2** Cherished; beloved: Freedom is a *precious* gift.

pre·cip·i·ta·tion /pri·sip′ə·tā′shən/ *n.* **1** The falling of rain, snow, sleet, hail, etc., on the earth; also, the amount that falls. **2** The process of separating a solid substance from a solution.

pre·cise /pri·sīs′/ *adj.* **1** Exact; accurate. **2** Very careful; strict about rules: *precise* about her diction. **3** Particular; exact: the *precise* moment.

pre·dict·a·ble /pri·dikt′ə·bəl/ *adj.* Capable of being predicted, known, or declared in advance.—**pre·dict′a·bly** *adv.*

pre·dic·tion /pri·dik′shən/ *n.* **1** The act of stating or foretelling what will happen. **2** The thing that is stated or foretold; a prophecy: a *prediction* about the future.

pre·dom·i·nant /pri·dom′ə·nənt/ *adj.* Superior in power, effect, etc.; prevailing; prominent.—**pre·dom′i·nant·ly** *adv.*

pref·er·a·ble /pref′ər·ə·bəl *or* pref′rə·bəl/ *adj.* Fit or worthy to be chosen; more desirable.

pre·lim·i·nar·y /pri·lim′ə·ner′ē/ *adj., n., pl.* **pre·lim·i·nar·ies** **1** *adj.* Preceding the main event or part, etc.: *preliminary* meeting. **2** *n.* Something that comes before or precedes as an introductory step.

prep·a·ra·tion /prep′ə·rā′shən/ *n.* **1** The act of preparing or being prepared; readiness. **2** Something done in order to get ready: party *preparations.* **3** Something made or prepared.

pre·scrip·tion /pri·skrip′shən/ *n.* **1** A doctor's formula for the preparation and use of a medicine. **2** The medicine itself. **3** Anything prescribed as a rule or direction: a *prescription* for success.

pres·i·dent /prez′ə·dənt/ *n.* **1** A person chosen to direct an organized body, as a college, club, etc.: Jane was elected class *president.* **2** (*often written* **President**) The chief executive of a nation.

pre·tend /pri·tend′/ *v.* **1** To make believe. **2** To give a false impression: to *pretend* to be sorry.

pre·tense /pri·tens′ *or* prē′tens/ *n.* A false act or show of something.

pri·ma·ry /prī′mer·ē/ *adj., n., pl.* **pri·ma·ries** **1** *adj.* First in time or order; basic. **2** *adj.* Most important; chief; main: a *primary* reason. **3** *n.* A preliminary election in which major parties choose their candidates for the main election: Did you vote for her in the *primary?*

pri·or /prī′ər/ *adj.* Coming before in time, order, or importance; earlier; previous: He cannot come because he has a *prior* engagement.

pri·or·i·ty /prī·ôr′ə·tē/ *n., pl.* **pri·or·i·ties** Something that is considered to be first in importance or in order: You must establish your *priorities.*

pris·on·er /priz′(ə)n·ər/ *n.* **1** A person confined in a prison. **2** A person who is held captive.

pri·vate /prī′vit/ **1** *adj.* Not intended for public use: a *private* park. **2** *adj.* Personal; intimate: *private* conversation. **3** *n.* A military rank. **4** *adj.* Secret; not known to the public: *private* information.

priv·i·lege /priv'ə·lij *or* priv'lij/ *n., v.* **priv·i·leged, priv·i·leg·ing** **1** *n.* A special benefit or right. **2** *v.* To grant a special benefit or right to. **3** *adj. use:* a *privileged* individual.

prob·a·bly /prob'ə·blē/ *adj.* Very likely.

pro·ce·dure /prə·sē'jər/ *n.* A way of proceeding; a method followed in doing something.

pro·ces·sion /prə·sesh'ən/ *n.* A line or body of persons or things proceeding in an orderly or formal succession. ► *Procession* comes from Latin *pro-,* "forward," and *cedere,* "to go."

prod·uct /prod'əkt/ *n.* **1** A thing made or produced by growth, labor, study, skill, etc.: a new cleaning *product.* **2** In math, the result obtained by multiplication.

pro·gress /*n.* prog'res, *v.* prə·gres'/ **1** *n.* A moving forward; an accomplishment or development: *progress* in your studies. **2** *v.* To move forward; to advance: to *progress* in your work. ► *Progress* comes from Latin *pro-,* "forward," and *gradi,* "to go."

proj·ect /*n.* proj'ekt, *v.* prə·jekt'/ **1** *n.* A special task or undertaking planned or devised: a school *project.* **2** *v.* To throw, cast, or extend forward or out: The stone *projects* from the wall. **3** *v.* To cast an image onto a surface: to *project* slides on a screen.

pro·jec·tor /prə·jek'tər/ *n.* A machine that casts or projects images, as slides or movies, onto a screen. ► *Projector* comes from Latin *pro-,* "forward," and *jacere,* "to throw."

prompt /prompt/ **1** *adj.* Right on time. **2** *adj.* Done without delay: Give *prompt* attention. **3** *v.* To urge or induce: to *prompt* a discussion.

pro·pel /prə·pel'/ *v.* **pro·pelled, pro·pel·ling** To drive, urge, or cause to move forward.

proph·et /prof'it/ *n.* **1** A person who speaks or writes about a divine or spiritual message. **2** A person who foretells the future. ► *Prophet* comes from the Greek word *prophetes,* "one who advocates."

pro·por·tion /prə·pôr'shən/ *n.* **1** The relative size, number, or degree between things; ratio: the *proportion* of food to people. **2** Balance: The flowers are in *proportion* to the vase. **3** A share or amount: a large *proportion* of people. **4** In math, the relationship of four numbers when the quotient of one pair equals the quotient of the other pair: $10 \div 5 = 4 \div 2$ is a *proportion.*

pros·e·cute /pros'ə·kyo͞ot/ *v.* **pros·e·cut·ed, pros·e·cut·ing** To put on trial for breaking the law: to *prosecute* a criminal.

pro·to·plasm /prō'tə·plaz'əm/ *n.* A thick grayish substance essential in all plant and animal cells, regarded as the physical basis for life.

pro·trude /prō·tro͞od'/ *v.* **pro·trud·ed, pro·trud·ing** To project; to jut out; to bulge. ► *Protrude* comes from Latin *pro-,* "forward," and *trudere,* "to thrust."

pro·vide /prə·vīd'/ *v.* **pro·vid·ed, pro·vid·ing** **1** To prepare beforehand: to *provide* for an emergency. **2** To supply, give, equip, or furnish: to *provide* medicine. ► *Provide* comes from Latin *pro-,* "forward," and *videre,* "to see."

prowl /proul/ *v.* To move about in a sly way.

psalm /säm/ *n.* A hymn or poem of praise. ► *Psalm* comes from Greek *psalmos,* "the plucking of a harp."

psy·chol·o·gy /sī·kol'ə·jē/ *n., pl.* **psy·chol·o·gies** The study of the mind or of mental states or behavior. ► *Psychology* comes from Greek *psyche,* "soul," and *-logy,* "study of."

pulse /puls/ **1** *n.* The regular throbbing of the arteries caused by contractions of the heart. **2** *n.* Any regular throbbing.

pu·ri·fy /pyo͝or'ə·fī/ *v.* **pu·ri·fied, pu·ri·fy·ing** To make or become clean or pure: The water has been *purified.*

act, āte, câre, ärt; egg, ēven; if, īce; on, ōver, ôr; bo͝ok, fo͞od; up, tûrn; ə=a in *ago,* e in *listen,* i in *giraffe,* o in *pilot,* u in *circus;* yo͞o=u in *music;* oil; out; chair; sing; shop; thank; that; zh in *treasure.*

pur·suit /pər·s(y)o͞ot′/ *n.* **1** A chase. **2** Any regular occupation, hobby, or sport: Tennis and photography are only two of her many *pursuits.* **3** An effort to attain something: the *pursuit* of freedom.

pyr·a·mid /pir′ə·mid/ *n.* **1** A solid geometrical figure having a flat base with three triangular sides that meet at the top. **2** Any of the huge monuments shaped like a pyramid in which ancient Egyptian rulers were buried.

Q

quad·ri·lat·er·al /kwod′rə·lat′ər·əl/ **1** *n.* Any closed figure or shape bounded by four straight lines. **2** *adj.* Four-sided.

qual·i·fy /kwol′ə·fī/ *v.* **qual·i·fied, qual·i·fy·ing** To have the needed ability; to be suitable, as for a job, a school, etc.

qui·et /kwī′ət/ **1** *adj.* Having or making little or no noise: a *quiet* machine. **2** *adj.* Without stress; calm: a *quiet* activity. **3** *v.* To make quiet: I *quieted* the crying child. *Syn.*: silence.

quite /kwīt/ *adv.* **1** Completely; very much. **2** Really; truly: *quite* capable.

R

ra·cial /rā′shəl/ *adj.* Of or having to do with race, ancestry, or origin.

ra·di·us /rā′dē·əs/ *n., pl.* **ra·di·i** **1** A straight line extending from the center of a circle to the circumference. **2** A circular area or boundary measured by the length of the radius: a *radius* of 20 miles. *Alternate plural:* **radiuses.** ▶ *Radius* is a Latin word meaning "ray" or "spoke."

ras·cal /ras′kəl/ *n.* **1** An unprincipled or dishonest person. **2** A mischievous child or animal. *Syn.*: scoundrel.

rasp·ber·ry /raz′ber′ē/ *n., pl.* **rasp·ber·ries** **1** A small, soft, round, red or black fruit, full of seeds. **2** The prickly bush on which this fruit grows.

re·al·ize /rē′əl·īz/ *v.* **re·al·ized, re·al·iz·ing** **1** To grasp, understand, or appreciate clearly and fully. **2** To achieve: to *realize* success.

rea·son·a·ble /rē′zən·ə·bəl/ *adj.* **1** Having, using, or exhibiting reason or fairness; sensible. **2** Moderate or fair in price.

reb·el *n.* or **re·bel** *v./n.* reb′əl, *v.* ri·bel′/ *n., v.* **re·belled, re·bel·ling** **1** *n.* An individual who resists or refuses to submit to authority, a governing power, etc., and fights against it. **2** *adj. use:* a *rebel* army. **3** *v.* To rise up against an authority, a governing power, etc.

4 *v.* To resist or feel opposition toward: He *rebelled* against the dress code.

re·ces·sive /ri·ses′iv/ *adj.* **1** Tending to go or move back; receding. **2** Less active or strong than an opposing hereditary characteristic or trait: a *recessive* gene.

rec·og·nize /rek′əg·nīz/ *v.* **rec·og·nized, rec·og·niz·ing** **1** To identify or to be aware of someone or something as having been previously seen or known. **2** To express appreciation for: to *recognize* his abilities. **3** To acknowledge or accept; to realize: to *recognize* the problem.

rec·om·mend /rek′ə·mend′/ *v.* **1** To praise or speak in favor of: I *recommend* this book. **2** To advise or suggest: She *recommended* that we call the police.

re·cord /*v.* ri·kôrd′, *n., adj.* rek′ərd/ **1** *v.* To write down information for future use. **2** *v.* To show or indicate: The thermometer *recorded* a temperature of 102°. **3** *v.* To store sound on a tape or disk. **4** *n.* A disk that can be played on a phonograph. **5** *n.* Preserved information about things that have happened: school *records.* **6** *n.* The greatest achievement of its kind, as in sports. **7** *adj.* Better or greater than all others: a *record* rainfall.—**break the record** To do or be better than the best that has been achieved.

rec·tan·gle /rek′tang′gəl/ *n.* A parallelogram all of whose angles are right angles.

re·cur /ri·kûr′/ *v.* **re·curred, re·cur·ring** To happen or occur over and over at regular intervals.—**re·cur′rence** *n.*

re·duc·tion /ri·duk′shən/ *n.* **1** The act or condition of reducing or making less. **2** Anything that has been reduced or made less: a price *reduction.* **3** The amount by which something is reduced or made less: a 5% *reduction* in expenses.

ref·er·ence /ref′ər·əns *or* ref′rəns/ *n.* **1** The act of referring or mentioning: in *reference* to your suggestion. **2** Something, as a statement, passage, etc., that is a source of information. **3** Something that provides information: A dictionary is a book of *reference.* **4** *adj. use:* a *reference* book.

re·fin·er·y /ri·fī′nər·ē/ *n., pl.* **re·fin·er·ies** An establishment where crude materials are refined or purified: an oil *refinery.*

re·fract /ri·frakt′/ *v.* To cause refraction, or the shifting of the direction of a ray of light or other energy as it passes from one substance into another: Light is *refracted* when it passes from air into water.

refrigerate   **retract**

re·frig·er·ate /ri·frij′ə·rāt/ *v.* **re·frig·er·at·ed, re·frig·er·at·ing** To make or keep very cold.

ref·uge /ref′yo͞oj/ *n.* Shelter or protection from danger, trouble, etc. *Syn.:* sanctuary.

reg·u·lar /reg′yə·lər/ *adj.* **1** Even, smooth, or balanced: a *regular* pattern. **2** Usual; habitual: a *regular* routine. **3** Always happening at the same time: *regular* meetings. **4** In grammar, having or following the most common forms and endings: *regular* verbs.

reg·u·lar·i·ty /reg′yə·lar′ə·tē/ *n., pl.* **reg·u·lar·i·ties** The condition or quality of being regular, steady, or systematic.

reign /rān/ **1** *v.* To rule or govern. **2** *n.* The period or time during which a sovereign rules or governs.

rel·a·tive /rel′ə·tiv/ **1** *n.* A member of one's family, connected by blood or marriage. **2** *adj.* Having meaning only in relation to something else: The words *high* and *low* have *relative* meanings.

re·li·a·ble /ri·lī′ə·bəl/ *adj.* Able to be trusted; dependable.—**re·li·a·bly** *adv.* ▶ *Reliable* comes from Latin *re-*, "back," and *ligare,* "to bind or tie."

re·me·di·al /ri·mē′dē·əl/ *adj.* Serving to remedy, relieve, or make better.

rem·e·dy /rem′ə·dē/ *n., pl.* **rem·e·dies,** *v.* **rem·e·died, rem·e·dy·ing** **1** *n.* Something that cures, relieves, or corrects. **2** *v.* To cure, relieve, or make right: A hearty meal *remedied* our hunger.

ren·o·vate /ren′ə·vāt/ *v.* **ren·o·vat·ed, ren·o·vat·ing** To make like new; to repair.

re·or·gan·ize /rē·ôr′gən·īz/ *v.* **re·or·gan·ized, re·or·gan·iz·ing** To organize again or rearrange in a certain order.

re·pel /ri·pel′/ *v.* **re·pelled, re·pel·ling** **1** To force or drive back. **2** To cause someone to draw back in disgust.

rep·li·ca /rep′lə·kə/ *n.* **1** A copy or reproduction of a work of art, especially by the original artist. **2** Any close or exact copy or reproduction of something: At the museum, we saw a *replica* of an Egyptian tomb.

res·cue /res′kyo͞o/ *v.* **res·cued, res·cu·ing,** *n.* **1** *v.* To save or free from danger, confinement, etc. **2** *n.* The act of saving from danger, confinement, etc.

re·sem·blance /ri·zem′bləns/ *n.* The quality or state of being similar, especially in appearance; likeness.

re·side /ri·zīd′/ *v.* **re·sid·ed, re·sid·ing** To make one's home; to dwell; to live.

res·i·dence /rez′ə·dəns/ *n.* The place where a person lives; home; dwelling.

res·i·den·tial /rez′ə·den′shəl/ *adj.* Of or pertaining to a home or homes.

re·sis·tance /ri·zis′təns/ *n.* **1** The act of resisting, opposing, or withstanding: *resistance* to change. **2** The power or force of one thing resisting or opposing another: a metal's *resistance* to rust.

re·spect·ful /ri·spekt′fəl/ *adj.* Showing respect in a manner that exhibits regard, honor, or consideration; polite.—**re·spect′ful·ly** *adv.*

re·spec·tive·ly /ri·spek′tiv·lē/ *adv.* In the order given: The red and the yellow books belong to Eva and Meredith *respectively.*

re·spon·si·ble /ri·spon′sə·bəl/ *adj.* **1** Obliged to take care of, as a duty, trust, etc. **2** Deserving credit or blame; accountable: *responsible* for the damage. **3** Having to do with trust or importance. **4** Reliable; trustworthy: A baby sitter should be a *responsible* person.

res·tau·rant /res′tə·ränt *or* res′tränt *or* res′tər·ənt/ *n.* A public place where meals are sold and served.

res·to·ra·tion /res′tə·rā′shən/ *n.* **1** The act of restoring or bringing back to a former or original state or condition: *restoration* of health. **2** Something that is restored: Sturbridge Village is an interesting *restoration* of a Colonial town.

re·tract /ri·trakt′/ *v.* **1** To pull in or to draw back into: The turtle *retracted* into its shell. **2** To take back: to *retract* a statement.

---

act, āte, câre, ärt;   egg, ēven;   if, īce;   on, ōver, ôr;   bo͞ok, fo͞od;   up, tûrn;
ə=a in *ago,* e in *listen,* i in *giraffe,* o in *pilot,* u in *circus;*   yo͞o=u in *music;*   oil;   out;
chair; sing; shop; thank; that; zh in *treasure.*

reveal

scribble

re·veal /ri·vēl′/ v. 1 To make known: to *reveal* a secret. 2 To make visible: The door opened to *reveal* a crowd of people.

re·verse /ri·vûrs′/ adj., v. **re·versed, re·vers·ing,** n. 1 adj. Having the back or rear part facing the observer: the *reverse* side of a fabric. 2 v. To turn inside out or upside down: to *reverse* a sleeping bag. 3 n. The back or rear side of something: the *reverse* of a page. 4 v. To turn in the opposite direction: to *reverse* a car. 5 v. To change into something completely different or the opposite of: to *reverse* a verdict. 6 n. (usually pl.) A change for the worse; a misfortune: to suffer *reverses*.

re·vers·i·ble /ri·vûr′sə·bəl/ adj. 1 Finished on both sides so that either side may be the outside: My jacket is *reversible*. 2 Able to go either forward or backward: a *reversible* chemical process.

re·vert /ri·vûrt′/ v. To go or return to a former condition, habit, belief, etc.: He *reverted* to his former attitude.

re·vise /ri·vīz′/ v. **re·vised, re·vis·ing** 1 To amend, correct, or change: to *revise* an essay. 2 To change: We had to *revise* our vacation plans three times.

rev·o·lu·tion·ar·y /rev′ə·lōo′shən·er′ē/ adj., n., pl. **rev·o·lu·tion·ar·ies** 1 adj. Having to do with or causing a revolution or revolt: *revolutionary* speech. 2 adj. Causing or creating a radical change: a *revolutionary* discovery. 3 n. A person that participates in a revolt. 4 adj. Rotating or revolving: *revolutionary* motion. 5 n. (written **Revolutionary**) Of or having to do with the war for American independence.

rhi·noc·e·ros /rī·nos′ər·əs/ n., pl. **rhi·noc·e·ros·es** A large, heavy, thick-skinned, plant-eating mammal, found in Africa and Asia, having one or two upright horns on its snout: People liked the *rhinoceros* in the zoo. *Alternate plural:* **rhinoceros.** ► *Rhinoceros* comes from Greek *rhino-,* "nose," and *keras,* "horn."

rhythm /rith′əm/ n. 1 The repetition of a beat or accent in a uniform or patterned way: *rhythm* of drums. 2 The pattern or arrangement of musical sounds or of the syllables in poetry. ► *Rhythm* comes from the Greek word *rhythmos,* "a flowing," which comes from *rhein,* "to flow."

ri·val /rī′vəl/ n., v. **ri·valed, ri·val·ing** 1 n. A competitor; a foe. 2 adj. use: a *rival* chess player. 3 v. To try to excel or outdo: Ed *rivaled* Ann in spelling. 4 v. To be the equal of: Nothing can *rival* skiing down a mountain. *Syn.:* foe. *Alternate spellings:* **rivalled, rivalling.**

ro·tate /rō′tāt/ v. **ro·tat·ed, ro·tat·ing** 1 To turn or cause to turn on an axis. 2 To alternate: Farmers *rotate* crops.

ru·mor /rōo′mər/ 1 n. Information that is not necessarily true but is spread from one person to another; gossip. 2 v. To tell as a rumor.

s

sanc·tu·ar·y /sangk′chōo·er′ē/ n., pl. **sanc·tu·ar·ies** 1 A holy or sacred place, especially a church or the place in a church around the main altar. 2 A haven or shelter for people or animals. *Syn.:* refuge.

sat·el·lite /sat′ə·līt/ n. 1 A celestial body that orbits or follows a planet or star, such as the moon. 2 An object launched by means of a rocket into an orbit around a celestial body, and used for research, communications, and weather prediction. 3 A small country that is politically and economically controlled by another more powerful country.

sat·u·rate /sach′ə·rāt/ v. **sat·u·rat·ed, sat·u·rat·ing** 1 To soak or fill thoroughly or completely: The rain *saturated* my coat. 2 To cause to absorb a substance so that no more can be added or taken in: to *saturate* a solution with sugar.

scen·er·y /sē′nər·ē/ n. 1 The natural features of a landscape. 2 Materials used on a stage to represent various scenes.

scrap¹ /skrap/ n., v. **scrapped, scrap·ping** 1 n. A small piece; fragment. 2 v. To throw out or abandon as useless: The rain caused us to *scrap* our plans to visit the park.

scrap² /skrap/ v. **scrapped, scrap·ping,** n. 1 v. To fight or quarrel. 2 n. A quarrel.

scrib·ble /skrib′əl/ v. **scrib·bled, scrib·bling,** n. 1 v. To write in a hasty or careless way: to *scribble* a quick note. 2 v. To make meaningless marks on paper; to doodle. 3 n. Careless or uncontrolled writing.

sec·on·dar·y /sek′ən·der′ē/ *adj.* **1** Coming next after that which is first or primary: *secondary* school. **2** Derived or originating from that which is primary or basic: *secondary* sources.

seg·ment /seg′mənt/ **1** *n.* A section, piece, or part: a *segment* of the pie. **2** *v.* To cut or divide into sections, pieces, or parts. **3** *n.* A section separated from a figure, especially a circular one, by a line. **4** *n.* A section of a line.

seis·mo·graph /sīz′mə·graf/ *n.* An instrument that records the length, direction, and intensity of earthquakes and other vibrations in the earth.

seize /sēz/ *v.* **seized, seiz·ing** **1** To take hold of suddenly or with force; to grasp. **2** To capture or arrest: to *seize* a thief. **3** To capture or take possession of by force. **4** To take advantage of an opportunity: to *seize* a chance.

sem·i·fi·nal·ist /sem′ē·fī′nəl·ist/ *n.* A person who participates in the next-to-last round or match in a contest.

sense /sens/ *n., v.* **sensed, sens·ing** **1** *n.* One of the powers by which an organism becomes aware of things; sight, hearing, touch, smell, or taste. **2** *n.* An awareness or understanding: a *sense* of justice. **3** *v.* To become aware of: to *sense* danger. **4** *n.* (*often pl.*) Good judgment: to come to your *senses*. **5** *n.* The meaning of something, as a word, phrase, or sentence.

sen·si·ble /sen′sə·bəl/ *adj.* Having or showing good sense or good judgment.

sen·si·tive /sen′sə·tiv/ *adj.* **1** Easily upset or angered; touchy: a *sensitive* personality. **2** Tender or painful: *sensitive* skin. **3** Capable of feeling, reacting, appreciating, etc., quickly or easily: My eyes are *sensitive* to light.

sep·a·rate /*v.* sep′ə·rāt, *adj.* sep′ər·ət *or* sep′rət/ *v.* **sep·a·rat·ed, sep·a·rat·ing,** *adj.* **1** *v.* To move or pull apart; to divide.

2 *adj.* Not connected; detached: in *separate* countries. **3** *adj.* Not shared; individual: My sister and I have *separate* rooms. **4** *v.* To keep apart by being between; to divide: The river *separates* the two towns.

shriv·el /shriv′əl/ *v.* **shriv·eled, shriv·el·ing** To wither; to shrink and dry up. *Alternate spellings:* **shrivelled, shrivelling.**

shrub·ber·y /shrub′ər·ē/ *n., pl.* **shrub·ber·ies** A group of shrubs or bushes, such as those in a garden or around a lawn.

sig·nal /sig′nəl/ *n., v.* **sig·naled, sig·nal·ing** **1** *n.* Something that serves to warn, direct, or give instruction, as a light, gesture, etc. **2** *v.* To make a signal. **3** *n.* An electric current transmitted or received: a radio *signal*. **4** *v.* To make known by a signal: The bell *signals* lunch. *Alternate spellings:* **signalled, signalling.**

sig·ni·fy /sig′nə·fī/ *v.* **sig·ni·fied, sig·ni·fy·ing** **1** To make known or express by signs, words, or actions. **2** To be an indication of: The tolling bell *signified* victory.

si·lence /sī′ləns/ *n., v.* **si·lenced, si·lenc·ing** **1** *n.* Stillness; quiet: *silence* of the night. **2** *n.* A period of remaining silent, without noise or talking. **3** *v.* To make quiet: to *silence* a bell. **4** *v.* To suppress: to *silence* gossip.

sil·hou·ette /sil′oo·et′/ *n., v.* **sil·hou·et·ted, sil·hou·et·ting** **1** *n.* A portrait of a person or object in outline form, cut from a dark paper or filled in with a dark color. **2** *n.* The outline of a person or thing shown against a light or a light background. **3** *v.* To show or appear in silhouette.

sim·i·lar /sim′ə·lər/ *adj.* Very much alike, but not completely the same. *Syn.:* alike.

---

act, āte, câre, ärt;   egg, ēven;   if, īce;   on, ōver, ôr;   bŏŏk, fōōd;   up, tûrn;
ə=a in *ago,* e in *listen,* i in *giraffe,* o in *pilot,* u in *circus;*   yōō=u in *music;*   oil;   out;
chair; sing; shop; thank; that; zh in *treasure.*

sim·pli·fy /sim′plə·fī/ *v.* **sim·pli·fied, sim·pli·fy·ing** To make less complicated; to streamline: to *simplify* plans.

si·mul·ta·ne·ous /sī′məl·tā′nē·əs/ *adj.* Existing or done at the same time.

si·phon /sī′fən/ **1** *n.* A bent tube that is used to transfer liquid out of one container into another by means of air pressure and gravity. **2** *v.* To draw out using a siphon.

site /sīt/ *n.* The place where something is or was situated or located: Cooperstown, New York, is the *site* of the Baseball Hall of Fame.

skel·e·tal /skel′ə·təl/ *adj.* Of, having to do with, forming, or resembling a skeleton.

sliv·er /sliv′ər/ **1** *n.* A long, slender piece cut or broken off something; splinter. **2** *v.* To cut, split, or break into slivers.

sol·emn /sol′əm/ *adj.* **1** Majestic; impressive: a *solemn* event. **2** Serious; earnest: a *solemn* mood. **3** Having a religious character; sacred: a *solemn* ritual. **4** Somber; gloomy: a *solemn* person.

so·lem·ni·ty /sə·lem′nə·tē/ *n., pl.* **so·lem·ni·ties** The state or character of being solemn or serious.

soothe /sooth/ *v.* **soothed, sooth·ing 1** To calm; to relieve: to *soothe* a crying child. **2** To have a calming or relieving effect: Quiet music *soothes* me. **3** *adj. use:* a *soothing* melody.

soph·o·more /sof′(ə·)môr/ *n.* A student in the second year of high school or college.

spa·cious /spā′shəs/ *adj.* Having lots of open space; roomy: a *spacious* apartment.

spe·cial /spesh′əl/ *adj.* **1** Of a particular or distinctive nature. **2** Having a particular purpose or function: a *special* lock. **3** Great; very dear: a *special* relative.

spe·cial·ize /spesh′əl·īz/ *v.* **spe·cial·ized, spe·cial·iz·ing 1** To concentrate on or pursue one particular activity or subject. **2** *adj. use:* a *specialized* instrument.— **spe′cial·ist** *n.*

spec·i·fy /spes′ə·fī/ *v.* **spec·i·fied, spec·i·fy·ing** To indicate definitely and specifically: *Specify* the exact color.

spec·tac·u·lar /spek·tak′yə·lər/ *adj.* **1** Amazing to see: a *spectacular* view. **2** Very elaborate; on a grand scale: a *spectacular* circus.

spec·ta·tor /spek′tā·tər/ *n.* A person who watches an event but does not take part in it; observer.

spec·u·la·tion /spek′yə·lā′shən/ *n.* **1** The act of speculating, meditating, or forming theories about something. **2** An unproved the-

ory or guess: *speculation* about life on other planets. **3** A risky investment of money: real estate *speculation*.

sphere /sfir/ *n.* **1** A surface curved evenly around a single center point; globe; ball. **2** A range, scope, or field: a *sphere* of knowledge.

spi·nal /spī′nəl/ *adj.* Of or having to do with the spine or backbone.

spir·it /spir′it/ *n.* **1** The life-giving or inner force of a human being, as the mind or the soul. **2** A divine or supreme being. **3** A supernatural being, as a ghost, goblin, etc. **4** Liveliness; vigor; courage: a person of *spirit*. **5** *(pl.)* Feeling or mood: in good *spirits*. **6** Vigorous sense of devotion or loyalty: team *spirit*.

sprawl /sprôl/ *v.* **1** To sit or lie with legs and arms spread out. **2** To spread out: The city *sprawls* over three counties.

sta·di·um /stā′dē·əm/ *n., pl.* **sta·di·ums** A large structure with tiers of seats for spectators built around a playing field. *Alternate plural:* **stadia.** ► *Stadium* is a Latin spelling of the Greek word *stadion,* "a length of 600 feet."

sta·tion·ar·y /stā′shən·er′ē/ *adj.* Staying or keeping in one place; not moving or movable. *Syn.:* immobile.

sta·tion·er·y /stā′shən·er′ē/ *n.* Materials used in writing, especially letter paper and envelopes.

stat·ue /stach′oo/ *n.* A likeness of a person, animal, etc., that is carved, molded, or cast; figurine.

stat·ute /stach′oot/ *n.* A rule or law, usually presented in a formal document: Village *statutes* prohibit camping in public parks.

ste·nog·ra·pher /stə·nog′rə·fər/ *n.* A person who takes dictation, usually in shorthand, a rapid type of writing that uses symbols to stand for letters, words, or phrases.

ster·il·ize /ster′əl·īz/ *v.* **ster·il·ized, ster·il·iz·ing** To free from bacteria or germs, usually by heating to a high temperature: to *sterilize* an infant's bottle.

stom·ach /stum′ək/ *n.* A bag or pouch in the digestive tract used for storing, diluting, and digesting food.

strait /strāt/ *n.* **1** A narrow body of water connecting two larger bodies of water. **2** *(often pl.)* A condition of distress, trouble, etc.: in dire *straits*.

strat·e·gy /strat′ə·jē/ *n., pl.* **strat·e·gies** The careful planning and working out of a course of action in order to achieve some goal.

strength /streng(k)th/ *n.* **1** The quality of being strong; bodily or mental power or force. **2** The ability to resist a force or strain without bending or breaking. **3** Effectiveness: the *strength* of a drug.

stren·u·ous /stren′yoo·əs/ *adj.* Requiring much effort, energy, or work: a *strenuous* activity. *Syn.*: rugged, exhausting.

stun /stun/ *v.* **stunned, stun·ning** **1** To knock unconscious; to make dizzy. **2** To shock or astonish.

stun·ning /stun′ing/ *adj.* **1** Causing unconsciousness. **2** Extremely beautiful, stylish, etc.: a *stunning* outfit.

stu·pe·fy /st(y)oo′pə·fī/ *v.* **stu·pe·fied, stu·pe·fy·ing** To dull the senses or the capabilities of: *stupefied* with fright.

sub·merge /səb·mûrj′/ *v.* **sub·merged, sub·merg·ing** **1** To put or sink below the surface of water or any liquid. **2** To cover with water: The valley was *submerged* by the flood.

sub·scrip·tion /səb·skrip′shən/ *n.* An agreement that a person will receive a certain number of issues of a publication, etc.

sub·si·dize /sub′sə·dīz/ *v.* **sub·si·dized, sub·si·diz·ing** To support, aid, or assist with money, as a grant, etc.

sub·stan·tial /səb·stan′shəl/ *adj.* **1** Having substance or being of an actual, material, or real quality: *substantial* evidence. **2** Of a solid, firm, or strong quality: a *substantial* fabric. **3** Of ample amount, quantity, size, etc.; considerable: *substantial* progress.— **sub·stan′tial·ly** *adv.*

sub·sti·tute /sub′stə·t(y)oot/ *n., v.* **sub·sti·tut·ed, sub·sti·tut·ing** **1** *n.* A person or thing that takes the place of someone or something else; an alternate. **2** *v.* To be or act as a substitute or alternate. **3** *v.* To replace or use in place of: to *substitute* milk for cream.

sub·tle /sut′(ə)l/ *adj.* **sub·tler, sub·tlest** **1** Not obvious; hard to comprehend: I only noticed a *subtle* difference. **2** Delicate: a *subtle* taste.

sub·trac·tion /səb·trak′shən/ *n.* The act of removing or taking away, especially a part from a whole or one number from another in arithmetic; deduction.

sub·urb /sub′ûrb/ *n.* **1** An area, as a town, village, etc., that is close to a large city. **2** *(pl.)* The area outside a city; outskirts: Many people commute from the *suburbs*.

suc·cumb /sə·kum′/ *v.* **1** To give in or give way to force; to yield: The governor did not *succumb* to the demands. **2** To yield to disease, age, etc.; to die.

sul·len /sul′ən/ *adj.* Gloomily silent; resentful; ill-humored. *Syn.*: sulky: Paul was very *sullen* tonight.

su·per·fi·cial /soo′pər·fish′əl/ *adj.* **1** Of, on, or affecting only the surface; not deep: a *superficial* cut. **2** Concerned with what is on the surface or obvious; not profound; shallow: a *superficial* remark.—**su′per·fi′cial·ly** *adv.*

su·per·sti·tious /soo′pər·stish′əs/ *adj.* Having to do with superstition or the unreasoning fear or belief that certain objects, places, or actions have power over the normal course of nature: Paul is a *superstitious* person.— **su′per·sti′tious·ly** *adv.*

su·per·vise /soo′pər·viz/ *v.* **su·per·vised, su·per·vis·ing** To oversee or manage: Gail will *supervise* the group today.

sup·press /sə·pres′/ *v.* **1** To put an end to or subdue by force: to *suppress* a revolt. **2** To keep in; to repress; to keep from becoming known: to *suppress* a laugh. ► *Suppress* comes from Latin *sup- (sub-)*, "under," and *premere*, "to press."

sur·ger·y /sûr′jər·ē/ *n.* **1** The branch of medicine that is concerned with the repair or removal of diseased parts of the body: heart *surgery*. **2** A surgical operation: She had *surgery* done on her foot. **3** A room or place for surgical operations: They wheeled the patient into *surgery*.

sur·mise /sər·mīz′/ *n., v.* **sur·mised, sur·mis·ing** **1** *n.* An opinion based on a small amount of evidence. **2** *v.* To form such an opinion; to guess: to *surmise* that a problem exists.

---

act, āte, câre, ärt; egg, ēven; if, īce; on, ōver, ôr; book, food; up, tûrn;
ə=**a** in *ago*, **e** in *listen*, **i** in *giraffe*, **o** in *pilot*, **u** in *circus*; y**oo**=**u** in *music*; oil; out;
chair; sing; shop; thank; that; zh in *treasure*.

surprise

sur·prise /sə(r)·prīz'/ *v.* **sur·prised, sur·pris·ing,** *n.* **1** *v.* To shock or astonish by doing something unexpected. **2** *adj. use: surprising* results. **3** *n.* The feeling caused by something unexpected; astonishment. **4** *n.* Something that causes surprise. **5** *adj. use:* a *surprise* party.

sur·vey /*n.* sûr'vā, *v.* sər·vā'/ **1** *n.* An examination or study: a *survey* of consumer needs. **2** *v.* To look over or examine, as from a height: to *survey* the situation. **3** *v.* To measure land and determine boundaries: *survey* the wilderness.

sus·pect /*v.* sə·spekt', *n.* sus'pekt/ **1** *v.* To believe something or someone is bad, wrong, or guilty without actual proof. **2** *n.* A person thought to be guilty of a crime. **3** *v.* To think something is likely: I *suspect* it will rain.

sus·pense /sə·spens'/ *n.* A state or condition in which there is a great deal of uncertainty or excitement about what is going to happen: I liked the detective story because it was filled with *suspense.*

sus·pi·cious /sə·spish'əs/ *adj.* **1** Tending to suspect; distrustful: a *suspicious* nature. **2** Likely to arouse suspicion; questionable: a *suspicious* alibi.—**sus·pi'cious·ly** *adv.*

syl·lab·i·ca·tion /si·lab'ə·kā'shən/ *n.* The division of a word into syllables.

syl·la·ble /sil'ə·bəl/ *n.* A word or part of a word that has one vowel sound.

sym·bol /sim'bəl/ *n.* **1** Something that stands for something else: A heart is a *symbol* of love. **2** A mark or sign that has meaning, as letters, numbers, etc. *Syn.:* token.

sym·bol·ize /sim'bəl·īz/ *v.* **sym·bol·ized, sym·bol·iz·ing** To be a symbol or sign of; to represent: The white dove often *symbolizes* peace.

sym·met·ri·cal /si·met'ri·kəl/ *adj.* Having symmetry; arranged in such a way that every element in one half is balanced by a matching element in the other half; balanced: A snowflake is *symmetrical.*

sym·pa·thet·ic /sim'pə·thet'ik/ *adj.* **1** Showing sympathy or sharing someone else's emotions: *sympathetic* to her problems. **2** Showing approval; appreciative: a *sympathetic* audience. *Ant.:* antipathetic /an'ti·pə·thet'ik/—**sym'pa·thet'i·cal·ly** *adv.*

sym·pa·thize /sim'pə·thīz/ *v.* **sym·pa·thized, sym·pa·thiz·ing** **1** To share someone else's feelings: I *sympathize* with your problem. **2** To have or express compassion or understanding.

symp·tom /sim'təm/ *n.* Evidence of the existence of something; sign: Fever is a *symptom* of influenza.

syn·a·gogue /sin'ə·gôg/ *n.* A Jewish temple; a place of meeting for Jewish worship and religious instruction. ► *Synagogue* comes from Greek *syn-,* "together," and *agoge,* "gathering."

syn·chro·nize /sing'krə·nīz/ *v.* **syn·chro·nized, syn·chro·niz·ing** **1** To occur, coincide, or agree in time or speed. **2** To make timepieces indicate the same time: to *synchronize* your watches.

syn·o·nym /sin'ə·nim/ *n.* A word that has the same or almost the same meaning as another.

syn·op·sis /si·nop'sis/ *n., pl.* **syn·op·ses** /si·nop'sēz/ A brief summary that presents the main points of a story, play, etc.: The critic gave a *synopsis* of the movie.

syn·thet·ic /sin·thet'ik/ **1** *adj.* Made, usually by a chemical process, rather than occurring naturally; artificial: *synthetic* fuels. **2** *n.* Something synthetic: Nylon is a *synthetic.*—**syn·thet'i·cal·ly** *adv.* ► *Synthetic* comes from Greek *syn-,* "together," and *tithenai,* "to put."

T

tan·gent /tan'jənt/ **1** *adj.* Touching a curve at a single point but not crossing it. **2** *n.* A line that is tangent to a curve. **3** *n.* In a right triangle, the ratio of the side opposite a given angle to the side next to the angle.—**go off on a tangent** To move suddenly from one course of action or thought to another: During his speech, the senator *went off on a tangent* and talked about his vacation.

tel·e·gram /tel'ə·gram/ *n.* A message sent by telegraph.

telegraph   **traceable**

tel·e·graph /tel′ə·graf/ **1** *n.* A device for sending and receiving messages by means of a series of electrical pulses. **2** *v.* To send or receive a message by this device.

tel·e·vise /tel′ə·vīz/ *v.* **tel·e·vised, tel·e·vis·ing** To broadcast by means of television.

tem·per·a·men·tal /tem′prə·men′təl *or* tem′pər·ə·men′təl/ *adj.* **1** Of or having to do with temperament or disposition. **2** Easily excited or upset: Artists are often accused of being *temperamental.*

tem·per·a·ture /tem′pər·ə·chər *or* tem′prə·chər/ *n.* **1** The degree of warmth or coldness of an object or substance, as measured on a scale: The *temperature* of the air was 0° C. **2** Excessive body heat, especially in a human being; fever: The sick child had a high *temperature.*

tem·po·rar·y /tem′pə·rer′ē/ *adj.* Not lasting for a long time: a *temporary* job.

ten·den·cy /ten′dən·sē/ *n., pl.* **ten·den·cies** An inclination or leaning toward some condition, action, etc.: The actor had a *tendency* to forget his lines.

ten·don /ten′dən/ *n.* A band of tough tissue that holds a muscle and a bone together.

ter·mi·nate /tûr′mə·nāt/ *v.* **ter·mi·nat·ed, ter·mi·nat·ing** To bring to an end; to stop: The class *terminates* at noon.

ter·ri·fy /ter′ə·fī/ *v.* **ter·ri·fied, ter·ri·fy·ing** To fill with tremendous fear: The boy was *terrified* by the wasps.

the·o·rem /thē′ər·əm *or* thir′əm/ *n.* **1** A proposal, statement, or proposition that can be proved or is accepted as true. **2** In mathe-matics, a proposition that has been proved or is accepted as true.

the·o·ry /thē′ə·rē *or* thir′ē/ *n., pl.* **the·o·ries** **1** An idea that seems to explain a set of circumstances: the *theory* of gravity. **2** A set of principles upon which a branch of knowledge is based, as math, science, etc.: geometry *theories.* **3** An unproven opinion: It's only a *theory.*

ther·mal /thûr′məl/ *adj.* **1** Pertaining to, us-ing, or caused by heat. **2** Designed to pre-vent loss of body heat: *thermal* socks.

ther·mom·e·ter /thər·mom′ə·tər/ *n.* An in-strument for measuring temperature.

ther·mo·nu·cle·ar /thûr′mō·n(y)ōō′klē·ər/ *adj.* Of, pertaining to, or using a nuclear-fusion reaction at a high temperature, as in a hydrogen bomb.

ther·mos /thûr′məs/ *n.* (*also written* **Ther-mos**) A bottle or jug that keeps liquids hot or cold; a vacuum bottle: a trademark.

ther·mo·stat /thûr′mə·stat/ *n.* A device that establishes and maintains a certain temper-ature automatically.

thor·ough /thûr′ō/ *adj.* Complete, detailed, and careful in every respect: a *thorough* search.—**thor′ough·ly** *adv.*

threat·en /thret′(ə)n/ *v.* **1** To make or utter a threat or warning; to promise to hurt or punish. **2** To make such a warning or promise against. **3** To menace: Drought *threatened* the crops. **4** To give a warning; to signal: The skies *threatened* rain. *Syn.*: ominous. ► *Threaten* comes from the Old English word *threatian,* "to press or threaten."

throb /throb/ *v.* **throbbed, throb·bing** To beat with increased force or rapidity; to pul-sate.

through·out /thrōō·out′/ *adv., prep.* In or to every part of; all about: The noise was heard *throughout* the house.

tire·some /tīr′səm/ *adj.* Tedious; boring.

to·ken /tō′kən/ **1** *n.* Something meant to in-dicate or represent; symbol; sign: He gave flowers as a *token* of his respect. **2** *adj.* Done, given, or present merely to fulfill an obligation: a *token* smile. **3** *n.* A stamped piece of metal used in place of money, as for a fare.

trace·a·ble /trā′sə·bəl/ *adj.* Able to be traced or followed: *traceable* evidence.

---

act, āte, câre, ärt; egg, ēven; if, īce; on, ōver, ôr; bŏŏk, fŏŏd; up, tûrn;
ə=a in *ago*, e in *listen*, i in *giraffe*, o in *pilot*, u in *circus;* yŏŏ=u in *music;* oil; out;
  chair; sing; shop; thank; that; zh in *treasure.*

trait

vein

trait /trāt/ *n.* A particular quality or characteristic: a genetic *trait*.

trans·late /trans·lāt′ *or* tranz′lāt/ *v.* **trans·lat·ed, trans·lat·ing** To change something written or spoken from one language into another: She *translated* the story into Spanish.

treas·ur·y /trezh′ər·ē/ *n., pl.* **treas·ur·ies** 1 A place where the funds of a government, business, club, etc., are deposited, kept, and paid out: How much money is in the club's *treasury*? 2 (*written* **Treasury**) The department of the United States government that manages and distributes the country's money.

tre·men·dous /tri·men′dəs/ *adj.* 1 Enormous; huge. 2 Dreadful; terrible: a *tremendous* storm. 3 Wonderful: It was a *tremendous* performance. *Syn.:* huge, enormous, immense.

trib·u·tar·y /trib′yə·ter′ē/ *n., pl.* **trib·u·tar·ies** A stream feeding or flowing into a larger body of water: The Arkansas River is a *tributary* of the Mississippi.

triv·i·a /triv′ē·ə/ *n. pl.* Insignificant, inconsequential, or unimportant matters: The magazine contains a great deal of *trivia*.

trust·wor·thy /trust′wûr′thē/ *adj.* Worthy of confidence or trust; reliable: a *trustworthy* friend. ► *Trustworthy* comes from Old English *treowe*, "faithful, true," and *wyrthe*, "worthy."

twelfth or **12th** /twelfth/ 1 *adj.* Next after the eleventh. 2 *n.* The one that is next after the eleventh. 3 *adj.* Being one of twelve equal parts: a *twelfth* of the pie.

ty·ran·ni·cal /ti·ran′i·kəl/ *adj.* Unjustly cruel, harsh, or severe: Ivan the Terrible was a *tyrannical* ruler.

tyr·an·ny /tir′ə·nē/ *n., pl.* **tyr·an·nies** 1 A government wherein a sole ruler has absolute power. 2 Any oppressive, absolute control.

U

um·pire /um′pīr/ *n., v.* **um·pired, um·pir·ing** 1 *n.* A person who rules on plays in a sports contest, particularly baseball. 2 *v.* To act as an umpire of a game.

u·ni·fy /yoo′nə·fī/ *v.* **u·ni·fied, u·ni·fy·ing** To bring together; to unite.

un·nec·es·sar·y /un·nes′ə·ser′ē/ *adj.* Not needed or required; needless.

un·prof·it·a·ble /un·prof′it·ə·bəl/ *adj.* Yielding no profit or gain: an *unprofitable* business; an *unprofitable* search.

un·rav·el /un·rav′əl/ *v.* **un·rav·eled, un·rav·el·ing** 1 To separate or pull out the threads of, as from something knitted or tangled. 2 To solve or explain: to *unravel* a mystery. *Alternate spellings:* **unravelled, unravelling.**

un·re·li·a·ble /un′ri·lī′ə·bəl/ *adj.* Not dependable, trustworthy, or reliable: Our old car was *unreliable*.

un·u·su·al /un·yoo′zhoo·əl/ *adj.* Uncommon; not ordinary.—**un·u′su·al·ly** *adv.*

urge /ûrj/ *v.* **urged, urg·ing,** *n.* 1 *v.* To push or force along; to coax with vigor: to *urge* a team on. 2 *v.* To plead with or try to persuade; to advocate strongly. 3 *n.* A strong desire to do something: an *urge* to go back to the beach. *Syn.:* *v.* encourage.

ur·gent /ûr′jənt/ *adj.* Requiring immediate action or attention; insistent: an *urgent* request.—**ur′gent·ly** *adv.*

u·til·i·tar·i·an /yoo·til′ə·târ′ē·ən/ *adj.* Concerning usefulness or practicality rather than beauty: *utilitarian* clothing.

u·til·ize /yoo′təl·īz/ *v.* **u·til·ized, u·til·iz·ing** To make good use of.

V

va·cant /vā′kənt/ *adj.* 1 Not used; empty; not occupied or taken. 2 Lacking or appearing to lack thought, interest, or intelligence.—**va′cant·ly** *adv.*

val·ley /val′ē/ *n., pl.* **val·leys** 1 A low area between mountains or hills. 2 An area drained or watered by a river and its tributaries.

val·u·a·ble /val′y(oo·)ə·bəl/ 1 *adj.* Having worth, especially having a high value or price. 2 *n.* (*usually pl.*) Something worth a great deal, as jewelry, antiques, etc.

veg·e·ta·ble /vej′(ə)·tə·bəl/ *n.* 1 A plant or part of a plant used for food: Corn is a *vegetable*. 2 *adj.* use: *vegetable* juice.

ve·hi·cle /vē′i·kəl/ 1 *n.* Any device with wheels or runners that is used to carry something or someone, as a car, bus, etc. 2 A means or way of expressing, presenting, or making something known: The debate was a *vehicle* for the candidates to express their ideas.

vein /vān/ *n.* 1 One of the systems of branching vessels that carry blood from parts of the body to the heart. 2 One of the branching ribs forming the structure of a leaf or an insect's wing. 3 A deposit of ore or of a mineral substance found in the earth: a *vein* of coal.

ven·geance /ven′jəns/ *n.* Punishment, harm, etc., inflicted on a person by another who has been harmed by him or her; revenge: The victim swore *vengeance.*

ven·tri·cle /ven′trə·kəl/ *n.* One of the two lower chambers or sections of the heart.

ver·dict /vûr′dikt/ *n.* **1** The decision of a jury after a trial: The *verdict* was not guilty. **2** A decision; judgment: What is your *verdict* on my cooking?

ver·sa·tile /vûr′sə·til/ *adj.* **1** Capable of doing many things well: Peter is a very *versatile* individual. **2** Having many uses: a *versatile* tool.

verse /vûrs/ *n.* **1** Poetry. **2** A poem. **3** A stanza or single line of a poem: Do you remember the last *verse* of the poem?

ver·sion /vûr′zhən/ *n.* **1** A particular or personal account of something, possibly inaccurate: the child's *version* of the fairy tale. **2** A particular variety or form of something: a modern *version* of the play.

ver·te·bra /vûr′tə·brə/ *n., pl.* **ver·te·brae** One of the bones forming the spinal column. *Alternate plural:* **vertebras.**

ver·ti·cal /vûr′ti·kəl/ *adj.* Upright; forming right angles with horizontal lines: a *vertical* line.

vet·er·an /vet′ər·ən *or* vet′rən/ *n.* **1** A person who has served in the armed forces: Paul is a *veteran* of World War II. **2** A person with long experience in something. **3** *adj. use:* a *veteran* entertainer.

vi·cious /vish′əs/ *adj.* **1** Spiteful; mean; malicious. **2** Violent; fierce: a *vicious* attack. **3** Savage; ferocious: a *vicious* animal.— **vi′cious·ly** *adv.*

vig·or·ous /vig′ər·əs/ *adj.* **1** Full of energy or vigor: a *vigorous* person. **2** Performed with energy or vigor; strenuous: a *vigorous* hike. *Syn.:* energetic.

vi·tal /vīt′(ə)l/ *adj.* **1** Necessary or essential to life. **2** Of essential or critical importance: a *vital* decision. **3** Energetic; lively: a *vital* person.

vi·tal·i·ty /vī·tal′ə·tē/ *n.* **1** Energy or vigor. **2** The capacity for survival or continuation: *vitality* of a society.

vo·cab·u·lar·y /vō·kab′yə·ler′ē/ *n., pl.* **vo·cab·u·lar·ies** **1** The total number of words that an individual knows and can use: He has a large *vocabulary.* **2** The language

used by a specific group or in a particular field: the *vocabulary* of science. **3** All the words in a language.

vol·un·tar·y /vol′ən·ter′ē/ *adj.* **1** Given, made, done, etc., by a person's own will or choice; not forced: *voluntary* membership. **2** Undertaken by volunteers rather than by paid individuals.

W

waive /wāv/ *v.* **waived, waiv·ing 1** To agree to give up a right, claim, etc.: to *waive* one's claim to an inheritance. **2** To delay or postpone.

with·draw /with·drô′ *or* with·drô′/ *v.* **with·drew, with·drawn, with·draw·ing 1** To take away or remove: I *withdrew* money from the bank. **2** To move back or to take back: to *withdraw* from a room; to *withdraw* a question.

with·drawn /with·drôn′ *or* with·drôn′/ **1** Past participle of **withdraw. 2** *adj.* Reserved; quiet; isolated: The runner looked tired and *withdrawn* after losing the race.

with·hold /with·hōld′ *or* with·hōld′/ *v.* **with·held, with·hold·ing** To hold or keep back: Please *withhold* your questions until the end of the lecture.

with·in /with·in′ *or* with·in′/ **1** *adv.* In or into the interior or inner part; inside; indoors. **2** *prep.* Inside: Dale finished the test *within* an hour's time.

with·stand /with·stand′ *or* with·stand′/ *v.* **with·stood, with·stand·ing** To stand up against; to hold up under; to resist: to *withstand* pressure.

wor·ri·some /wûr′i·səm/ *adj.* **1** Causing worry; troubling: a *worrisome* cough. **2** Worrying often: a *worrisome* person.

wretch·ed /rech′id/ *adj.* **1** Unhappy or miserable: to feel *wretched.* **2** Causing discomfort, misery, or grief: a *wretched* hut. **3** Wicked or mean: a *wretched* villain. **4** Poor; unsatisfactory: a *wretched* excuse.

Y

yolk /yōk/ *n.* The yellow part of an egg.

Z

zo·ol·o·gy /zō·ol′ə·jē/ *n.* The science that deals with animals, their classification, structure, development, and habitats.

---

act, āte, câre, ärt;   egg, ēven;   if, īce;   on, ōver, ôr;   bŏŏk, fōōd;   up, tûrn;
ə=a in *ago,* e in *listen,* i in *giraffe,* o in *pilot,* u in *circus;*   yōō=u in *music;*   oil;   out;
chair;   sing;   shop;   thank;   that;   zh in *treasure.*

SPELLING THESAURUS

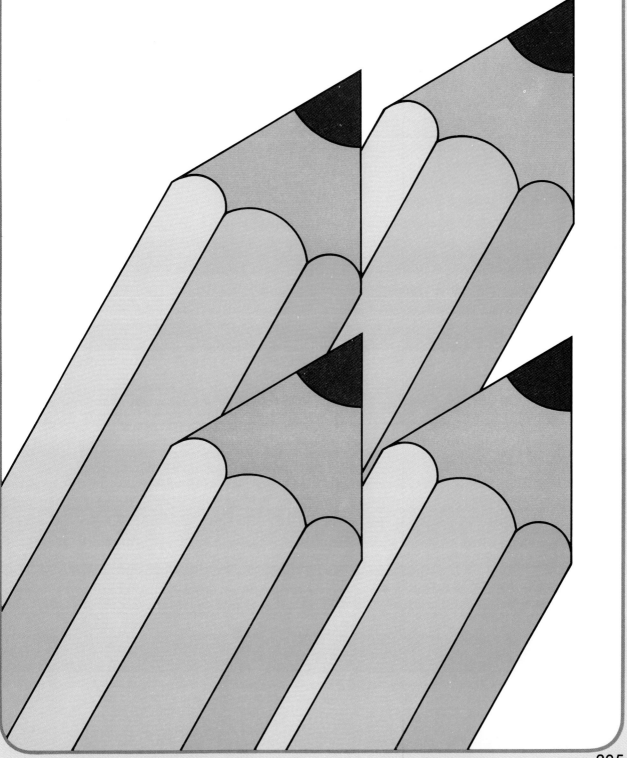

What Is a Thesaurus?

Do you find when you write that sometimes you use the same words over and over again? Have you ever thought if you had a word list, your writing would be more interesting?

A **thesaurus** is a book that lists words and their synonyms. Like a dictionary, a thesaurus lists words in alphabetical order. Each of these words is called an **entry word.** A list of synonyms follows the entry words. Sometimes a thesaurus lists antonyms.

Look at the parts of this thesaurus entry for the adjective *generous.*

The **entry word** is in red letters. It is followed by the part of speech and a definition. An **example sentence** shows how the word can be used.

> generous *adj.* Sharing; unselfish. The generous man donated a kidney to his ill daughter.

Synonyms for the entry word are in *slanted* letters. Each synonym is followed by a definition and an example sentence.

> *bountiful* Unselfish and free in giving; liberal. Scrooge was a fictional miser who became *bountiful.*
> *charitable* Giving help of any kind freely to the poor and unfortunate. The *charitable* woman did volunteer work at the local hospital.
> *lavish* Large or abundant. The entertainer gave the waiter a *lavish* tip.
> *liberal* Very large; lavish. An anonymous donor made a *liberal* gift to the university.

If an **antonym** is given, it is printed in dark letters.

> **ANTONYMS: miserly, selfish, stingy**

How to Use Your Spelling Thesaurus

Suppose you are writing a story about a person who made a generous contribution. You read over your work and see you have used the word *generous* too many times. You decide to use the Spelling Thesaurus to find some synonyms. Follow these steps.

1. Look for the word in the Thesaurus Index. The Index lists every word in the Spelling Thesaurus.

2. Find the word in the Index. This is what you will find:

    generous *adj.*

    The red print tells you that *generous* is an entry word.

3. Turn to the correct page in the Spelling Thesaurus and read the entry carefully. Choose the synonym with the exact shade of meaning you want. Not every synonym will fit in the context of your story.

Remember: Each word has a slightly different meaning. Look at the sample entry for *generous* on page 206. Which synonym for *generous* makes most sense in a story about someone making a generous contribution?

- Sometimes you may find a word is listed in the Index like this:

    lavish generous *adj.*

    This means you will find the word *lavish* listed as a synonym under the entry word *generous*. Since *lavish* is not printed in red, it is not an entry word. If you look for *lavish* in the Spelling Thesaurus as an entry word under the letter *L,* you will not find it!

- You will also see lines in the Index that look like this:

    miserly generous *adj.*

    This means that *miserly* is listed as an antonym under the entry word *generous.*

A

abandon cancel *v.*
abbreviate *v.*
abhorrent precious *adj.*
abnormal unusual *adj.*
abode residence *n.*
abominable obnoxious *adj.*
absolute imaginary *adj.*
absorbed intent *adj.*
absurd *adj.*
abundant *adj.*
abuse persecute *v.*
accessible *adj.*
accident disaster *n.*
accord controversy *n.*
accumulate *v.*
actual imaginary *adj.*
adaptable cumbersome *adj.*
adequate deficient *adj.*
admirable impressive *adj.*
adored precious *adj.*
adversary foe *n.*
advise *v.*
advocate advise *v.*
affected artificial *adj.*
affected naive *adj.*
aggravate irritate *v.*
aggressive enthusiastic *adj.*
agitated apprehensive *adj.*
agony ecstasy *n.*
agreeable pleasant *adj.*
agreeable sullen *adj.*
agreement controversy *n.*
alert observant *adj.*
alien unusual *adj.*
ally foe *n.*
aloof *adj.*
amass accumulate *v.*
amiable pleasant *adj.*
amiable sullen *adj.*
ample abundant *adj.*
amplify magnify *v.*
amusement diversion *n.*
anguish ecstasy *n.*
annihilate *v.*

annihilate renovate *v.*
annoy irritate *v.*
annoyance nuisance *n.*
antagonist foe *n.*
anxious apprehensive *adj.*
appall terrify *v.*
appalling *adj.*
apparent *adj.*
appealing gruesome *adj.*
appease irritate *v.*
appraise gauge *v.*
appreciate realize *v.*
apprehend realize *v.*
apprehensive *adj.*
apt liable *adj.*
artificial *adj.*
artless naive *adj.*
assemble accumulate *v.*
associate foe *n.*
astound surprise *v.*
asylum refuge *n.*
atrocious appalling *adj.*
atrocious vicious *adj.*
attainable accessible *adj.*
attentive observant *adj.*
available accessible *adj.*
average *adj.*
average unusual *adj.*
avid enthusiastic *adj.*
awe surprise *v.*
awesome impressive *adj.*

B

baffle perplex *v.*
banish expel *v.*
barrier obstacle *n.*
basic complicated *adj.*
beauteous exquisite *adj.*
beauteous gruesome *adj.*
believable outrageous *adj.*
belligerent *adj.*
beloved precious *adj.*
beneficial *adj.*
bewilder perplex *v.*
bleak solemn *adj.*
bliss ecstasy *n.*
blockade obstacle *n.*
blunder error *n.*
boldness nerve *n.*
boring tiresome *adj.*

bountiful abundant *adj.*
bountiful generous *adj.*
bravery nerve *n.*
brilliant *adj.*
brittle frail *adj.*
bulky cumbersome *adj.*

C

calamity disaster *n.*
camouflage disguise *n.*
cancel *v.*
capable efficient *adj.*
captivate fascinate *v.*
captivity *n.*
catastrophe disaster *n.*
cautious *adj.*
charitable generous *adj.*
cheerful solemn *adj.*
cherished precious *adj.*
clarify perplex *v.*
coarse *adj.*
combative belligerent *adj.*
comfort terrify *v.*
communicative aloof *adj.*
compact magnify *v.*
competent efficient *adj.*
competitor foe *n.*
complex complicated *adj.*
complicated *adj.*
complimentary vicious *adj.*
comprehend realize *v.*
compress abbreviate *v.*
compress magnify *v.*
comrade foe *n.*
concealed apparent *adj.*
conceive realize *v.*
concentrate magnify *v.*
concentrated intent *adj.*
concoct devise *v.*
condense magnify *v.*
conduct control *v.*
confident suspicious *adj.*
confinement captivity *n.*
conflict controversy *n.*
confuse **perplex** *v.*
conquer suppress *v.*
conscientious responsible *adj.*
considerate courteous *adj.*
consolidate unify *v.*

208

constructive beneficial *adj.*
contemplate deliberate *v.*
contender foe *n.*
contestant foe *n.*
contract magnify *v.*
control *v.*
controversy *n.*
cordial aloof *adj.*
cordial pleasant *adj.*
cordial sullen *adj.*
counsel advise *v.*
courteous *adj.*
cowardice nerve *n.*
create devise *v.*
creative inventive *adj.*
cultivated elegant *adj.*
cultured elegant *adj.*
cumbersome *adj.*
curious unusual *adj.*
customary regular *adj.*

D

dawdle loiter *v.*
debate controversy *n.*
debate deliberate *v.*
decisive hesitant *adj.*
deficient *adj.*
definite apparent *adj.*
definite hesitant *adj.*
dejected solemn *adj.*
deliberate *v.*
demolish annihilate *v.*
demolish renovate *v.*
dependable responsible *adj.*
deport expel *v.*
depressed solemn *adj.*
desolation ecstasy *n.*
detached aloof *adj.*
detention captivity *n.*
detestable obnoxious *adj.*
detestable precious *adj.*
devise *v.*
dignified elegant *adj.*
disagreeable pleasant *adj.*
disagreement controversy *n.*
disaster *n.*
discharge expel *v.*
disconnect unify *v.*
discontinue cancel *v.*

disengage unify *v.*
disguise *n.*
disinterested enthusiastic *adj.*
dismal solemn *adj.*
dismaying appalling *adj.*
dispensable essential *adj.*
dispense accumulate *v.*
disposition tendency *n.*
dispute controversy *n.*
disrespectful courteous *adj.*
distinguished average *adj.*
distraction diversion *n.*
distribute accumulate *v.*
distrustful suspicious *adj.*
disunite unify *v.*
diversion *n.*
dominant primary *adj.*
doubtful hesitant *adj.*
doubtful suspicious *adj.*
doubtless hesitant *adj.*
dread nerve *n.*
drivel jargon *n.*
dumfound surprise *v.*
dutiful courteous *adj.*
dwelling residence *n.*

E

ecstasy *n.*
effective efficient *adj.*
efficient *adj.*
elaborate complicated *adj.*
elation ecstasy *n.*
elegant *adj.*
elementary complicated *adj.*
eliminate annihilate *v.*
eliminate renovate *v.*
enchant fascinate *v.*
endanger jeopardize *v.*
endurance *n.*
energetic *adj.*
engaged intent *adj.*
engineer devise *v.*
enlarge abbreviate *v.*
enlarge magnify *v.*
enthrall fascinate *v.*
enthusiastic *adj.*
eradicate annihilate *v.*

error *n.*
essential *adj.*
essential minor *adj.*
esteemed precious *adj.*
estimable impressive *adj.*
estimate gauge *v.*
evaluate gauge *v.*
even-tempered sensitive *adj.*
everyday exquisite *adj.*
evident apparent *adj.*
exaggerate magnify *v.*
exceptional average *adj.*
excessive deficient *adj.*
exciting tiresome *adj.*
exile expel *v.*
expel *v.*
exquisite *adj.*
exquisite gruesome *adj.*
extend abbreviate *v.*
extend magnify *v.*
exterminate annihilate *v.*
extraordinary average *adj.*
extraordinary unusual *adj.*
exuberance ecstasy *n.*

F

facility flair *n.*
faculty flair *n.*
fancied imaginary *adj.*
fantastic outrageous *adj.*
fascinate *v.*
fearful apprehensive *adj.*
fearless apprehensive *adj.*
feeble frail *adj.*
ferocious belligerent *adj.*
fictitious artificial *adj.*
flair *n.*
flimsy frail *adj.*
foe *n.*
foreboding ominous *adj.*
foremost primary *adj.*
fortitude nerve *n.*
fragile frail *adj.*
fragment scrap *n.*
frail *adj.*
freedom captivity *n.*
frictionless coarse *adj.*
fundamental complicated *adj.*

likable obnoxious *adj.*
likable pleasant *adj.*
likely liable *adj.*
linger loiter *v.*
listless energetic *adj.*
liveliness spirit *n.*
loathsome gruesome *adj.*
loathsome precious *adj.*
lodging residence *n.*
logical absurd *adj.*
logical outrageous *adj.*
loiter *v.*
lose suppress *v.*
lounge loiter *v.*
lovable obnoxious *adj.*
lusterless brilliant *adj.*

M

magnificent brilliant *adj.*
magnify *v.*
major minor *adj.*
malicious vicious *adj.*
manageable cumber-
some *adj.*
mask disguise *n.*
masquerade disguise *n.*
mediocre inventive *adj.*
meditate deliberate *v.*
melancholy ecstasy *n.*
melancholy solemn *adj.*
menacing ominous *adj.*
merge unify *v.*
mimic imitate *v.*
minor *adj.*
minor essential *adj.*
mirror imitate *v.*
miscalculate gauge *v.*
mischievous *adj.*
miserly generous *adj.*
misery ecstasy *n.*
misestimate gauge *v.*
misevaluate gauge *v.*
misjudge gauge *v.*
mistake error *n.*
mob horde *n.*
mock imitate *v.*
mockery *n.*
monotonous tiresome *adj.*
morsel scrap *n.*
multitude horde *n.*
mystify perplex *v.*

N

naive *adj.*
neglectful cautious *adj.*
nerve *n.*
noble vicious *adj.*
nonaggressive belligerent *adj.*
noncombative belligerent *adj.*
nonessential essential
adj.
nonessential minor *adj.*
nonsense jargon *n.*
nonthreatening omi-
nous *adj.*
nonviolent belligerent
adj.
normal average *adj.*
normal unusual *adj.*
noteworthy average *adj.*
nuisance *n.*
numerous abundant *adj.*

O

obnoxious *adj.*
obscure brilliant *adj.*
observant *adj.*
obstacle *n.*
obstruction obstacle *n.*
obtainable accessible *adj.*
obvious apparent *adj.*
offensive belligerent *adj.*
offensive elegant *adj.*
offensive obnoxious *adj.*
ominous *adj.*
opponent foe *n.*
oppress persecute *v.*
optimistic solemn *adj.*
ordinary unusual *adj.*
original inventive *adj.*
originate devise *v.*
outrageous *adj.*

P

pacify irritate *v.*
panic terrify *v.*
particle scrap *n.*
pastime diversion *n.*
peaceful belligerent *adj.*
peculiar unusual *adj.*

perpetuate cancel *v.*
perplex *v.*
persecute *v.*
perseverance endurance *n.*
persist cancel *v.*
persistence endurance *n.*
perturbed apprehensive
adj.
pest nuisance *n.*
petrify terrify *v.*
pleasant *adj.*
plentiful abundant *adj.*
polished coarse *adj.*
polished elegant *adj.*
ponder deliberate *v.*
positive beneficial *adj.*
prankish mischievous
adj.
prattle jargon *n.*
precious *adj.*
predominant primary *adj.*
premier primary *adj.*
preoccupied intent *adj.*
preserve refuge *n.*
primary *adj.*
prime primary *adj.*
prolong abbreviate *v.*
prolong cancel *v.*
promising ominous *adj.*
prone liable *adj.*
proneness tendency *n.*
propose advise *v.*
provoke irritate *v.*
prudent cautious *adj.*

Q

qualified efficient *adj.*

R

rapture ecstasy *n.*
rate gauge *v.*
reachable accessible *adj.*
realize *v.*
reasonable outrageous
adj.
reassure terrify *v.*
reckless cautious *adj.*
recognize realize *v.*
recommend advise *v.*
recondition renovate *v.*
reconstruct annihilate
v.

unenthusiastic enthusiastic *adj.*
ungracious courteous *adj.*
unguarded cautious *adj.*
unhabitual regular *adj.*
unhandy cumbersome *adj.*
unify v.
unimaginative inventive *adj.*
unimportant minor *adj.*
unimportant primary *adj.*
unimposing impressive *adj.*
unimpressive impressive *adj.*
uninventive inventive *adj.*
unite unify *v.*
unlikable pleasant *adj.*
unlikely liable *adj.*
unmanageable cumbersome *adj.*
unmenacing ominous *adj.*
unmistakable apparent *adj.*
unobservant observant *adj.*

unobtainable accessible *adj.*
unoriginal inventive *adj.*
unperturbed apprehensive *adj.*
unpleasant pleasant *adj.*
unreasonable absurd *adj.*
unreliable responsible *adj.*
unrenowned brilliant *adj.*
unreserved aloof *adj.*
unresolved hesitant *adj.*
unrestrained aloof *adj.*
unrestraint captivity *n.*
unsophisticated naive *adj.*
unsuited efficient *adj.*
unsuspicious suspicious *adj.*
untangle perplex *v.*
untrustworthy responsible *adj.*
unusual adj.
unusual regular *adj.*
unwavering hesitant *adj.*
unwieldy cumbersome *adj.*
useless beneficial *adj.*

usual unusual *adj.*

V

valor nerve *n.*
vanquish suppress *v.*
vex irritate *v.*
vexation nuisance *n.*
vicious adj.
victimize persecute *v.*
vigor spirit *n.*
vigorous energetic *adj.*
vigorous frail *adj.*
vile vicious *adj.*
virtuous vicious *adj.*
vital energetic *adj.*
vital essential *adj.*
vital minor *adj.*
vitality spirit *n.*
void cancel *v.*
vulgar elegant *adj.*

W

wary cautious *adj.*
wary suspicious *adj.*
wavering hesitant *adj.*
wearisome tiresome *adj.*
wieldy cumbersome *adj.*
withdrawn aloof *adj.*
worthless beneficial *adj.*
wretched vicious *adj.*
wretchedness ecstasy *n.*

A

abbreviate *v.* To shorten or condense. The teacher decided to abbreviate the lesson, as time was running out.

compress To press together; condense; squeeze. The machine *compressed* the air and pumped it into a scuba tank.

reduce To make less in size or amount. The Congress passed a bill designed to *reduce* crime.

summarize To make a summary of; sum up. The film reviewer *summarized* the movie's plot.

ANTONYMS: enlarge, extend, prolong

absurd *adj.* Unreasonable; ridiculous; illogical. Dana's absurd explanation for not having her homework was that a goat ate it.

illogical Showing a lack of sound reasoning. Since it was too dark to see clearly, the witness's claim was *illogical*.

irrational Not able to reason or understand. The child spilled his cereal in an *irrational* fit of anger.

ridiculous Deserving ridicule or laughter because of absurdity or silliness. The hat looked *ridiculous* on the dog.

unreasonable Not reasonable or sensible. The management felt that the union was being *unreasonable* in its demands.

ANTONYMS: logical, sensible

abundant *adj.* Not scarce; plentiful; ample. The monsoon brings abundant rainfall to India in June.

ample Plentiful. The squirrel had stored *ample* food, which lasted through the winter.

bountiful Numerous; plentiful. The Thanksgiving baskets were *bountiful*.

numerous Very many. The books in the library were so *numerous* that some had to be stacked on the floor.

plentiful Existing in great quantity; more than enough. The corn crop was *plentiful* this year, and so the price of corn was low.

ANTONYMS: inadequate, insufficient, sparse

accessible *adj.* Capable of being reached; obtainable. The health center entrance was accessible from Grand Avenue.

attainable Capable of being gained or arrived at by hard work; achievable. Physical fitness is an *attainable* goal if you exercise regularly.

available That can be used or had. There were thirty more tickets *available* for the planetarium show.

obtainable Capable of being obtained or acquired, especially by effort. Rod felt that first prize in the singing contest was *obtainable* if he practiced enough.

reachable Capable of being reached. The mountain climbers kept going because they were convinced that the summit was *reachable*.

ANTONYMS: inaccessible, unattainable, unavailable, unobtainable, unreachable

accumulate *v.* To collect or gather. She accumulated a large collection of arrowheads.

amass To heap up, especially as wealth or possessions for oneself. The Rockefellers *amassed* a fortune through the oil industry.

assemble To come or bring together; collect. The soccer team *assembled* for team pictures.

hoard To save and store away, often greedily. Some people *hoard* food in case of disaster.

ANTONYMS: dispense, distribute, scatter

advise *v.* To make suggestions; to give advice. "I'd advise you to study for the test tomorrow," our teacher said.

advocate To speak or write in favor of; defend; support. Doctors *advocate* plenty of rest, exercise, and nourishing food.

counsel To give advice. The financial advisor *counseled* them on the best way to invest their money.

propose To put forward for acceptance or consideration. The student council member *proposed* that the meeting be adjourned.

recommend To suggest. The radio announcer *recommended* taking the subway to the stadium because of the heavy traffic on the highways.

aloof *adj.* Reserved or distant in manner. Although the children tried to be friendly with it, the cat remained aloof.

detached Not favoring a certain side; impartial. Because his children played on opposing teams, the father tried to be *detached* about the game.

reserved Keeping one's feelings, thoughts, and affairs to oneself. While his sister was outgoing, Paul was *reserved*.

restrained Held back; repressed. The symphony music went from the rich, robust brass section to the *restrained* flute section.

subdued Held back; less intense. We all wondered why Alicia, who was usually carefree, was so *subdued*.

withdrawn Reserved; quiet; isolated. Andy was *withdrawn* when strangers came to the house.

ANTONYMS: reconstruct, re-create, reestablish, renew, renovate, restore

annihilate *v.* To destroy utterly and completely. Pompeii was annihilated when Mount Vesuvius erupted in A.D. 79.

demolish To tear down completely; wreck; ruin. The wrecking crew *demolished* the abandoned building.

eliminate To get rid of. The athlete decided to *eliminate* junk food from her diet.

eradicate To remove or get rid of completely. The goal of the research group was to *eradicate* cancer.

exterminate To destroy (living things) entirely; kill. Scientists hoped to find a poison that would *exterminate* the harmful apple maggots.

ANTONYMS: reconstruct, recreate, reestablish, renew, renovate, restore

appalling *adj.* Causing dismay; shocking; frightful. His ignorance about the Bill of Rights was appalling.

atrocious Very bad in any way. The co-

median's taste in clothing is *atrocious*.

dismaying Alarming. The lack of enthusiasm at the school rally was *dismaying*.

shocking Causing an unpleasant surprise. Friday's newspaper had a *shocking* story about drinking and driving.
See also **apprehensive.**

apparent *adj.* Obvious. It was apparent that Mike wouldn't finish the computer program before class was over.

definite Known for certain. It is *definite* that our match will be canceled because of the rain.

evident Easily seen or understood; obvious. The billowing smoke made it *evident* that activity inside the volcano had increased.

obvious Easily perceived; clear; visible. Her fine handiwork was *obvious* in every detail of the wooden cabinet.

unconcealed Not hidden; open. Jason had an *unconcealed* dislike for snakes.

unmistakable That cannot be mistaken or misunderstood; clear. The basketball team's *unmistakable* improvement was due to the new coach.

ANTONYMS: concealed, indefinite, unapparent

apprehensive *adj.* Uneasy or fearful about something that might occur; worried. Chuck had been apprehensive about his dental appointment, but his checkup was perfect.

tated about the unnatural, still heat.

anxious Worried; uneasy. Lorraine felt *anxious* about her grandfather being in the hospital.

fearful Full of fear; frightened. Matt was *fearful* that the truck had backed over his skateboard.

perturbed Disturbed greatly; alarmed; agitated. Jenny was *perturbed* by the stealthy footsteps outside until she realized they were being made by her dog.

ANTONYMS: fearless, relaxed, unperturbed

artificial *adj.* Not natural or genuine; false; affected. David's wrestling opponent gave him an artificial smile before the match began.

affected Not natural. The child asked for the toy in a whiny, *affected* voice.

fictitious Not genuine; false; made up. To avoid being recognized, the actor made dinner reservations under a *fictitious* name.

insincere Not expressing true feelings; not sincere or genuine. My friend is very honest; she never makes *insincere* comments.

theatrical Dramatic. My sister's reaction to the car's dented fender was very *theatrical*.

ANTONYMS: genuine, sincere, straightforward, unaffected

average *adj.* Typical; common; ordinary. Although his height was average, his jumping ability made him an excellent basketball player.

normal Agreeing with the usual standard; regular. What started out as a *normal* day turned into the most exciting day of Sandy's life.

standard Widely accepted; regularly used. The power brakes were *standard* equipment on the car.

typical Having qualities or features common to the whole group or class. A *typical* mummy took seventy days to embalm.

See also **regular**.

ANTONYMS: distinguished, exceptional, extraordinary, noteworthy

B

belligerent *adj.* Tending to fight; warlike; hostile. The belligerent dog growled fiercely at the mail carrier.

combative Eager or ready to fight. The Huns were a *combative* race of people who ravaged Europe about 1,500 years ago.

ferocious Extremely fierce or savage. The *ferocious* tiger stalked its prey through the tall grasses.

hostile Showing dislike; unfriendly. When Yvonne felt *hostile,* she would retreat to her room and write in her journal.

offensive Unpleasant or disagreeable. The *offensive* remark was followed quickly by an apology.

ANTONYMS: nonaggressive, noncombative, nonviolent, peaceful, serene

beneficial *adj.* Useful; helpful; worthwhile. The soft music had a beneficial effect after the noisiness at the construction site.

constructive Helping to improve or make better. The art teacher gave Ben some *constructive* suggestions for adding depth to his paintings.

positive Useful. Mercy Otis Warren and Lydia Darragh were two patriots who made *positive* contributions during the American Revolution.

ANTONYMS: harmful, injurious, useless, worthless

brilliant *adj.* Distinguished; splendid. For years, young readers have enjoyed the brilliant books of Scott O'Dell.

glorious Full of or deserving glory. The colorful dawn signaled the beginning of a *glorious* day.

illustrious Very famous; renowned. The *illustrious* paintings of Pierre Auguste Renoir are admired around the world.

magnificent Superb; excellent. Scott Joplin's *magnificent* and exciting music became known as ragtime.

superb Excellent; outstandingly good. The view of the valley from Half Dome in Yosemite National Park is *superb*.

tremendous Wonderful. Described as "the eighth wonder of the world," the Brooklyn Bridge was a *tremendous* engineering feat.

ANTONYMS: lusterless, obscure, unrenowned

C

cancel *v.* To call off or do away with. Because he was ill, the marching-band director canceled practice.

abandon To give up wholly; forfeit. Pioneers *abandoned* all hopes for privacy and luxury when they decided to journey west.

discontinue To stop having, using, or making; break off or end. After a week, the store *discontinued* the sale on running shoes.

terminate To bring to an end; to stop. They decided to *terminate* their lease on the apartment at the end of the month.

void To take away the legal force or effect of; annul. The man *voided* the check he had written and paid cash instead.

ANTONYMS: perpetuate, persist, prolong, sustain

captivity *n.* Imprisonment or confinement. The rare Golden Monkey had been born and raised in captivity.

confinement The act of keeping shut in. The prisoner's *confinement* lasted three years.

detention The act of holding in custody. Nancy caught up on all of her assignments during *detention* after school.

imprisonment Close confinement. The suspect was acquitted, and his *imprisonment* ended.

ANTONYMS: freedom, liberty, release, unrestraint

cautious *adj.* Very careful or watchful. The cautious driver managed to stop in time.

guarded Prudent; planned. My friend's *guarded* answers made me suspect that a surprise awaited me.

heedful Paying careful attention. Bicycle riders must be *heedful* of the oncoming traffic.

prudent Using or showing careful planning and good judgment. The successful stockbroker was *prudent* in her investments.

wary Watchful and suspicious; very careful. The *wary* opossum played dead when it saw the dog.

ANTONYMS: heedless, neglectful, reckless, unguarded

coarse *adj.* Rough; not fine or smooth. We wore coarse clothing for our hike through the bushes.

grainy Having many small bumps; rough. The table John made in woodshop had a very *grainy* surface.

granular Made up of, like, or containing grains or granules. Of the three kinds of rock, sedimentary rock is the most *granular*.

gritty Like, containing, or made of grit. The sandwiches we took to the beach had become *gritty*.

ANTONYMS: frictionless, polished, slick

complicated *adj.* Not simple; intricate; complex. Robert used his calculator to work out the complicated math problem.

complex Intricate; not simple. Cameron learned the *complex* steps of the dance.

elaborate Worked out or developed carefully and thoroughly. The class sketched out an *elaborate* plan before beginning work on the mural.

intricate Involved or complex. It took Lisa two weeks to complete the *intricate* jigsaw puzzle.

involved Complex; intricate. Roger decided to pick up his friend at the airport, rather than give him *involved* directions to his house.

ANTONYMS: basic, elementary, fundamental

control *v.* To have power or authority to direct, manage, or command. Ancient Greeks believed that gods and goddesses controlled the world.

conduct To direct or manage an action; to carry on. The president of the company *conducted* the meeting.

govern To rule or guide. The British once *governed* India.

regulate To control according to certain rules. The assembly line worker *regulated* which vegetables were suitable for canning.

superintend To be in charge of and direct; manage; supervise. Mr. Wornian's job was to *superintend* production of the silicon chips.

supervise To oversee or manage. The river guide *supervised* the loading of the rafts.

controversy *n.* A dispute or debate. The controversy was about whether or not the seventh graders would be allowed to go on the field trip with the eighth graders.

conflict A struggle, fight, or battle. The War of the Roses was a *conflict* between the Lancasters and the Yorks that lasted for thirty years.

debate The act of discussing or arguing for or against, especially in a formal way between persons taking opposite sides of a question. The governor and his challenger held a *debate* on ways to curb crime.

disagreement An angry dispute; quarrel. The twins had a *disagreement* over what they should name the kitten.

dispute An argument, debate, or quarrel. The *dispute* between the Hatfields and McCoys lasted so long that they forgot why it started.

ANTONYMS: accord, agreement, understanding

courteous *adj.* Considerate; respectful. Mr. Curcelli was impressed with the courteous service at the restaurant.

considerate Thoughtful of others; kind. *Considerate* neighbors brought casseroles to Mrs. Larsen when she returned home from the hospital.

dutiful Having or showing a sense of duty; obedient or respectful. The *dutiful* dog brought the newspaper to the porch every morning.

gracious thoughtful; polite. Our *gracious* host in Hawaii gave us a wonderful tour of Waikiki.

respectful Showing respect in a manner that exhibits regard, honor, or consideration; polite. In the Japanese culture, people are very *respectful* toward their elders.

ANTONYMS: disrespectful, impolite, inconsiderate, insolent, ungracious

cumbersome *adj.* Awkward or hard to move or manage; unwieldy. The giant turnip outfit she wore for the school play was cumbersome

bulky Having great size, especially so big and clumsy as to be hard to handle. The repair person brought a hand truck to move the *bulky* washing machine.

inconvenient Troublesome or bothersome. At first Paul found the crutches *inconvenient,* but he quickly adapted to them.

unhandy Not easy to use; awkward. Barbara found scissors *unhandy* until she switched to a left-handed pair.

unmanageable Incapable of being managed or controlled; unruly. When Bob first started skiing, the skis seemed completely *unmanageable.*

unwieldy Hard to handle or manage, usually because of size, weight, or shape; awkward. The *unwieldy* mattress kept bending in all directions as they carried it upstairs.

ANTONYMS: adaptable, manageable, unburdensome, uncomplicated, wieldy

D

deficient *adj.* Not complete; insufficient or inadequate; lacking. Her bones were weak because her diet was deficient in calcium.

inadequate Less than is needed or required; not adequate. We had to work in pairs because there was an *inadequate* number of microscopes.

incomplete Not complete; unfinished or imperfect. The viewer of Michelangelo's *incomplete* sculptures can almost see the figures trying to push out of the stone.

insufficient Not enough; not adequate. There were an *insufficient* number of players to start a touch football game.

ANTONYMS: adequate, excessive, sufficient

deliberate *v.* To think over carefully; to consider; to ponder. Lee deliberated about walking across town but decided to take the bus.

contemplate To meditate. Inga *contemplated* writing her essay on horses but decided to write about robots instead.

debate To try to decide; consider. Leroy *debated* whether to visit his grandmother on Thursday or on Friday.

meditate To think quietly and deeply over a period of time; to reflect. Maria *meditated* on her father's words about arguing with her brother.

ponder To consider carefully; puzzle over. The British Prime Minister Neville Chamberlain *pondered* whether to trust Adolf Hitler.

speculate To think seriously or wonderingly; form theories; conjecture. Molly *speculated* about what living on a space station would be like.

devise *v.* To figure out; to invent. The scientist in the movie devised a contraption that allowed travel through space and time.

concoct To make up; create. Maxwell *concocted* a story to lure Jason to the surprise party.

create To cause to come into existence; originate; make. Electric lights, phonographs, and movie cameras were just a few of the inventions *created* by Thomas Edison.

engineer To manage or accomplish cleverly or skillfully. In a famous folk tale, Rumpelstiltskin *engineers* a method for turning straw into gold.

improvise To make something from whatever materials are available. The hikers *improvised* a stretcher for their injured friend.

originate To begin or come into existence; to initiate. The representative from Texas *originated* the bill which was later passed into law.

disaster *n.* An event causing great distress or damage. The earthquake in Mexico City was a terrible disaster.

accident An event that causes harm or injury, as a collision. Traffic was backed up for miles because of the *accident*.

calamity Any happening that causes great distress; a tragedy. The gloomy music on the television program warned the audience that a *calamity* was going to happen.

catastrophe A sudden tragic event. The *catastrophe* left 2,000 people homeless.

tragedy A sad or disastrous event. The sinking of the ocean liner *Titanic* was a *tragedy*.

disguise *n.* Something that hides or covers, as a costume or mask. Jeremy's disguise was so good that his own family didn't recognize him.

camouflage Any covering that hides or protects. Penguins have black backs and white fronts as a protective *camouflage*.

mask A covering used to hide or protect all or part of the face. Shelly wore a glittery *mask* to the costume party.

masquerade A costume for a party at which the guests wear masks and fancy clothing. Leonard devised a clown *masquerade* for the party.

diversion *n.* Distraction from attention to ordinary matters; recreation; relaxation; amusement. Playing his drum set was a great diversion for Mark.

amusement Something that amuses or diverts. Collecting antique irons was an *amusement* that Ms. Claison enjoyed.

distraction The act of distracting or diverting; that which draws away or diverts attention. The volleyball game being played outside was a *distraction* to the students in Mr. Risso's class.

pastime Something that makes time pass pleasantly, as a sport or recreation. His favorite *pastime* was gardening.

recreation Amusement, relaxation, or play, such as gardening, hiking, music, reading, dancing, or sports. Swimming is a popular form of *recreation*.

relaxation Recreation or amusement. He liked to read western novels for *relaxation*.

E

ecstasy *n.* Extraordinary happiness, pleasure, or delight. Holly was filled with ecstasy when she found out that her injured cat would survive.

bliss Great happiness or joy. His family was in *bliss* when the soldier returned from his year overseas.

elation A feeling of joy or triumph. Their *elation* at winning the football game lasted all day.

exuberance Joy and energy; high spirits. Mrs. Brady-Smith's family greeted her with *exuberance* when she arrived home from her long business trip.

rapture Very great or complete pleasure or delight. Marlene looked with *rapture* at the famous Sistine Chapel ceiling.

ANTONYMS: agony, anguish, desolation, melancholy, misery, wretchedness

efficient *adj.* Producing results with little effort or waste; capable. Crop rotation is a method that makes efficient use of farmland.

capable Having ability or skill; competent. The *capable* gas station attendant checked the oil and washed the windshield.

competent Possessing ability; capable. Judith, a *competent* worker, was promoted from salesclerk to floor manager.

effective Producing or able to produce the proper result. Larry hoped that his insect repellent would be *effective* during the camping trip.

qualified Suitable or competent, as for a particular occupation. The interviewer asked Mr. Lambert to explain what made him *qualified* for the job.

ANTONYMS: incapable, incompetent, ineffective, inefficient, unsuited

elegant *adj.* Refined; dignified; graceful. Lana thought the actress was the most elegant woman she had ever seen.

cultivated Improved and developed by study, exercise, or training. Her *cultivated* table manners were acquired at the boarding school.

cultured Having or showing culture or refinement. The *cultured* customer showed his good taste by buying one of the finest hand-knit sweaters.

dignified Having dignity; proud; calm and stately. The *dignified* judge had been on the Supreme Court for twenty years.

gracious Having good taste; refined. The visitors stayed in a *gracious* midtown hotel.

polished Cultured or refined, as of manner or style. The *polished* waiter led the customers through the fancy restaurant.

refined Free from vulgarity or coarseness; cultured. We all wanted to know how a *refined* girl such as

Innes came to be such a good hockey player.

ANTONYMS: indelicate, inelegant, offensive, tasteless, vulgar

endurance *n.* The ability to withstand hardship, strain, or stress. A marathon runner must have great endurance.

perseverance The act or habit of continuing to try to do something in spite of difficulties; persistence. Her *perseverance* on the difficult job impressed Raina's teacher.

persistence Determination. Dan's *persistence* and hard work landed him a position on the volleyball team.

stamina Vitality; vigor; strength. Flight attendants need *stamina* since they walk many miles during a flight.

energetic *adj.* Full of energy; lively. The brisk fall wind made Kate feel unusually energetic.

vigorous Full of energy or vigor. The *vigorous* stallion leaped the fence and galloped away.

vital Lively. Larry was thrilled to be feeling so *vital* after having been ill.

ANTONYMS: lazy, listless, sluggish

enthusiastic *adj.* Full of enthusiasm; excited or interested; eager. His teacher appreciated Jason's enthusiastic approach to learning.

aggressive Eager; forceful. The *aggressive* salesperson almost convinced me to buy the car he was selling.

avid Eager. The class had an *avid* discussion about what the legal voting age should be.

ANTONYMS: disinterested, unenthusiastic

error *n.* A mistake. The french horn player hoped her error was not heard.

blunder A stupid mistake. She made a *blunder* when she squirted hair gel instead of toothpaste onto her toothbrush.

inaccuracy A mistake. Banks cannot accept *inaccuracies* in cashing checks.

mistake An error or blunder. I made a *mistake* when I called Brian by his twin brother's name.

essential *adj.* Absolutely necessary. Good nutrition is essential for healthy bodies.

indispensable Absolutely necessary; vital. Eric could have done without many of the things he considered *indispensable*.

required Necessary. Sixteen is the *required* age to get a driver's license in California.

vital Necessary or indispensable. The heart is a *vital* organ.

ANTONYMS: dispensable, minor, nonessential, replaceable

expel *v.* To dismiss or banish. The football player was expelled from the game for unnecessary roughness.

banish To drive away; get rid of; dispel; dismiss. Heather tried to *banish* the suspicious thoughts from her mind.

deport To expel (a person, usually an alien) from a country by legal order; banish. The accused criminal was *deported* to his homeland, where he would be tried.

discharge To dismiss. Several employees were *discharged* when the company had to cut back on its staff.

exile To send (someone) away from his or her native land and forbid a return; banish. The author was *exiled* because his books criticized his country.

exquisite *adj.* Very beautiful. The forest scenery for the play was exquisite.

beauteous Beautiful. The Whitehall rose was considered the most *beauteous* flower in the show.

glamorous Full of glamor; charming, beautiful, or fascinating. Once a year *glamorous* movie stars are presented awards for their work in film.

gorgeous Very beautiful. The white sand and the aqua ocean looked *gorgeous*.

handsome Attractive, especially in a dignified way. The young man looked *handsome* in his tuxedo.

stunning Extremely beautiful, stylish. The *stunning* car on the display floor attracted every customer's eye.

ANTONYMS: everyday, gruesome, homely, repulsive, revolting

F

fascinate *v.* To attract, charm, or interest; to hold the attention of. Marla was fascinated by the experiment in which the peeled egg was sucked through the small neck of the bottle.

captivate To enchant or charm, as by beauty or excellence. The piano recital *captivated* the audience.

enchant To charm; delight. The friendly baby *enchanted* everyone at the party.

enthrall To keep spellbound. The sight of the Statue of Liberty *enthralled* the immigrants.

hypnotize To charm; to enthrall. The cat seemed *hypnotized* by its reflection in the mirror.

intrigue To arouse the interest or curiosity of. The anthropologist was *intrigued* with the Aztec culture.

flair *n.* A natural ability, talent, or skill; knack. Doug had a flair for singing.

facility Ease or skill in performance. The boy threw the newspapers with *facility*.

faculty A natural or acquired ability or talent. Mark Twain's *faculty* for writing stories in everyday language was admired and soon copied.

genius An extremely high degree of mental power or talent. Pablo Picasso had a *genius* for painting.

knack Ability or skill; talent. The principal had a *knack* for settling disagreements to everyone's satisfaction.

foe *n.* An enemy or rival. The United States and Germany were bitter foes during World War II.

adversary An enemy or opponent. The politician stepped up his campaign against his *adversary*.

antagonist A person who fights or contends with another; adversary. The *antagonist* in the quarrel was sent to the principal's office.

competitor A person who competes, as in games or business; a rival. The paper-making company felt that its recycling methods were better than those of its *competitor*.

frail   hesitant

contender A person who engages in a competition or contest. In the movie, an unknown young man trains to be a *contender* in a marathon.

contestant A person who enters a contest or competition. My mother was a *contestant* on a television game show.

opponent A person who opposes or competes with another, as in sports, a contest, and so on; a rival. The professional tennis player had to maintain her concentration to beat her *opponent*.

rival A competitor; an opponent. Julie had been my *rival* in sports for as long as I could remember.

ANTONYMS: ally, associate, comrade

frail *adj.* Physically weak; in delicate health. The tree branch looked too frail to hold a swing.

brittle Likely to break or snap; fragile. Mrs. Jepson tried to spread cheese on the *brittle* cracker, but it snapped.

feeble Lacking strength; weak. The *feeble* colt rose unsteadily to its feet.

flimsy Ready to fall apart or tear; easily damaged or broken. The *flimsy* shed was blown over during the storm.

fragile Easily shattered or damaged; delicate. The *fragile* glass figure was smashed on the stone floor.

ANTONYMS: hardy, resistant, unbreakable, vigorous

G

gauge *v.* To appraise, judge, or estimate. Contestants gauged the number of marbles in the barrel to see who would win the trip.

appraise To estimate the amount, quality, or worth of. The art collector *appraised* the painting at ten thousand dollars.

estimate To make a close guess about (as to size, number, or cost). The entertainment committee *estimated* that two hundred students would come to the dance.

evaluate To judge value or determine worth. Mr. Goodman checked content, style, and mechanics when he *evaluated* our English papers.

rate To assign a value or grade to. I *rate* E. L. Konigsburg's books among the best I've read.

ANTONYMS: miscalculate, misestimate, misevaluate, misjudge

generous *adj.* Sharing; unselfish. The generous man donated a kidney to his ill daughter.

bountiful Unselfish and free in giving; liberal. Scrooge was a fictional miser who became *bountiful*.

charitable Giving help of any kind freely to the poor and unfortunate. The *charitable* woman did volunteer work at the local hospital.

lavish Large or abundant. The entertainer gave the waiter a *lavish* tip.

liberal Very large; lavish. An anonymous donor made a *liberal* gift to the university.

ANTONYMS: miserly, selfish, stingy

gruesome *adj.* Horrible, especially in a disgusting way. During the French Revolution the gruesome guillotine was set up in the town square.

ghastly Horrible; terrifying. The *ghastly* creature advanced upon the hero in the movie.

grisly Causing fear or horror. They shivered in their sleeping bags when they heard the *grisly* tale.

loathsome Detestable; repulsive; abhorrent. Three *loathsome* women begin the story in Shakespeare's play *Macbeth*.

repulsive Disgusting or horrifying. The mold on the vegetables looked *repulsive*.

revolting Disgusting. The piles of trash on the park lawn were *revolting* to see.

ANTONYMS: appealing, beauteous, exquisite, handsome

H

hesitant *adj.* Uncertain; doubtful; undecided. The small boy was hesitant about going down the slide.

doubtful Uncertain or undecided. Because of the overcast weather, they were *doubtful* about going water skiing.

indecisive Not able to decide; wavering. We were *indecisive* about what movie to see.

unresolved Undecided. The question of what to do about the stray puppy was *unresolved*.

wavering Uncertain or undecided. The electrician was *wavering* about the best way to fix the dryer.

ANTONYMS: decisive, definite, doubtless, resolved, unwavering

horde *n.* A large group; a mass or crowd. In 1986 a horde of people went to New York City to celebrate the centennial of the Statue of Liberty.

legion A great number; multitude. A *legion* of fans tramped into the stadium to watch the football game.

mob A large or disorderly crowd. In 1789 a *mob* stormed the gates of the Bastille, a fortress in France.

multitude A great number of persons or things; crowd; throng. Mr. and Mrs. Gomez were stunned by the *multitude* of friends that surprised them with a party.

throng A great crowd; multitude. The *throng* of students crowded into the auditorium.

I

imaginary *adj.* Existing only in the mind or imagination; unreal. Young Sarah had an imaginary playmate named Matilda.

fancied Imagined; unreal. The inventor was elated about the *fancied* success of his time machine.

illusive Coming from or causing an illusion; not real; deceptive. On a hot day you may see an *illusive* puddle of water on the road ahead.

insubstantial Not real; in the imagination. Her *insubstantial* fears floated away when her father arrived home safe.

ANTONYMS: absolute, actual, substantial

imitate *v.* To attempt to act or look the same as; to copy; to mimic. The famous comedian imitated people who were in the news.

impersonate To mimic or copy. My father likes to *impersonate* famous actors from his youth.

mimic To copy the speech or actions of, usually in order to make fun of someone. It makes mom laugh when my baby sister *mimics* me!

mirror To reflect or show an image of. The mime *mirrored* every move the tourist made.

mock To mimic or ridicule. Instead of listening to his warning, the crowd began to *mock* him.

impressive *adj.* Producing strong admiration; awesome; imposing. Buckingham Palace in London, England, is an impressive building.

admirable Worthy of being admired or regarded with wonder, pleasure, or approval. The cast gave an *admirable* performance of *Our Town*.

awesome Causing awe. The thunderstorm was *awesome* from the airplane.

estimable Worthy of respect and esteem. The *estimable* university was over six hundred years old.

imposing Awesome, as in appearance, manner, or size. The car turned the corner and came upon the *imposing* mansion.

See also **unusual.**

ANTONYMS: insignificant, unimposing, unimpressive

intent *adj.* Having one's efforts or attention firmly fixed on something. The owl fixed the camper with an intent stare.

absorbed Engaged completely or completely attentive. The *absorbed* child refused to stop reading the book.

concentrated Having one's entire attention focused on something. The mother gave her misbehaving son a *concentrated* glare.

engaged Busy; occupied. The dog was so *engaged* with its bone that it didn't notice the cat.

preoccupied Interested or occupied fully. The *preoccupied* athlete could not forget the mistakes she had made during yesterday's game.

ANTONYMS: inattentive, unabsorbed, unengaged

inventive *adj.* Skillful at or showing imagination or originality. Alexander Graham Bell was an exceptionally inventive man.

creative Having the ability or power to bring into existence, originate, or make. The *creative* artist specialized in sculpture.

imaginative Full of or demonstrating imagination, or the power to form mental pictures, see things in new ways, or create new ideas. The *imaginative* photographer was known for using double exposures to create new images.

ingenious Skillful or clever. The man thought of an *ingenious* scheme for making money.

original Created totally by one's own mind and work. The models at the fashion show wore *original* dresses created by a famous designer.

ANTONYMS: mediocre, uncreative, unimaginative, uninventive, unoriginal

irritate *v.* To annoy or make angry; to bother. It irritated Kyle when his dog chewed up his shoes.

aggravate To provoke to anger. The hovering yellow jackets *aggravated* us during our picnic.

annoy To bother; to anger. Leslie *annoyed* her sister by borrowing her sweater without asking.

incense To make angry; enrage. The chef became *incensed* when he saw that the roast had burned.

provoke To make angry or resentful. John tried to *provoke* me by whistling the same tune all night.

vex To aggravate or annoy. The two-hour wait in line *vexed* everyone.

ANTONYMS: appease, pacify

J

jargon *n.* Confused or meaningless talk or writing; gibberish. The computer jargon in the manual did not make sense to me.

drivel Foolish talk or writing. Ms. Durham thought that the guest speaker's theories were a lot of *drivel*.

gibberish Rapid and senseless talk or chatter. The baby's *gibberish* made us laugh.

nonsense Words or actions that are meaningless or silly; foolishness. My sister sometimes talks *nonsense* in her sleep.

prattle Foolish or childish talk. We tried to understand the child's *prattle* because she looked so serious.

jeopardize *v.* To endanger; to risk. Lorraine decided not to jeopardize her health by going to school with a fever.

endanger To expose to danger. Drunk drivers *endanger* everyone on the road.

hazard To put in danger; risk. Lifeguards *hazard* their lives to save people.

imperil To place in peril; put in danger. Forests are *imperiled* when people don't put out their campfires.

risk To expose to a chance of injury or loss. Firefighters *risk* injuries when entering burning buildings.

L

liable *adj.* Likely; apt. Martin was liable to miss the school bus if he didn't hurry.

apt Having a natural tendency; likely. "The cat is *apt* to scratch you if you keep teasing it," warned Lloyd.

inclined Having a preference or tendency. Mr. Vogt was *inclined* to look on the bright side of things.

likely Having or showing a tendency or possibility to do or be; apt. Donna was *likely* to get a good grade in the class if she kept up with her work.

prone Given or inclined; disposed. Tim was *prone* to forgetting his locker combination.

ANTONYM: unlikely

loiter *v.* To linger or pass time idly. The newspaper carriers loiter around the stationery store while they wait for their papers.

dawdle To waste time; idle. The supervisor asked the students to stop *dawdling* in the hallway.

idle To waste (time) doing nothing. Peg was determined not to *idle* away another weekend.

linger To stay on as if unwilling to go. The fans *lingered* outside the concert hall, hoping to catch a glimpse of their singing idol.

lounge To pass time in a lazy manner; loaf. The couple *lounged* around the swimming pool all afternoon.

M

magnify *v.* To make something look bigger than its real size; to enlarge. Students in the science class magnified onion cells to learn about their structure.

amplify To enlarge or increase in power, amount, etc. The band *amplified* its sound so that it could be heard throughout the huge stadium.

enlarge To make or become larger; expand. Mrs. Easley used the overhead projector to *enlarge* the diagram.

exaggerate To make something appear larger than it really is. The political cartoonist *exaggerated* the features of the people in the drawing.

extend To stretch out. The artist *extended* the fence in the painting to give the picture more depth.

ANTONYMS: **compact, compress, concentrate, condense, contract**

minor *adj.* Of less importance or not important. The film critic found some minor flaws in the movie but gave it an excellent review.

inconsequential Unimportant. Dave tried to persuade himself that his errors in the game were *inconsequential*.

insignificant Unimportant. Toby tried not to get annoyed about *insignificant* matters.

nonessential Not essential; not really needed. Sharon cut some *nonessential* dialogue out of her story.

trivial Of little value or importance; insignificant. The secretary quickly took care of the *trivial* tasks before moving on to her major assignments.

unimportant Not important or significant. Ms. Humes told us that the length of our essays was *unimportant* as long as we covered the topic.

ANTONYMS: **essential, major, significant, vital**

mischievous *adj.* Full of mischief. The identical twins were always playing mischievous tricks.

high-spirited Having a courageous, vigorous, or fiery spirit. The babysitter finally got the *high-spirited* child to settle down and go to sleep.

prankish Playful. Caroline was a *prankish* girl who always managed to cheer people up.

roguish Playfully mischievous. Tom's *roguish* antics got him into trouble more than once.

mockery *n.* Ridicule. Lance, who had often made fun of people, found out how much mockery hurt when it was used against him.

jeering Bitter sarcasm. The *jeering* of the audience stopped when the speaker left the stage.

ridicule Words or actions intended to make another person or thing seem foolish. The politician was held up to *ridicule* for his statement.

scoffing Mocking disbelief. Her friend's *scoffing* only made Mary determined to find the fact in her book.

taunting Scorn; sarcasm. The pitcher tried not to be distracted by the crowd's *taunting*.

N

naive *adj.* Unaffected; innocent. Antonia was afraid she would sound naive if she asked the question.

artless Without cunning; simple; natural. *Artless* questions often have complicated answers.

innocent Showing a lack of worldly wisdom; simple. The house guests were charmed by the *innocent* child.

unaffected Natural, simple, and sincere. Tish was a wonderfully *unaffected* person.

unsophisticated Not sophisticated; simple, natural, or innocent; inexperienced in worldly things. Kevin's father tried to convince him that it was fine for a thirteen-year-old to be *unsophisticated*.

ANTONYMS: affected, insincere, sophisticated

nerve *n.* Courage; firmness, especially in a difficult situation. Tom had the nerve to ask for a raise.

boldness Courage; daring. Lancelot's *boldness* in battle was praised in many poems and stories.

bravery Valor; courage; fearlessness. Odysseus showed *bravery* and cleverness in his escape from the Cyclops.

fortitude Courage to meet and endure pain, hardship, or danger. Crossing an unknown sea and settling in an untamed land required *fortitude* from the Pilgrims.

valor Great courage or bravery, especially in war. My father received the Purple Heart for *valor*.

ANTONYMS: cowardice, dread, timidity

nuisance *n.* A bothersome or annoying person or situation. The television was a nuisance while I was trying to do my homework.

annoyance Something that bothers. His new glasses were an *annoyance* that Jared was trying to get used to.

pest An irritating or annoying person or thing. Aaron decided that his sister wasn't such a *pest* after all.

vexation A person or thing that irritates or annoys. My mother calls my uncle a *vexation* when he talks about politics.

obnoxious *adj.* Causing strong dislike; hateful; offensive. We were overwhelmed by an obnoxious odor when the river overflowed.

abominable Very bad or disgusting. The health conditions of the people in the Middle Ages were *abominable*.

detestable Deserving to be strongly disliked or disapproved; abominable. "IT" was the *detestable* villain in

Madeleine L'Engle's book *A Wrinkle in Time*.

hateful Arousing or worthy of hatred. The traitor's betrayal of his country for money was *hateful*.

offensive Unpleasant or disagreeable. Naomi wanted to apologize for her *offensive* remark.

ANTONYMS: inoffensive, likable, lovable

observant *adj.* Quick to observe or notice; alert; attentive. The observant birdwatcher was able to identify twelve different kinds of birds in one morning.

alert Very watchful and ready, as for sudden action. The police officer was *alert* for any signs of danger.

attentive Giving or showing attention, interest, or notice. Although Roger was very *attentive*, he couldn't figure out how Bob did the card trick.

heedful Attentive and careful. The hiking group was told to be *heedful* about where they walked.

ANTONYMS: inattentive, unalert, unaware, unobservant

obstacle *n.* Something that prevents or hinders; obstruction. The bicycle rider swerved around the obstacle in the road.

barrier Something that blocks the way or stops movement, as a wall, fence, or dam. Gary and Greg set up a *barrier* dividing their room in half.

blockade Anything that hinders or obstructs. The police set up a *blockade* around the open manhole.

hindrance A person or thing that hinders or gets in the way; an obstruction. The new copying machine was a *hindrance* because it broke down so often.

obstruction Something that obstructs; barrier; hindrance. The apartment building residents considered the skyscraper an unsightly *obstruction* to their view.

ominous *adj.* Threatening or foreboding, like a bad omen. The loud thunder and jagged lightning seemed ominous to the detective.

foreboding Marked by a feeling that something bad is going to happen. We walked up the foreboding dark driveway with a strong sense of fear.

menacing Threatening, as with evil or harm. The massive, *menacing* monster in the closet turned out to be a bathrobe when Ray turned on the light.

sinister Threatening evil, trouble, or bad luck. There was something *sinister* about the old house in the woods, where the crime had happened long ago.

threatening Marked by a sign or indication of something bad or unfavorable to come; menacing. The deer sniffed the air worriedly, as if it sensed something *threatening* nearby.

ANTONYMS: heartening, nonthreatening, promising, soothing, unmenacing

outrageous *adj.* Unbelievable. Chris didn't blink at Carlos's outrageous plan.

fantastic Amazing; unbelievable. Marilyn had a *fantastic* ability to talk me into going along with her crazy ideas.

incredible So strange, unusual, or extraordinary as to be unbelievable. Thor Heyerdahl and his small crew made an *incredible* journey across the Pacific Ocean in a frail craft named Kon-Tiki.

unbelievable Not to be believed; incredible. When the baseball game was over, our opponents had beaten us by an *unbelievable* twenty runs.

ANTONYMS: believable, logical, reasonable

P

perplex *v.* To confuse or bewilder. The assignment perplexed Wayne until he asked the teacher for help.

baffle To confuse; bewilder. Larry *baffled* his friends and co-workers when he turned down the promotion.

bewilder To baffle or confuse; to puzzle. All the signs and complicated exits on the Los Angeles Freeway *bewildered* the tourist.

confuse To bewilder; mix up. Trying to keep track of the days during summer vacation always *confuses* me.

mystify To puzzle, bewilder, or baffle. The strange message that was left on our answering machine *mystified* us.

ANTONYMS: clarify, untangle

persecute *v.* To mistreat or oppress. The Pilgrims were persecuted for their religious beliefs.

abuse To treat harshly or cruelly. When people *abuse* animals, the Society for the Prevention of Cruelty to Animals often provides shelter.

oppress To burden or keep down by unjust use of force or authority. Throughout history, people who were *oppressed* by unfair rulers have revolted.

victimize To make a victim of. In George Orwell's famous book *1984,* the Big Brother government *victimized* people who questioned its actions.

pleasant *adj.* Agreeable or friendly in disposition or manner. Jennifer is one of those pleasant people who rarely becomes angry.

agreeable Giving pleasure; pleasing. The babysitter was relieved to discover that his charge was an *agreeable* child.

amiable Pleasing in disposition; agreeable; friendly. The *amiable* museum guide told us many interesting facts about the artists.

cordial Warm and hearty; sincere. The *cordial* hostess shook our hands at the end of the meeting.

genial Friendly and kind; cheerful. The *genial* doctor soon made Ted feel relaxed.

likable Pleasing; enjoyable. Fred, a *likable* student, was elected president of the class.

ANTONYMS: disagreeable, unenjoyable, unlikable, unpleasant

precious *adj.* Cherished; beloved. Al's great-aunt treasured the precious gift of a photograph album.

adored Loved and honored with great devotion. Grandparents are *adored* family members.

beloved Loved. Romeo and his *beloved* Juliet are two of William Shakespeare's most famous characters.

cherished Held dear; treated tenderly. The new father held his *cherished* young son in his arms.

esteemed Valued. May's *esteemed* bowling trophy held the place of honor on her dresser.

ANTONYMS: abhorrent, detestable, hateful, loathsome

primary *adj.* Most important; chief; main. The primary function of the pupil is to control the amount of light that enters your eye.

dominant Commanding; controlling; most important of all. The political party having the most members in Congress is the *dominant* party.

foremost First in place, time, rank, or order; chief. The Tour de France is the world's *foremost* bicycle endurance race.

predominant Superior in power, effect, etc.; prevailing; prominent. Shipping and tourism are the *predominant* industries in Vancouver, British Columbia.

premier First in rank or position; principal. The *premier* leader in many companies is the chairman of the board of directors.

prime First in rank or importance; chief. The *prime* purpose for the meeting between the leaders of the world was to discuss human rights.

ANTONYMS: inferior, subordinate, unimportant

R

realize *v.* To grasp, understand, or appreciate clearly and fully. I didn't realize it was autumn until I had to rake up the leaves from our old oak.

appreciate To recognize the value of something. Janna learned to *appreciate* football from her father, who had played professionally.

apprehend To understand or comprehend. Charlene *apprehends* the difference between "its" and "it's."

comprehend To understand; grasp. Finding the Rosetta Stone helped anthro-

pologists *comprehend* ancient Egyptian picture-writing, or hieroglyphics.

conceive To imagine; to understand. Frank tried to *conceive* how to make the characters in his paintings look three-dimensional.

recognize To acknowledge or accept. Although Jim *recognized* his problem, he couldn't think of a solution.

refuge *n.* Shelter or protection from danger or trouble. We took refuge in the cellar when we heard the tornado warnings.

asylum A place of safety; shelter. The refugees sought *asylum* in the United States.

haven A safe place; shelter. The charitable institution offered a *haven* for the homeless.

preserve An area set apart for the protection of something, as wildlife or forests. The government set aside the small island as a wildlife *preserve*.

sanctuary A haven or shelter for people or animals. Hundreds of wild birds nest at the bird *sanctuary*.

regular *adj.* Usual; habitual. Eating lunch at her desk was a regular routine for the busy executive.

customary Based on custom; usual. In social tennis, it is *customary* to spin a racket to see who will serve first.

habitual Expected from habit; usual. We took our *habitual* route to school.

routine Habitual; customary. Carrie had her *routine* snack before going to gymnastics practice.

See also **average.**

ANTONYMS: irregular, uncustomary, unhabitual, unusual

renovate *v.* To make like new; to repair. The Pedersons have renovated their Victorian house to its original 1890's appearance.

recondition To overhaul; put back into good condition. Rob worked for several weekends to *recondition* a used bicycle.

refresh To make fresh or vigorous again; revive. Breathing the cool night air *refreshed* us all.

renew To make new or as if new again; restore. Mr. Murphy *renews* antique furniture for a living.

restore To bring back to a former or original condition. It took experts a long time to *restore* the priceless painting.
ANTONYMS: annihilate, demolish, eliminate

residence *n.* The place where a person lives; home; dwelling. The President's official residence is the White House.

abode The place where one lives or stays; home; dwelling. My uncle drawled, "Welcome to my humble *abode.*"

dwelling A place where someone lives; a house or other home. The geography and weather in an area often determine what kinds of *dwellings* are built there.

habitation A dwelling place. The soldier had no idea where his next *habitation* would be.

lodging A small dwelling, as a house or cabin, where a person may stay, as for a vacation. Many national parks offer *lodging* for visitors.

responsible *adj.* Reliable; trustworthy. The most responsible player was chosen team captain.

conscientious Careful and reliable. Angela was *conscientious* about getting her work done on time.

dependable Worthy of trust; reliable. The *dependable* babysitter never had trouble getting work.

reliable Able to be trusted; dependable. Whenever we wanted somebody *reliable* to keep score, we called Michael.

trustworthy Worthy of confidence; reliable. The *trustworthy* engineer eased the train into the depot.
ANTONYMS: irresponsible, undependable, unreliable, untrustworthy

S

scrap *n.* A small piece; fragment. The important scrap of paper fluttered unnoticed off the table.

fragment A broken-off part or incomplete piece; a chip. Jessie glued the

broken *fragment* back onto the flowerpot.

morsel A small piece or bit. Tim had to beg Bill for just a *morsel* of his sandwich.

particle A very small part, piece, or amount; speck. The *particles* of pollen in the air made Ed's allergies worse.

shred A bit; particle. By the time the party was over, there wasn't a *shred* of food in the house.

sensitive *adj.* Easily upset or angered; touchy. Evelyn is sensitive about what others think of her.

high-strung Very nervous. The trainer was very careful with the *high-strung* horse.

temperamental Easily excited or upset. The *temperamental* director stormed angrily out of the room.

thin-skinned Easily hurt or insulted; touchy. The *thin-skinned* quarterback flinched when the crowd booed his performance.

touchy Easily offended or hurt; irritable. Erin was *touchy* about her very short haircut.
ANTONYMS: insensitive, even-tempered, thick-skinned

solemn *adj.* Somber; gloomy. The solemn family sat in the waiting room hoping for good news.

bleak Gloomy; dismal. Once the members drew up a budget, their financial situation did not seem so *bleak.*

dejected Low in spirits; unhappy; downcast. The *dejected* child sat on the bench with her broken toy.

depressed Gloomy or sad. Everyone felt *depressed* when the rain continued for ten days.

dismal Sad and miserable. Allan was *dismal* when his dog ran away.

melancholy Gloomy; sad; depressed. The sad song on the radio put Anna in a *melancholy* mood.
ANTONYMS: cheerful, lighthearted, optimistic

spirit *n.* Liveliness; vigor; courage. Randall's spirit makes people gather around him at a party.

liveliness Vitality. Our dog's *liveliness* sometimes exhausted us.

vigor Active strength or force of mind or body; healthy energy. Elaine woke up refreshed and full of *vigor*.

vitality Energy or vigor. The talent scout was very impressed by the athlete's *vitality*.

ANTONYMS: idleness, inactivity, inertia, languor

sullen *adj.* Gloomily silent; resentful; ill-humored. Kirk tried to cheer up his sullen brother.

ill-humored Irritable. I went to bed too late and woke up *ill-humored*.

resentful Full of or tending to feel resentment. Carol was *resentful* when Karen beat her for the lead in the school play.

sulky Gloomily cross or ill-humored. Lee was *sulky* because he thought everyone had forgotten his birthday.

surly Rude and ill-humored; cross; gruff. The teacher found it difficult to be patient with the *surly* student.

ANTONYMS: agreeable, amiable, cordial, genial, good-natured

suppress *v.* To put an end to or subdue by force. The king suppressed all opposition within the country.

conquer To defeat or win control of by use of force, as in war. The Spanish conquistadors *conquered* the Aztecs in Mexico.

subdue To gain power over, as by force; conquer. During the late 1400's, countries first began using cannons to *subdue* their enemies.

vanquish To defeat or overcome. The Greeks *vanquished* the Trojans in the Trojan War.

ANTONYMS: lose, surrender

surprise *v.* To shock or astonish by doing something unexpected. Loretta will surprise her mother by cleaning her room without being asked.

astound To stun with amazement. Joseph *astounded* his family when he won first prize in the speech contest.

awe To fill or inspire with awe. The beauty of the Egyptian pyramids *awes* almost every visitor.

dumfound To strike speechless with surprise; astonish; amaze. The unexpect-

ed visit of their long-lost relative *dumfounded* the Lyles.

stun To shock or astonish. The assassination of President John F. Kennedy *stunned* the world.

suspicious *adj.* Tending to suspect; distrustful. The cat was suspicious of the new baby.

distrustful Feeling or showing distrust; doubtful. World peace will be difficult to attain as long as countries are *distrustful* of one another.

doubtful Uncertain or undecided. The police were *doubtful* about the suspect's story.

skeptical Not believing readily; inclined to question or doubt. In the 1400's, people were *skeptical* of Copernicus's theory that the earth revolved around the sun.

wary Watchful and distrustful; very careful; cautious. The young woman was *wary* of the frog's claim that he was a prince.

ANTONYMS: confident, trusting, unsuspicious

T

tendency *n.* An inclination or leaning toward some condition or action. Yolanda's tendency to daydream concerned her parents.

disposition A leaning or inclination. Mr. Randolph had a *disposition* to worry about unimportant things.

inclination A leaning toward a certain condition, action, etc. People have an *inclination* to refuse desserts when they are on a diet.

proneness Inclination. Her *proneness* to put things off caused her to be too late to buy a concert ticket.

terrify *v.* To fill with tremendous fear. The Frankenstein monster mask terrified the young child.

appall To fill with dismay, horror, or shock. The tarantula *appalled* the camper as she watched it walk across her sleeping bag.

panic To be filled with fear and terror. The skydiver *panicked* when it was his turn to jump out of the plane.

petrify To make rigid or motionless with fear or surprise. We were *petrified* when the tree fell on our house during the storm.
ANTONYMS: comfort, reassure, soothe

tiresome *adj.* Tedious; boring. After awhile, Lynn found watching television tiresome.

boring Dull or tedious. Julie enjoyed science fiction books, but Yvette thought they were *boring*.

monotonous Boring because of lack of variety or change. Because it was *monotonous*, Jerry and Rick took turns playing catch with the dog.

tedious Long, dull, and wearisome. Weeding the garden is a *tedious* job.

wearisome Causing fatigue; tedious. The most *wearisome* part of Ms. Carlson's job was the two-hour daily commute.
ANTONYMS: exciting, stimulating, thrilling

U

unify *v.* To bring together; to unite. President Lincoln wanted to unify the North and the South.

consolidate To combine or unite. The store manager decided to *consolidate* three departments onto one floor.

integrate To fit or bring together into a whole. The artist *integrated* different historic scenes into a mural.

merge To combine or be combined so as to lose separate identity. The two banks *merged*, hoping to streamline services and increase business.

unite To join together so as to form a unit; combine. Canada and the United States *united* to construct the St. Lawrence Seaway.
ANTONYMS: disconnect, disengage, disunite, separate

unusual *adj.* Uncommon; not ordinary. The unusual design on Mac's skateboard was a spiral within a star.

abnormal Not normal; irregular. One hundred degrees is an *abnormal* body temperature.

alien Very strange. The idea of eating a peanut butter and tomato sandwich was *alien* to me, but my father insisted it was delicious.

curious Odd or strange. In the story *Alice in Wonderland*, Alice falls into a very *curious* world.

extraordinary Remarkable. Jason's entry was the most *extraordinary* science exhibit the judges had seen.

peculiar Odd or strange. John's high-jumping technique was very *peculiar*, but he beat the rest of us every time.

See also **impressive**.

ANTONYMS: average, normal, ordinary, regular, usual

V

vicious *adj.* Spiteful; mean; malicious. Who could be responsible for such a vicious rumor?

atrocious Terribly wicked, criminal, vile, or cruel; barbaric. The Goths were an *atrocious*, uncivilized people who attacked poorly protected cities.

malicious Showing or having malice or the desire to harm or injure; spiteful. *Malicious* gossip can hurt or ruin a person's reputation.

spiteful Filled with spite. Lance immediately regretted his *spiteful* comment.

vile Evil; low; depraved. The *vile* criminal was sent to a maximum-security prison.

wretched Wicked or mean. Steve was selected to play the *wretched* villain in the school play.

ANTONYMS: complimentary, genial, noble, righteous, virtuous

WRITER'S GUIDE

WRITER'S GUIDE

SPELLING RULES

Unit 1: Prefixes and Suffixes

- A **prefix** is a word part that is added to the beginning of a word to change its meaning or part of speech.

Prefix	Example
a-	*aloft*
be-	*belittle*
with-	*withhold*

- A **suffix** is a word part that is added to the end of a word to change its meaning or part of speech.

Suffix	Example
-hood	*likelihood*
-some	*handsome*
-wise	*otherwise*

Unit 2: The Sound /ə/

The weak vowel sound schwa /ə/ may be spelled with these letters in the final syllable.

- with **a,** as in *incidental*

- with **e,** as in *intruder*

- with **o,** as in *competitor*

- with **ou,** as in *tremendous*

- The sound /y/ may be heard before /ər/. In /yər/, /y/ is spelled with i.

  famil<u>i</u>ar   pecul<u>i</u>ar

- In many words that end with /əs/, a vowel letter precedes <u>ous</u>.

  stren<u>u</u>ous   outrag<u>e</u>ous

Unit 3: Confusing Pronunciations

- To spell correctly words with different pronunciations, pronounce each syllable in the words. Do not add or leave out syllables or sounds.

  con·grat·u·la·tions   kin·der·gar·ten

Unit 4: The /ə/ and Shifting Accents

- To spell a word with /ə/, think of another word with the same root. You can often hear the vowel sound clearly in the second word.

    disp<u>o</u>sition   disp<u>o</u>se

Unit 5: More Shifting Accents

- When you are uncertain of the spelling of a word, remember that a related word can often help you.

    custody   custodian

Unit 7: Plurals

- Some English words that are borrowed from Latin or Greek have two plural forms.

Original Form	English Form
antennae	antennas
indices	indexes

- For some Latin and Greek words, the original forms of the plurals are preferred.

Singular	Plural
alumnus	alumni
datum	data

- To form the plural of a noun that ends with a vowel and *y*, add *s*.

    essay—essays   attorney—attorneys

- To form the plural of a noun that ends with a consonant and *y*, change *y* to *i* and add *es*.

    theory—theories   mystery—mysteries

Unit 8: Words with *-ery* and *-ary*

- The suffix *-ary* can be added to a root or base word to form an adjective.

    revolution—revolutionary

- The suffix *-ery* can be added to a root or base word to form a noun.

Suffix	Meaning	Example
-ery	"a place where something is done"	refinery
	"the act or art of"	archery

Unit 9: **Homophones**

- **Homophones** are words that sound alike but are spelled differently and have different meanings. To spell correctly a word that is a homophone, think about the meaning of the word.

     My father is the *counsel* to the President's *council*.

Unit 10: **Easily Confused Words**

- To spell a word that can be easily confused, pronounce the word carefully and think about its meaning.

     A *statute* is a bill or law.
     A *statue* is a sculpture.

- The sound /ə/ in *remedy* changes to /ē/ in the accented syllable of *remedial*.

Unit 11: **Inflectional Endings**

If a word ends with one vowel followed by one consonant, double the final consonant before adding *ed* and *ing* if:

- it is a one-syllable word.

     drag   dragged   dragging

- it is a two-syllable word and the accent is on the final syllable.

     propel   propelled   propelling

Do not double the final consonant before adding *ed* or *ing* if:

- it is a word with one vowel and one consonant and the first syllable is accented.

     signal   signaled   signaling

- it is a verb that ends with two consonants or with two vowels and a consonant.

  sprawl   sprawled   sprawling
  reveal   revealed   revealing

Unit 13: Words with Greek Roots

- Many English words were borrowed from ancient Greek. The word *sphere*, for example, comes from the Greek word *sphaira,* which means "ball."

Unit 14: More Words with Greek Roots

- Many words used by scientists have origins in the Greek language, although they are not Greek words. For example, *dehydrate* is formed with the Greek root *hydr,* which means "water."

Unit 15: Verb Suffixes

- The suffixes *-ify* and *-ate* are often added to a root or base word to form a verb.

  just + ify = justify   abbrevi + ate = abbreviate

Unit 16: More Shifting Accents

When a suffix is added to some words, there is a shift in the accented syllable. Listening for the shift in the accented syllable in the second word will help you spell the first word. Here are some examples.

- The sound /ə/ in *remedy* changes to /ē/ in the accented syllable of *remedial.*

- The "silent" *n* in *condemn* is sounded when the accent shifts in *condemnation.*

Unit 17: Mathematics Words

- Words used in the study of mathematics were borrowed from many ancient civilizations. The word *algebra* comes from the two Arabic words: *al,* "the," and *jabr,* "reduction of fractions."

Unit 19: Tricky Spellings

- To spell correctly words with tricky spellings, remember the key letter combinations.

  do<u>ugh</u>nut   g<u>au</u>ge

Unit 20: Latin Prefixes

Here are five Latin prefixes and their meanings.

Prefix	Meaning	Example
ab-	"away from"	*abrupt*
ad-	"to"	*adhesive*
ex-	"out from"	*exception*
pro-	"forward"	*projector*
sub-	"merge"	*submerge*

Unit 21: Words with Latin Roots

Here are two Latin roots and their meanings.

Root	Meaning	Example
duct	"lead"	conduct
tract	"pull"	attraction

Unit 22: More Latin Roots

Here are two more Latin roots and their meanings.

Root	Meaning	Example
script	"write"	description
vers	"turn"	reverse

Unit 23: Synonyms and Antonyms

- A **synonym** is a word that has the same or almost the same meaning as another word.

  donation—contribution
  apparent—evident

- An **antonym** has the opposite meaning of another word.

  irritate—soothe
  counterfeit—authentic

Unit 25: Words with -*ant* and -*ent*

Here are two ways to spell /ənt/ at the end of words.

- with -**ant,** as in *hesitant*
- with -**ent,** as in *frequent*

Unit 26: Words That End with /īz/

- The suffix -*ize* can be added to a noun or an adjective to form a verb.

  critic (n.)—criticize (v.)
  sterile (adj.)—sterilize (v.)

- Most of the verbs that end with the sounds /īz/ are spelled with *ize*. In some words /īz/ is spelled *yze*.

  paralyze   analyze

Unit 27: Science Words

- Most words used in the study of science come from Latin or Greek: *bacteria, plasma.*

Unit 28: Syllable Patterns

- When a word has two consonant letters between two vowel sounds, divide the word between the consonants. Remember, however, that you should never divide a consonant digraph.

  bal·lot   ras·cal   broth·er

- When a word has one consonant letter between two vowel sounds, divide *before* the consonant if the first vowel sound is long;

  fo·cus   si·lence

  divide *after* the consonant if the first vowel sound is short and the first syllable is accented.

  piv·ot   crev·ice

- When a word has a prefix or a suffix, separate the prefix or suffix from the base word before dividing the base word.

  dis·honor·able   mis·direct

WRITER'S GUIDE

Unit 29: Double-Letter Spellings

- Double consonant letters can result from **assimilation,** or the changing of a sound in a word to make the word easier to pronounce. Assimilation often occurs when a prefix that ends with a consonant is added to a base word that begins with a consonant. The final consonant of the prefix is changed so that it is the same as the first consonant of the base word.

Unit 31: Words with /əns/ or /ens/

- Usually, if you can find an English verb in the word, the word will end with *-ance.*

     resist   resistance

- Usually, if you can think of a related adjective, the noun will end with *-ence.*

     innocent   innocence

- Most words ending in /əns/ or /ens/ are spelled with the letters *ence* rather than *ense.* You must memorize the words that end with *ense.*

     defense   suspense

Unit 32: Adjective Suffixes

- The adjective suffixes *-ible* and *-able* add the meaning "able to" to verbs and to some root words, as in *divisible* and *changeable.*
- The adjective suffix *-ive* adds the meaning "tending to, or having the quality of" to verbs and root words, as in *impressive* and *sensitive.*

Here are some rules for adding *-ible, -able,* and *-ive* to form adjectives.

- If a word ends with *e,* drop the final *e* before adding a suffix beginning with a vowel letter. However, if a word ends with *ce* or *ge* and the suffix begins with *a,* keep the final *e* to spell the sounds /s/ and /j/.

     like—likable   trace—traceable

- When a word ends with a consonant and *y,* change the *y* to *i* before adding the suffix.

     rely   reliable

Unit 33: /shəl/ and /shəs/ Endings

- If a base word ends with the sound /n/ before /shəl/, the spelling is most often *tial*.

    residential   potential

- If a base word ends with *ce* as in *race,* but not *nce* as in *confidence,* the spelling is usually *cial*.

    race   racial

- All words that end with the sounds /fishəl/ are spelled with *cial*.

    artificial   superficial

- If a base word ends with *ce* (not *nce*), /shəs/ is spelled *cious*.

    malice—malicious   space—spacious

Unit 34: Words from Greek

Here are the spellings and pronunciations of some English words from Greek.

- **ch** is pronounced /k/, as in *chaos*.

- **ph** is pronounced /f/, as in *prophet*.

- **ps** is pronounced /s/, as in *psalm*.

- **rh** at the beginning of a word is pronounced /r/, as in *rhythm*.

- **th** is pronounced /th/, as in *marathon*.

Unit 35: Multisyllabic Words

- To spell an unfamiliar multisyllabic word, divide it into its smaller word parts. Think of the meaning of the root and prefix or suffix. Remember the spelling and pronunciation of each smaller part to help you recall the word.

    un·usual·ly   semi·final·ist

TROUBLESOME WORDS TO SPELL

already	have	quite	today
am	haven't	receive	together
and	hello	remember	tomorrow
are	her	right	tonight
awhile	here	school	too
because	I'll	some	two
before	I'm	sometimes	until
can't	isn't	stationery	very
close	it's	suppose	want
couldn't	know	teacher	we
cousin	letter	Thanksgiving	went
didn't	maybe	that's	we're
don't	Mr.	their	won't
down	Mrs.	there	would
everybody	name	there's	write
football	now	they're	writing
for	off	think	you
friend	our	thought	your
from	outside	time	you're
Halloween	pretty	to	yours

LANGUAGE: A Glossary of Terms and Examples

Grammar

Sentences

- A **sentence** is a group of words that expresses a complete thought. Every sentence begins with a capital letter and ends with a punctuation mark.

- A **declarative sentence** makes a statement. It ends with a period (.).
    This airport is a busy place.

- An **interrogative sentence** asks a question and ends with a question mark (?).
    Is my flight on time?

- An **imperative sentence** gives a command or makes a request. It ends with a period (.).
    Please give me a window seat.

- An **exclamatory sentence** expresses strong feeling or surprise. It ends with an exclamation point (!).
    How excited I am!

- The **subject** of a sentence is the part about which something is said. All the words that make up the subject are called the **complete subject.**
    Everyone in the club is an excellent swimmer.

- The **predicate** of the sentence is the part that says something about the subject. All the words that make up the predicate are called the **complete predicate.**
    The truck driver pulled up to the restaurant parking lot.

Nouns

- A **noun** is a word used to name a person, place, thing, or idea.

- A **common noun** names any person, place, thing, or idea. Common nouns are not capitalized unless they come at the beginning of a sentence.

    umpire   delicatessen   cactus

- A **proper noun** names a particular person, place, thing, or idea. Proper nouns are always capitalized.

    Hank Aaron   San Francisco   August

- A **singular noun** names one person, place, thing, or idea.

- A **plural noun** names more than one person, place, thing, or idea.

- To form the plurals of most nouns, add *s*.

    pier—piers   alien—aliens   incident—incidents

- To form the plurals of nouns ending in *s, ss, zz, x, sh,* or *ch,* add *es*.

    excess—excesses   hatch—hatches   ax—axes

- To form the plurals of nouns ending in *y* preceded by a consonant, change the *y* to *i* and add *es*.

    locality—localities   photocopy—photocopies

- To form the plurals of nouns ending in *y* preceded by a vowel, add only *s*.

    essay—essays   valley—valleys   decoy—decoys

- To form the plurals of some nouns ending in *o*, add *s*. Add *es* to some others.

    solo—solos   hero—heroes   embryo—embryos

- To form the plurals of some nouns ending in *f* or *fe,* change the *f* to *v* and add *s* or *es*.

    life—lives   half—halves

- The plurals of some nouns are formed by a vowel change within the singular form or by an addition to the singular form.

    goose—geese   child—children   ox—oxen

- Some nouns have the same form for singular and plural.

    moose   deer   sheep

- A few nouns have only a plural form.

    scissors   politics   slacks

- A **possessive noun** shows ownership.

- To form the possessive of a singular noun, add an apostrophe and *s*. To form the possessive of a plural noun ending with *s*, add only an apostrophe.

    Earl's bike   the attorneys' cases

- To form the possessive of a plural noun that does not end with *s*, add an apostrophe and *s*.

    children's clothing   sheep's wool

Verbs

- A **verb** is a word used to express an action or state of being.

    walk   flew   sleeps   became

- An **action verb** expresses physical or mental action.

    drowned   admitted   controlled

- A **linking verb** connects the subject of a sentence to a noun, a pronoun, or an adjective in the predicate. It does not show action.

    is   are   was   were   seems   feels   sounds

- A **verb phrase** is a verb that consists of more than one word.

    was unraveling   had been canceled   are invading

- The **main verb** is the verb in a verb phrase that expresses action or being.

    was <u>unraveling</u>   had been <u>canceled</u>   are <u>invading</u>

- A **helping verb** is used with the main verb to express tense, person, or number.

    <u>was</u> unraveling   <u>had been</u> canceled   <u>are</u> invading

Verb Tenses

- The time expressed by a verb is its **tense.**

- The **present tense** expresses action that is taking place now.

    The problem <u>perplexes</u> Mai.   Mai <u>analyzes</u> the problem.

- The **past tense** expresses action that took place at some *definite time in the past.*

    The problem <u>perplexed</u> me this morning.

Regular and Irregular Verbs

- The three basic forms of a verb are its **principal parts.** These principal parts are the **present,** the **past,** and the **past participle.**

- The past and past participle of **regular verbs** are formed by adding *d* or *ed* to the present form. The past and past participle of regular verbs ending in a consonant followed by *y* are formed by changing the *y* to *i* and adding *ed*.

Present	Past	Past Participle
attempt(s)	attempted	(has, have, had) attempted
modify(ies)	modified	(has, have, had) modified

- The past and past participle forms of **irregular verbs** are not formed by adding *d* or *ed* to their present forms. Their past and past participles are formed in a variety of ways, as shown below.

Present	Past	Past Participle
go(es)	went	gone
ride(s)	rode	ridden
swim(s)	swam	swum

Adjectives

- An **adjective** is a word used to describe a noun or a pronoun.

  That man has a courteous manner.

- The **positive degree** of an adjective is used when only *one* thing is being described.

  The puppy is cute.   This meal is delicious.

- The **comparative degree** of an adjective is used when *two* things or ideas are being compared. To compare two things, add *er*.

  My dog is friskier after a bath than before I bathe it.

  Some adjectives of two syllables and most adjectives of three or more syllables use the word *more* to form their comparative forms.

  Its coat looks even more magnificent when it's clean.

- The **superlative degree** of an adjective is used when *three or more* things are being compared. Add *est* to form the superlative form.

  At the dog show, it'll have the shiniest coat of all.

  Some adjectives of two syllables and most adjectives of three or more syllables use the word *most* to form their superlative forms.

  I'll be complimented on the *most* professional job of all.

- A **participle** is a word that looks like a verb form but is used as an adjective.

  My groomed pet will be a shining example of my hard work.

Adverbs

- An **adverb** is a word used to modify a verb, an adjective, or another adverb. Adverbs answer the questions *where, when, how, how often,* and *to what extent.*

    <u>Yesterday</u> I ran in the track meet. (modifies the verb *ran*)
    That movie is <u>extremely</u> sad. (modifies the adjective *sad*)
    He played <u>very</u> well. (modifies the adverb *well*)

- You can often form an adverb by adding *ly* to an adjective. When you add *ly,* you usually do not change the spelling of the word.

    frequent—frequently   elegant—elegantly

- When a word ends with *ble, ly* takes the place of *le.*

    reliable—reliably   comparable—comparably

- When a word ends with *ic,* add *ally* to form the adverb.

    frantic—frantically   magic—magically

- The **positive degree** of an adverb is used when *one* action is being described.

    Eileen ran the course <u>swiftly</u>.

- The **comparative degree** of an adverb is used to compare two actions.

    Suzanne ran the course <u>more swiftly</u> than Eileen.

- The **superlative degree** of an adverb is used when three or more actions are being compared.

    Alice ran the course the <u>most swiftly</u> of all.

Pronouns

- A **pronoun** is a word used in place of one or more nouns.

    Shelley is taking piano lessons. <u>She</u> practices every day.

- A **possessive pronoun** takes the place of a possessive noun or a possessive noun phrase. The words *my, mine, your, yours, his, her, hers, its, our, ours, their,* and *theirs* are possessive pronouns.

Agreement

● A verb must agree with its subject in number. If the subject of a sentence is singular, it takes a singular verb. If the subject is plural, it takes a plural verb.

> The <u>writers</u> <u>revise</u> manuscripts often.

> The <u>writer</u> <u>revises</u> manuscripts often.

● Some plural nouns take a singular verb.

> <u>Genetics</u> <u>is</u> the study of the biology of heredity.

Vocabulary

Synonyms

● **Synonyms** are words that have the same or nearly the same meaning. Here are some synonym pairs.

> ample—plenty   sulky—sullen

Antonyms

● **Antonyms** are words with opposite meanings. Here are some antonym pairs.

> convenient—inconvenient   rejection—acceptance

Homophones

● **Homophones** are words that sound alike but have different meanings and are often spelled differently. Here are some homophone pairs.

> peer—pier   council—counsel

Homographs

● **Homographs** are words that are spelled alike but have different meanings and sometimes different word histories.

> We tried to <u>console</u> Mike when he lost the race.
> Please put the <u>console</u> next to the wall.

Prefixes

- A **prefix** is a word part that is added to the beginning of a word to change its meaning or part of speech.

  <u>super</u>power   <u>mis</u>fortune   <u>be</u>little

Suffixes

- A **suffix** is a word that is added to the end of a word to change its meaning or part of speech.

  imagin<u>ary</u>   terri<u>fy</u>   commit<u>ment</u>

DICTIONARY: A Glossary of Terms and Examples

Alphabetical Order

- The order of letters from A to Z is called **alphabetical order.** Words in a dictionary are listed in alphabetical order. These words are in alphabetical order.

  exposure

  exquisite

  familiar

  favorite

Guide Words

- There are two **guide words** at the top of each dictionary page. The word on the left is the first word on the page. The word on the right is the last word on the page. All the other words on the page are in alphabetical order between the guide words.

evidence   exquisite

ev·i·dence /ev′ə·dəns/ *n.*   **1** That which tends to prove or disprove the truth of something; proof: *evidence* of a crime.

signs of or demonstrate: to *exhibit* fatigue. **5** *n.* Something given as evidence in a court of law.

Entry Word

- On a dictionary page, an **entry word** is a word in dark print that is followed by its meaning. Entry words appear in alphabetical order.

  ex·cep·tion /ik·sep′shən/ *n.*   **1** An exclusion. **2** Something that does not conform to the general pattern: an *exception* to the rule.
  ex·cess /*n.* ek′ses *or* ik·ses′, *adj.* ek′ses/ **1** *n.* An amount, degree, or supply of something beyond what is needed or proper: an *excess* of anger. **2** *adj.* Over what is usual, allowed, or needed: Don't carry *excess* weight while hiking.
  ex·clu·sive /iks·kloo′siv/ *adj.*   **1** Resisting the admission of outsiders to association, membership, etc.: an *exclusive* circle of friends. **2** Excluding all others from a part or share; belonging to only one: *exclusive* rights. **3** Complete; total; undivided: *exclusive* attention.

Pronunciation

- A **pronunciation** follows each entry word. Special spelling and symbols, called **diacritical marks,** show how to pronounce each word.

> **ex·qui·site** /eks′kwi·zit *or* ik·skwiz′it/ *adj.*
> **1** Very fine or delicate: an *exquisite* necklace.   **2** Very beautiful: an *exquisite* dress.
> **3** Of rare excellence; admirable: *exquisite* taste.

Part of Speech

- A **part of speech** tells whether the word is a noun, a verb, or some other part of speech. The names are abbreviated.

Definition

- A **definition** tells what a word means in the dictionary. Many words have more than one definition. Sometimes an example sentence follows the definition.

Example

- An **example** shows you how to use the word.

Pronunciation Key

- A **pronunciation key** explaining the diacritical marks appears at the beginning of a dictionary. A brief key is often found at the bottom of a dictionary page as well.

---

act, āte, câre, ärt;   egg, ēven;   if, īce;   on, ōver, ôr;   bo͝ok, fo͞od;   up, tûrn;
ə=a in *ago,* e in *listen,* i in *giraffe,* o in *pilot,* u in *circus;*   yo͞o=u in *music;* oil;   out;
chair;   sing;   shop;   thank;   that;   zh in *treasure.*

Syllables

- Most words are made up of several parts called **syllables.** Each syllable has a vowel sound.
- In a word with two or more syllables in the dictionary, the **accent mark** (′) in the pronunciation shows which syllable is said with the most force.
- The syllable with the accent mark is called the **accented syllable.**
- A **secondary accent** shows a syllable that is said with less force.

Etymology

- An **etymology** is a word history. It explains how a word came into our language. It also tells how the meaning and spelling of a word has changed and developed. Some dictionaries provide etymologies. They often use a special symbol such as an arrow to show where the etymology begins.

> **flu·ent** /floo'ənt/ *adj.* **1** Capable of speaking or writing with smoothness or ease. **2** Spoken or written with smoothness or ease; effortless: She speaks *fluent* Chinese.—**flu'ent·ly** *adv.* ▶ *Fluent* comes from the Latin verb *fluere,* "to flow."

Idiom

- An **idiom** is an expression that has a specialized meaning. The meaning of an idiom is usually quite different from the meaning of the separate words.

> **re·cord** /*v.* ri·kôrd', *n., adj.* rek'ərd/ **1** *v.* To write down information for future use. **2** *v.* To show or indicate: The thermometer *recorded* a temperature of 102°. **3** *v.* To store sound on a tape or disk. **4** *n.* A disk that can be played on a phonograph. **5** *n.* Preserved information about things that have happened: school *records.* **6** *n.* The greatest achievement of its kind, as in sports. **7** *adj.* Better or greater than all others: a *record* rainfall.—**break the record** To do or be better than the best that has been achieved.

COMPOSITION

Guides for the Writing Process

Prewriting

Use this checklist to plan your writing.

- Choose a topic.

- Choose a purpose for writing.

- Ask yourself questions about your topic.

- Choose a prewriting plan that works best for the form of writing you have chosen.

- Add more ideas as you think of them.

- Read over your plan.

- Begin to put your ideas in order.

Here are some prewriting plans.

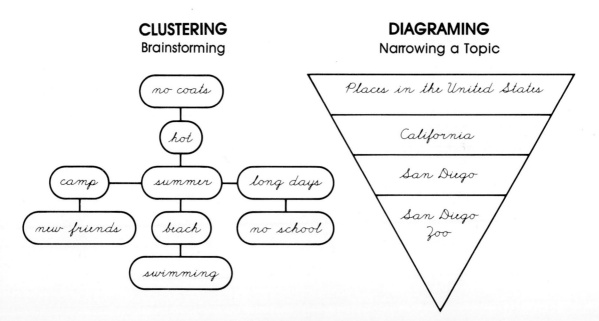

CLUSTERING
Brainstorming

no coats

hot

camp — summer — long days

new friends   beach   no school

swimming

DIAGRAMING
Narrowing a Topic

Places in the United States

California

San Diego

San Diego Zoo

CHARTING
Organizing Facts

Who	What	When	Where	Why
Anne	mows lawn	week-ends	local homes	to earn money
José	feeds horses	every day	the ranch	to help family
Ray	waters plants	once a week	in house	likes growing things

OUTLINING
Organizing Research

Dinosaurs

Kinds of
A. Lizard-hipped
  1. Brontosaurus
  2. Tyrannosaurus
B. Bird-hipped
  1. Stegosaurus
  2. Triceratops

Living Habits
A. Lived in swamps
B. Got food from plants

MAPPING
Drawing a Plan

Beginning

Val wants to be on the U.S. Olympic Swim Team.

She wants to practice every day for hours at a time.

Middle

Val wins many local and state races.

Val signs up for a national race to qualify for the Olympic team.

One week before the race, Val gets the flu.

Ending

Val must stay in bed. She cannot practice.

On race day, Val does swim. She finishes third. She makes team.

Composing

Use this checklist as you write.

- Read over your plan.

- Think about your purpose and audience.

- Use your plan to put your ideas on paper quickly.

- Do not worry about spelling, punctuation, or grammar at this time.

- Remember that you may get more ideas as you write.

- Add more new ideas as you think of them.

Revising

Use this checklist when you edit and proofread your work.

Editing

- Read over your work.

- Be sure your audience has enough information.

- Be sure the order of your sentences makes sense.

- Check that each sentence is a complete thought.

- Be sure each paragraph has a clear topic sentence.

- Check that all the detail sentences support the main idea.

- Be sure the words are lively and interesting.

Proofreading

- Be sure you used capital letters correctly.

- Be sure you used punctuation marks correctly.

- Check the spelling of each word.

- Be sure you used each word correctly.

- Be sure the grammar is correct.

- Be sure the first line of each paragraph is indented.

- Be sure your handwriting is neat and readable.

Editing and Proofreading Marks

- Use **editing and proofreading marks** when you revise your writing. These marks help you see the changes you want to make.
- Remember you can go back and change words or sentences as many times as you want or need to.

> The school fair will be held next
> <u>t</u>uesday afternoon. All students are
> going to attend⊙ There will be a ^*writing* contest
> and a crafts show. Science projects will
> also be displayed. Teachers ^ families,
> and friends will be invited. The
> school band will play ˇThe Star-Spangled
> Banner. ˇThen the principal and the ~~and the~~
> coach will give a speech. ⟨Prises⟩ *Prizes* will be
> given for the best compositions and
> drawings. ¶The fair has always been
> a highlight of the /school year. Plans
> are already being made for the fair
> next year. It will ⟨place⟩ take ⟨in⟩
> tr
> April instead of in May.

Editing and Proofreading Marks	
≡	capitalize
⊙	make a period
∧	add something
⸋	add a comma
ˇˇ	add quotation marks
ℯ	take something away
◯	spell correctly
¶	indent the paragraph
/	make a lowercase letter
∼ tr	transpose

A Glossary of Terms and Examples

Kinds of Sentences

- A **sentence** is a group of words that expresses a complete thought. Every sentence begins with a capital letter and ends with a punctuation mark.
- A **declarative sentence** makes a statement. It ends with a period (.).

  This sandwich is delicious.

- An **interrogative sentence** asks a question and ends with a question mark (?).

  When are you leaving?

- An **imperative sentence** gives a command or makes a request. It ends with a period (.).

  Call me at five o'clock.

- An **exclamatory sentence** expresses strong feeling or surprise. It ends with an exclamation point (!).

  How nice of you to come!

Paragraph

- A **paragraph** is a group of sentences that develops a single topic. The single topic is the **main idea** of the paragraph.
- The **topic sentence** expresses the main idea of a paragraph.
- **Detail sentences** support, explain, or expand the topic sentence.
- The first sentence in a paragraph is indented.

Descriptive Paragraph

- A **descriptive paragraph** describes a person, place, or thing.
- The **topic sentence** often gives a general impression of the subject.
- **Detail sentences** must support the topic sentence. They should be arranged in some kind of logical order.
- Using vivid descriptive words helps set the **tone** for this type of paragraph. The tone is the mood of the paragraph.
- Where appropriate, words that help the reader *see, hear, smell, touch,* and *feel* are used in a description.
- Using personality traits as well as physical characteristics when describing people and animals adds to a description.
- Comparisons can make descriptions more vivid.

Here is an example of a descriptive paragraph.

> When I approached the narrow glass doors with the plain, wooden frames, I prepared myself to be disappointed in the fabled Grand Hotel. After one step inside, however, my senses were assuring me that all the stories about it were true. Rows of lush palm trees bent to greet me like green-liveried servants. Live parrots cawed and whistled above my head amid the babble of running water. The bellhops, in sparkling white uniforms with gold braid, pushed along heaving carts full of bags and satchels of every size and description. I twirled around slowly, drinking in the scene and wondering how anything so exotic could have such a plain brown wrapper.

How-to Paragraph

- A paragraph that tells the reader how to do something is called a **how-to paragraph.**
- A how-to paragraph begins with a **topic sentence** that tells the process to be explained.
- The paragraph includes a list of the materials needed.
- **Detail sentences** explain the steps in the process in the correct order.

Here is an example of a how-to paragraph.

> Here is a quick and easy way to make a pillow. You will need material that measures 2 feet by 1 foot, a needle, thread, and stuffing. For the stuffing, use the stuffing from an old pillow, or old clean socks or stockings. First, fold the material in half so that it is 1 foot square. Make sure you fold the material inside out. Next, sew the edges together. Make your seam 1 inch from the edge. Leave a space of 3 inches unsewn along the last edge. Now turn the material right side out. Fill it with the stuffing. Last, sew up the 3-inch space and your pillow is finished!

Comparison Paragraph

- A paragraph that shows how two things are alike is a **paragraph of comparison.**
- Most paragraphs of comparison have no more than two subjects. Usually, no more than three qualities are compared.
- The **topic sentence** states the subjects to be discussed.
- Each quality is discussed in the *same order* in which it is introduced.

Here is an example of a paragraph of comparison.

> Running and swimming are similar in some ways. Both exercises are convenient. They are solitary, independent exercises that can be done according to your own needs and schedule. They don't require teammates, extensive equipment, or long training. Running and swimming have similar short- and long-term effects on the body. As you run or swim, you increase your heart rate, which helps the body burn calories faster. Over the long term, both running and swimming improve muscle tone.

Persuasive Paragraph

- The purpose of a **persuasive paragraph** is to convince the audience that the writer's opinion and reasons for it are correct and should be followed.
- The **topic sentence** states the issue and offers an opinion on the issue.
- The **supporting sentences** present the reasons for the opinion.
- The strongest reason is usually saved for last because the audience is most likely to remember the final reason.
- The **conclusion** of the paragraph is a restatement of the reasons and calls upon the audience to take action on the issue.

Here is an example of a persuasive paragraph.

> We need more bike paths here in Lima City. First of all, bike paths would offer the possibility of healthful exercise to people of all ages. They would be especially good for young people because many of them have bikes but no good place to ride them. Secondly, bike paths would provide places for instructors to teach bike safety and supervise beginners until they have learned to ride. Most importantly, however, bike paths would cut down on accidents by providing safe areas without cars and trucks to distract bikers and make them nervous. Please support the Youth Council's petition for bike paths that will offer healthful activity and perhaps save lives!

Friendly Letter

- **Friendly letters and social notes,** such as **invitations** and **thank you notes,** have five parts.
- The **heading** is in the upper right-hand corner. It contains the letter writer's address and the date. A comma is used between the city and the state and between the day and the year.
- The **salutation** begins at the left margin. It begins with a capital letter and is followed by a comma.
- The **body** is organized in paragraphs. Each paragraph is indented.
- The **closing** is in line with the heading at the end of the letter. The first word of the closing is capitalized. A comma follows the closing.
- The **signature** is in line with the closing.

Here is an example of a friendly letter.

Heading	115 Lee Street Seattle, WA 98109 April 21, 19——
Salutation	Dear Aunt Kay,
Body	Congratulations! I am very excited about my new cousin. As soon as she is old enough, I'll show little Katie my secret for shooting lay-up shots. She will be a basketball star before she can walk. Mom says we may be able to fly back to visit you this summer. Meanwhile, please be sure to take lots of pictures. I don't want to miss out on one of Katie's smiles.
Closing **Signature**	Lots of love, Andrea

Business Letter

- A **business letter** is written to accomplish a specific purpose: to make a request, place an order, or register a complaint. A business letter has six parts.
- The **heading** is in the upper right-hand corner. A comma is used between the city and the state and between the day and the year.
- The **inside address** starts at the left margin. It shows the name and address of the person or business receiving the letter.
- The **salutation** begins at the left margin. It begins with a capital letter and is followed by a colon.
- The **body** tells why you are writing the letter. It should give briefly and clearly all the facts that the receiver will need to answer the letter or fill an order.
- The **closing** at the end of the letter lines up with the heading. The first word of the closing is capitalized. A comma follows the closing.
- The **signature** is in a line with the closing. The signature includes the writer's full name.

Here is an example of a business letter.

Heading	151 Knoll St. Kansas City, Missouri 64118 May 9, 19––
Inside Address	Literacy Volunteers 194 N. Mill Road New Hope, New Jersey 08822
Salutation	Dear Sir or Madam:
Body	Please send me your pamphlet "Teaching English as a Second Language." I am tutoring a fellow student who has recently moved to the United States from Korea. If you have any other printed materials you think would be helpful, I would appreciate it if you would send them as well. Thank you for your help.
Closing	Sincerely,
Signature	*James Lott* James Lott

Journal

- A **journal** is a record of daily activities that serves as a reminder of personal happenings.
- Journal entries also provide useful source material for other original fiction or nonfiction compositions.
- Each journal entry starts with a day and a date.

Here is an example of a journal entry.

> *Wednesday, November 19—*
> *I got a great letter from Kelly today. He's coming home for*
> *Thanksgiving! I studied for tomorrow's math test. I hope I do well.*

Book Report

- One way of sharing information about a book is to write a **book report.** A book report gives enough information to enable a person to decide whether he or she would enjoy the book.
- The **summary** names the author and title of the book and briefly describes the plot of a fiction book or the contents of a nonfiction book.
- The **opinion** and **support** sections give the reader's opinion of the book and support that opinion with specific examples from the book.

Here is an example of a book report.

My Brother Sam Is Dead

One of the most exciting books I've read recently is a historical fiction novel called My Brother Sam Is Dead. The novel was written by James Lincoln Collier and Christopher Collier. It tells the story of Tim Meeker, a twelve-year-old boy who lived in Redding, Connecticut, during the time of the Revolutionary War. Tim's father is sympathetic to the Tories and loyal to the King of England. Tim's brother Sam is a rebel who joins the Patriots' Army to fight against the king. Tim is caught in the middle. I really enjoyed this book! Through Tim's experiences, I understood not only the historical and political effects of the war, but also how the war can affect a family.

Research Report

- A **research report** is a presentation of facts about a certain topic.
- An outline of the research notes helps organize the material before writing the report.
- Each heading of the outline serves as the topic sentence of a paragraph in the report.
- The subheadings and other facts from the notes help form the detail sentences supporting the main idea.
- A rough draft based on the outline is usually written.
- Transitional expressions or sentences are added where necessary.

Here is an introductory paragraph of a report.

> Imagine a beam of light that can measure distances to other planets, send signals into space, and split diamonds. It sounds like something out of a science-fiction movie, doesn't it? This beam of light is real. It's called a laser beam. Many of its uses are quite down-to-earth. Lasers are used to make delicate cuts in surgery, to cut and weld metal, to guide construction machinery, and to scan groceries at the checkout counter for price codes. In this report, you will find out what a laser beam is. You will also learn about the many extraordinary things a laser beam can do.

Story

- A **story** has a beginning, a middle, and an end.
- The **beginning** of the story gives the names of the characters and the setting.
- The **middle** of the story presents the problem and tells how the characters try to solve it. It usually tells how the main character grows and changes.
- The **ending** tells how the problem is solved.
- A story has a title. The first word and each important word begins with a capital letter.
- Many stories are told from a *first-person point of view,* meaning the person to whom the events happened is telling the story.

Here is an example of the beginning paragraph for a story.

<u>Journey into Another World</u>

I was worried. Seven miles seemed to be a long way to hike, even if it was all downhill. We'd be carrying packs and our required gallon of water per person. We'd need the water. After the sun came up we could expect temperatures up to 115°F, with no shade except where a rock ledge jutted out of the steep sides of the canyon. There was no alternative. We were at the rim of the Grand Canyon, and the rafts were waiting for us at Phantom Ranch on the Colorado River, seven long miles below. "There's no place to go but down," I thought, as I shouldered my pack and began the descent.

Conversation

- **Conversation** is a written dialogue between two or more persons.
- A new paragraph begins each time the speaker changes.
- The speaker's exact words are set off by quotation marks. If the quotation is divided into two parts by other words, the quotation marks are placed only around the quoted words.
- If the speaker's words continue for several sentences, the quotation does not close until the speaker is finished.
- Commas and periods go inside the closing quotation marks. Question marks and exclamation points go inside the closing quotation marks if the quotation itself is a question or an exclamation.

Here is an example of written conversation.

"Well?" Mom asked as Jed came through the door. "Did you go to football tryouts?"

Jed answered slowly, "Yes, I did." He put his books on the table.

Mom looked at him. "Well," she said, "Did you make the team?"

Jed suppressed a smile. Then he replied excitedly, "Coach says I'll be first-string this year."

"I knew you would!" said Mom. "So I planned your favorite dinner—chicken and baked potatoes."

News Story

- The purpose of a **news story** is to tell readers in a brief, factual, and interesting way about something that has happened.

- The **lead,** or first, paragraph or sentence of a news story contains the most essential information. The lead usually answers the questions *who, what, when, where, why,* and *how.*

- The paragraph or paragraphs that follow the lead give supporting details, arranged in the order of their importance.

- Some news stories include direct quotations from interviews.

- Every news story has a headline that sums up the main idea of the story.

Here is an example of a lead paragraph for a news story.

Vest-Pocket Park Becomes Reality

The phrase "meet you at the corner" now has a special meaning for residents of 113th and Semour Streets. Last Saturday, September 9, about one hundred and fifty friends and neighbors met at the corner to celebrate the completion of a park. The residents made the park themselves by clearing out an empty lot. Long-time resident Bill Shakes said, "For years this corner has been nothing but weeds and broken glass. It was a place to hurry by. Now it's a nice place to be."

Biography

- A **biography** is the story of a person's life written by someone else.

- A biography is written from the *third-person point of view.*

- A biography often starts with a person's birth and continues to his or her death.

- **Anecdotes** are short, entertaining accounts often included in biographies.

Here is an example of an introductory paragraph for a biography.

> Edgar Poe was born on January 1, 1809, in Boston, Massachusetts. He was the son of an American actor, David Poe, Jr., and an English actress, Elizabeth Arnold Poe. The baby's troubles began when his father walked out, never to return. In 1811, the two-year-old Edgar became an orphan when his mother died in Richmond, Virginia. Edgar was taken in by a childless couple named John and Frances Allan who raised him as their foster child and from whom he took the middle name Allan. It was from these tragic beginnings that Edgar Allan Poe drew his inspiration as a writer. His poems and stories endure as some of the most original and haunting works ever written.

Poetry/Rhymes

- In many poems, the words at the ends of some lines sound alike. This is called **rhyme.**
- A **rhyme scheme** in a poem is the pattern of the rhymes.
- Most poems have **rhythm,** or a regular beat.
- The pattern of beats in a poem is its **meter.**

Here is an example of a humorous poem.

> Though many people
> Say, "They're easy!"
> Computer programs
> Make me queasy.
>
> To push some buttons
> Is a risk—
> Perhaps you will
> Erase the disk!
>
> So give me pencil
> Give me paper
> It's not fast,
> But it is safer.

MECHANICS: A Glossary of Rules

Capitalization

Names and Titles of People, Places, and Organizations

- Capitalize names of people, including initials, titles, and abbreviations of titles.

  Dr. John D. Samuels   Ms. Elena J. Matthews

- Always capitalize the pronoun *I*.

  My brother and I are planning a trip.

- Capitalize geographical names and names of monuments, buildings, and organizations, as well as their abbreviations.

  Burlington, Iowa   Mason St.   Games, Inc.   Blvd. (Boulevard)

- Capitalize names of nationalities.

  Irish   Chinese   Polish

Names of Days, Months, and Holidays

- Capitalize all proper nouns and adjectives, including the names of days and months and their abbreviations.

  Wednesday   Thurs.   January   Dec.

- Capitalize important words in the name of a holiday.

  Fourth of July   Valentine's Day

Titles, Historical Events, and Languages

- Capitalize the first word, the last word, and all other important words in a title.

  The Last of the Mohicans   The Prince and the Pauper

- Capitalize historical and special events and periods.

  Industrial Revolution   the Middle Ages

- Capitalize names of languages.

  Italian   Japanese   Swahili

Punctuation

Period

- Place a period at the end of a declarative or an imperative sentence.

    The wind is chilly.   Wear a sweater.

- Place a period after most abbreviations.

    Sept.   U.S.A.   Tues.   Prof.   St.

- Place a period after an initial.

    John F. Kennedy   A.R. Lofft

- Place a period after a numeral or a letter in an outline.

    I. Sources of Energy
       A. The sun
          1. Fission

Question Mark and Exclamation Point

- Place a question mark at the end of an interrogative sentence.

    Have you heard the weather report?

- Place an exclamation point at the end of an exclamatory sentence.

    How frightened I am of tornadoes!

Comma

- Place a comma between the day and the year in a date. If the year is followed by more words in the sentence, place a comma after the year.

    On April 6, 1975, I made my first plane trip.

- Use a comma between the city and the state in an address. If the address or place name is in a sentence, put commas after the street address, between the city and state, and at the end of the address.

    We live at 752 Carrol Drive, Fulton, Maine.
    Is this 416 Dale Road, Durham, North Carolina?

- Place a comma after the greeting of a friendly letter or a social note and the closing of any letter.

  Dear Winnie,   Very truly yours,   Your friend,

- Place commas after every element but the last in a series.

  We ordered pizza, salad, and milk.

- Use a comma to set off quoted words from the rest of a sentence unless a question mark or exclamation point is needed.

  "I wonder," said Cory, "if I can learn to ski."

- Use commas to set off transitional expressions in a sentence.

  Woolens, however, are not worn in a warm climate.

Apostrophe

- Use an apostrophe for possessive nouns but not for possessive pronouns.

  Lewis's   diplomats'   people's
  his   theirs   yours

- Use an apostrophe to form contractions of pronouns and verbs and to form contractions of verbs with the adverb *not*.

  I'm   she'd   won't

Colon and Hyphen

- Use a colon after the greeting of a business letter.

  Dear Ms. Iversen: Dear Senator Forbes:

- Place a colon between the hour and the minute in the time of day.

  6:05 A.M.   9:30 A.M.

- Use a colon before a list or series of items, especially when the list follows expressions such as *the following* or *as follows*.

  Order the following: brushes, canvas, paint.

- Use a hyphen to divide a word at the end of a line.

  Tabby was attracted by the smell of spear-
  mint toothpaste.

Underlining and Quotation Marks

● Underline titles of books, plays, newspapers, magazines, movies, TV shows, records, works of art, musical compositions, and long poems.

> <u>The Adventures of Tom Sawyer</u> (book)
> <u>The News Chronicle</u> (newspaper)
> <u>Romeo and Juliet</u> (play)

● Place quotation marks around titles of songs, articles, short stories, chapters in books, and short poems.

> "Battle Hymn of the Republic" (song)
> "Crafts for Fun and Profit" (article))

● Place quotation marks around the exact words of a direct quotation. If the quotation is divided into two parts by other words, place quotation marks around the quoted words only.

> Mr. Bailey said, "The corn is ready to be harvested."
> "We must have the tractor repaired," she replied, "or we will not finish harvesting in time."

● If there are several sentences in a direct quotation, do not close the quotation until after the last sentence.

> "I'll buy the part I need today. It shouldn't be too expensive. Then I can repair the tractor," he said.

● Always place commas and periods inside the closing quotation marks. Place question marks and exclamation points inside the closing quotation marks if the quotation itself is a question or an exclamation.

> Mr. Bailey said, "We'll begin harvesting next week."
> "Wow! It's going to be hot!" his daughter exclaimed.
> Will the tractor be ready in time?" Betty asked.
> Did Mr. Clark say, "I have the part you need"?

● When you write conversation, begin a new paragraph every time the speaker changes.

> "Can we repair the tractor ourselves?" asked Betty.
> "I think so," answered Mr. Bailey. "We had the same problem about two years ago."

HANDWRITING: Letter Forms

Uppercase and Lowercase Manuscript Letters

Uppercase and Lowercase Cursive Letters

A B C D E F G H I
J K L M N O P 2 R
S T U V W X Y Z
a b c d e f g h i
j k l m n o p q r
s t u v w x y z

A B C D E F G H I
J K L M N O P 2 R
S T U V W X Y Z
a b c d e f g h i
j k l m n o p q r
s t u v w x y z

273